The Federal Government and Educational R & D

Richard A. Dershimer

Lexington Books
D.C. Heath and Company
Lexington, Massachusetts
Toronto

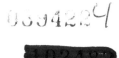

Library of Congress Cataloging in Publication Data

Dershimer, Richard A.
    The Federal Government and educational R&D.

    1. Educational Research–United States. 2. Federal aid to education
–United States. I. Title.
LB1028.D45   370'.78'073   74–293
ISBN 0-669-92700-7

Published simultaneously in Canada

Printed in the United States of America

International Standard Book Number: 0–669–92700–7

Library of Congress Catalog Card Number: 74–293

I dedicate this book first to Alice, then to
Joan, and now to Greta

Contents

**The Federal
Government
and Educational
R&D**

Lexington Books Politics of Education Series
Frederick M. Wirt, Editor

Michael W. Kirst, Ed., *State, School, and Politics: Research Directions*

Joel S. Berke, Michael W. Kirst, *Federal Aid to Education: Who Benefits? Who Governs?*

Al J. Smith, Anthony Downs, M. Leanne Lachman, *Achieving Effective Desegregation*

Kern Alexander, K. Forbis Jordan, *Constitutional Reform of School Finance*

George R. LaNoue, Bruce L.R. Smith, *The Politics of School Decentralization*

David J. Kirby, T. Robert Harris, Robert L. Crain, Christine H. Rossell, *Political Strategies in Northern School Desegregation*

Philip K. Piele, John Stuart Hall, *Budgets, Bonds, and Ballots: Voting Behavior in School Financial Elections*

John C. Hogan, *The Schools, the Courts, and the Public Interest*

Jerome T. Murphy, *State Education Agencies and Discretionary Funds: Grease the Squeaky Wheel*

Howard Hamilton, Sylvan Cohen, *Policy Making by Plebiscite: School Referenda*

Daniel J. Sullivan, *Public Aid to Nonpublic Schools*

James Hottois, Neal A. Milner, *The Sex Education Controversy: A Study of Politics, Education, and Morality*

Lauriston R. King, *The Washington Lobbyists for Higher Education*

Frederick M. Wirt, Ed., *The Polity of the School: New Research in Educational Politics*

Peter J. Cistone, Ed., *Understanding School Boards: Problems and Prospects*

Lawrence E. Gladieux, Thomas R. Wolanin, *Congress and the Colleges: The National Politics of Higher Education*

Dale Mann, *The Politics of Administrative Representation: School Administrators and Local Democracy*

Harrell R. Rodgers, Jr., Charles S. Bullock, III, *Coercion to Compliance: The Role of Law in Effectuating Social Change*

Richard A. Dershimer, *The Federal Government and Educational R&D*

Introduction

The title of this book needs some elaboration; words like "federal government" and "educational R&D" in addition to not being very exciting are not very descriptive. So let me begin this introduction by answering the question, "What is this book all about?"

From my personal and professional experience during those ten years that I was located in Washington, D.C., as Executive Officer of the American Educational Research Association, I learned that most of the men and women who make up the community of educational researchers and developers (definitions will come later) know precious little about how the federal government operates. In this respect, they differ very little from their counterparts in other behavioral and social sciences, or the practitioners and informed laypersons who make up the larger educational enterprise. And the converse is true: few bureaucrats realize how research communities operate. So it is the primary purpose of this book to better educate both groups.

The way I have chosen to do this is by reviewing and analyzing events in those government agencies responsible for supporting educational R&D over the years beginning with the advent of the Course Content Improvement Program in the National Science Foundation (NSF) and the Cooperative Research Program in the Office of Education to the formation of the National Institute of Education; this covers roughly from 1954 to 1972. But I have not been content with just a chronological description; nor have I settled for conventional explanations of those events. I have fashioned a conceptional framework that, while flaunting some conventional wisdom, allows me to better sort out and explain what was happening back then. This framework is a composite of work that has been done by political scientists and (surprisingly for me) economists. It can be found in Chapters 1 and 2.

The reader needs another kind of perspective, however, that which comes from an understanding of the larger forces and events that shifted national priorities in the 1950s and 1960s, that elevated public education into the national consciousness about social injustices and onto center stage in the federal government. President Johnson may have had the personal predisposition to favor public education as president but the fact that he acted on that predisposition is the result (and the cause) of subtle shifts in beliefs and opinions about what the federal government should do for public education. This is what makes up the substance of Chapter 3.

After the stage is set conceptually and historically, I describe in Chapters 4 through 8 some specific programs within selected bureaus. I concentrate on the Bureau of Research within the Office of Education because that is where most of the ideas ended up of those who espoused and promoted educational R&D. But I help the reader gain perspective by referring as often as possible to parallel actions or counter actions in educational R&D in other governmental agencies like NSF, the National Institute of Mental Health, and the Office of Economic Opportunity.

The reader also will discover that I chose to describe the activities of those bureaus by concentrating as much as possible on the actions of individuals. To many Americans, the bureaucracy may be a sea of faceless, nameless automatons; not to me. I was fortunate to have known many of the men and women bureaucrats and advisors of those years. In the final analysis, it was a human or a group of humans who did or did not do something about educational R&D. I am not interested in blaming, or necessarily applauding their decisions. But no description of how the federal bureaucracy influenced the field of educational research can be complete without mentioning these individuals and how they functioned.

For what purpose? What can we learn from the behavior of individuals most of whom are long gone from federal service and whose positions, programs, even their agencies have been eliminated? Further, even if all of these variables were still present, the events and forces to which these persons were responding would long since have passed into history. What generalizations are possible? Most of the answers to these questions are provided (I hope) in Chapter 1. I show that there are certain tendencies operating among bureaucrats, and there are norms within the system itself that persist over time. These norms will be carried from group to group. Bureaucracies are no different in this respect than other human organizations. To the extent that outsiders can understand how individual bureaucrats are influenced to that extent can they deal with the federal bureaucracy more rationally.

In the final chapter, I put my data and documents to one side to ruminate and speculate. There is something wrong with the way we are trying to use the social and behavioral sciences to change education, and what is wrong has to do both with the system in which we are all caught up and the notion of what scientific behavior is. I argue that unless we change certain aspects of both, the system and the tradition of science, that we are not likely to do things much differently in the future than we have in the past. These changes must occur before another wave of hope will sweep up to and over the federal machinery the way certain notions about research did in the late 1950s and early 1960s.

That provides an overview of the book but doesn't explain what kind of book it is. Is it a personal memoir or a report of systematic research? The answer lies somewhere halfway between. My decisions of what are significant from those years rest to a large extent on my personal experiences, my personal recollections. But I tried to avoid the biases and the inaccuracies and the myths that permeate memoirs by verifying, in documents or the memories of others, as much as I possibly could; hence the rather extensive footnotes and references. For example, yes, there were biases against "educationists" among the Keppel staff in USOE, that is a rather well known fact. But well known or not, I sought, and found, comments in print that confirm that fact.

Many other references have been included to encourage others to pick up where I leave off, to subject the federal agencies and federal bureaucrats to more intensive, hopefully more disciplined, inquiry. There still is the tendency, especially among that generation of researchers of which I was once regarded as one of the younger men, to play down the importance of the federal government. Many have said, in private, that the important work in educational research, if not development, takes place along those academic corridors hardly touched by federal influences. To me this is a head-in-the-sand attitude that can no longer be defended. I am not saying that there is a one-to-one relationship between what the government does and the response of researchers. And there are and may well continue to be individuals who can function effectively without using federal funds. But he or she will be housed in an institution surrounded by colleagues and dealing with students (or school systems) who interact with the federal government. As a field, we must continue to grow in our understanding of and the sophistication in dealing with federal agencies. This means that there must be a (growing) group within the educational R&D community that studies how the bureaucracy functions, and how policies and politics affect the performance of R&D. So this book is designed to encourage and be a spring board for further studies.

Now let me return to the necessary but unappetizing chore of providing some definitions. Hopefully the reader will understand the first term in my title—"the federal government." The other half of the equation, "educational R&D," cannot be passed over so quickly. But I shudder at the necessity of having to devise a useful (succinct) definition. I could go on at some length about what constitutes research and development in education and still not provide a useable set of inclusion-exclusion criteria. Should I include the work of Jean Piaget and Barbel Inhelder? Of Frank Skinner? Or studies of the effects of malnutrition on learning? Or the effects of parental attitudes toward upward mobility on school success of children? To all these questions the answers are, "Yes and No."

The fact is that we are describing a field of study, not a single discipline. Psychology, as broad as that term has become, can be identified by the activities of persons who have received (usually an advanced) degree in psychology. But no one receives a degree in educational research.

A field of study is made up of many interconnecting specialties. Both the membership in those specialties as well as the specialties themselves are constantly shifting. Jerome Bruner and J. McVickers Hunt published material in the mid-1960s that was read and debated with intense interest by educationists. Both have since drifted off to work that has relevance to far fewer researchers in education. Ten years ago policy studies was a specialty that appeared to have little if any relevance to education; today it is a growing specialty in the field. Because of these shifts a precise definition of educational R&D is not possible. It must suffice to say that the core of educational research remains those studies of the activities that take place in the institutions of learning in our society and leave it go at that.

As for development, we seem to have outgrown the disputes about whether or not there is such a phenomenon. A growing group of specialists today refer to themselves as educational developers. They talk about producing useable products and designing new technology, which means the equipment, materials, systems, and procedures employed by the professionals in educational institutions. In one sense, they are "applied" researchers; in another, they are engineers. Their focus is to use research methods to solve specific problems.

Enough for definitions. I hasten on to the more pleasant task of thanking the many hundreds of persons (or so it seems) who assisted me over the three years it took to produce this manuscript. So many of the bureaucrats themselves, persons like Lenora Lewis Smith, Kent Viehover, Ward Mason and Richard McVity, have helped me dig into files and otherwise find obscure documents. Others like Howard Hjelm and Thomas Clemens have read drafts of chapters and made valuable additions and corrections. To Gary Hanna, who has done all of these chores I owe additional thanks because of how he has shared his perceptions and views of the workings of government.

To David Clark, Frances Keppel, William Paisley, Sam Sieber, Roald Campbell, Fred Wirt, and Hendrik Gi deonse, I am indebted for help on the chapters they read in draft form and reacted to. To Stephen Bailey, I am especially indebted because he read and encouraged me with the complete document. It goes without saying that this is my work nevertheless.

Two institutions and their personnel must be singled out. The School of Education at Stanford generously provided me with space and privileges for two summers; without Dean Arthur Coladarci, his secretarial staff, and my assistant Gary Sikes, this book would have been much thinner and far less useful. I also thank William Russell, the present Executive Officer of AERA, for allowing me to use so many of the facilities of the central office.

Two more thanks are in order: First to the Spencer Foundation and Thomas James for having faith enough in my ability to say something worthwhile to grant me supporting funds for my work. But my last and most heartfelt thanks are reserved for Ruth Guttadauro, who continued to provide all the countless forms of help to me now as friend that she did for eight years as my secretary.

If I have omitted anyone, it is inadvertent and I extend my apologies and my deepest thanks to them now.

**The Federal
Government
and Educational
R&D**

1

The Bureaucratic-Professional Complex: The Federal Side

How can the reader best understand the events that are depicted in the middle sections of this book? There are references to dozens of persons and a couple of dozen programs in five agencies that spent altogether between the years 1955 and 1975 more than $2 billion. It is easy to become mesmerized by the details or swept up in the action and not recognize the messages that have the most importance for future events. These first two chapters are designed to highlight those messages.

What complicates matters is that conventional wisdom about how the federal government operates hinders understanding as much as it helps. Conventional wisdom, as used here, refers to such often-heard comments as these: "Educational research needs a more active constituency"; "Congress won't develop any interest in educational research; there aren't enough votes in it"; "Research and politics don't mix." The difficulty with these aphorisms is not their veracity (or lack of it) but that they are based on an outdated concept of how the federal government operates, one founded on a mixture of nineteenth-century pork-barrel politics and early twentieth-century liberalism.

Most critics of educational R&D fail to account for the changes that have come about in the bureaucratic and political nature of the federal government since World War II. In this brief span of a quarter of a century, there has been an unparalleled growth in the professionalization of the bureaucracy that has been both a cause and an effect of the growing importance of specialized knowledge in operating the government. As its size and complexity increased, new systems were needed for fiscal budgeting and accounting, management, and planning. And as the government became more involved in the economic and social life of the nation, it had to make the best possible use of the substantive knowledge in many fields. These developments have led to what Samuel H. Beer calls "technocratic politics."[1]

A signal characteristic of technocratic politics is the direction of the flow of the policy processes. In traditional politics, the source of policy is the public, the body politic. Their spokesmen articulate the public will to the political representatives who fashion it into operating policies for governmental action. The bureaucrat is acknowledged to influence this process but in circumscribed ways, Consequently, his importance to this system is quite limited.

Beer sees a quite different process operating today:

In technocratic policy making the pressures and proposals arise *within* government and its associated circles of professionals and technically trained cadres.[2]

1

In today's government, more and more it is the insiders who are expected to remain current with the problems of society and to propose solutions in those areas in which they have expert knowledge, whether they be bureaucrats or legislators. And because this calls for leadership, the men and women in Washington must then turn to the body politic to educate them or mobilize their support. They do this best when they work through those groups who have espoused those policies or who are most familiar with the workings of the agency involved.

These government workers and their associated circles of specialists make up what Beer calls the "professional-bureaucratic complex." The professional side consists of four groups: a research elite of various specialized fields; groups in the private sector who benefit from the government programs; counterparts to the federal bureaucrats at the local and state levels; and members of the House of Representatives and the Senate who espouse the causes of a particular complex.

Beer is not saying that technocratic politics is the only political style now operating within the federal government. In his brilliant essay, he describes four types of politics: porkbarrel, spillover, class, and technocratic. Each is best associated with a particular period of our history; technocratic politics, Beer believes, is the dominant mode of our times. Nevertheless, all are in use today at one time or another; their appropriateness is determined by the issues, the outside groups, and the agencies involved. Technocratic politics is singled out for more attention here because it has the most relevance to the events depicted in this story. Beer's contentions are supported by the evidence gathered for this volume. *Every research and development support program in education launched by the federal government was initiated by a small handful of persons, in other words, by a professional-bureaucratic complex.* And many of these remain in existence today not because of any widespread public demand but because elements in the complex still support them.

The purpose of this book now can be made more explicit: *to describe and assess the effectiveness of the professional-bureaucratic complex that has been responsible for launching and maintaining support for educational research and development.* In this chapter, we begin by examining first the characteristics of the bureaus and some of the key persons who staffed them. In Chapter 2, we examine who made up the professional side of the complex and then discuss some of the policies they generated and the processes they used.

Bureaus and Bureaucrats Supporting Educational R&D

By the 1960s four agencies of the federal government were supporting research and development activities aimed at improving public education in the country: the U.S. Office of Education (USOE); the National Science Foundation (NSF);

the National Institute of Mental Health (NIMH); and the Office of Economic Opportunity (OEO). In 1972, most of the R&D programs in USOE were shifted to the newly created National Institute of Education (NIE), and some of the efforts of the OEO were moved to the newly created Office of Child Development (OCD). So altogether we are interested in six agencies. Other government bureaus have sponsored R&D that is of interest to educational researchers—for example, computer-aided instruction and reading (Office of Naval Research, ONR), programmed instruction (Department of Defense, DOD), and child health (Institute of Child Health and Human Development, NCHHD)—but they will be given only passing reference. The focus clearly will be on USOE and NSF since that is where the bulk of the money has been spent during the years of this analysis, roughly 1965 to 1972.[3]

On first glance, these agencies seem to have more differences than similarities. USOE is an old-line agency, having been created in 1867. NSF and NIMH are post-World War II phenomena, and OEO is a product of the social concern of the 1960s. In USOE, research was grafted onto an operating agency; NSF and NIMH were created expressly to aid the development and application of new knowledge. OEO was established to help change some of the basic institutions of our society; USOE was considered to be well integrated into the educational enterprise.

Different though they are, all these organizations are bureaucracies. So let us examine that term so we can best understand its importance.

What is a Bureaucracy?

Most of the literature that answers this question is of little relevance to us. The study of bureaucracy typically is the study of large organizations; as Downs says, ". . . small organizations are excluded from the ranks of bureaus."[4] Yet the staffs that operated the R&D programs were small, consisting mostly of in-and-outers who devoted only a few years of their careers to the federal government. How then can we consider them and the bureaus in which they operated as anything but deviations or anomalies of the federal bureaucracy?

The fact is they existed, still exist today, and are as much a part of the federal scene as other better known agencies. In fact, any organization can be considered bureaucratic if its activities include the following:

1. Strives for "clear-cut division of integrated activities which are regarded as inherent in the office."[5]
2. Operates under criteria for hiring of personnel and their promotion that are "based at least partly upon some type of assessment of the way in which they have performed or can be expected to perform their organizational roles. . . ."[6]

3. Operates so that the major portion of its output is *not* evaluated in markets external to the organization.[7]
4. Establishes bi-lateral monopoly with its sponsor.[8]

The sponsor provides the bureau with a budget for a promise of a set of activities (and outputs) in which the sponsor has interest. The budget is shaped by the larger organization in which the bureau is housed. Specifically, the bureaus with which we are concerned look to the Congress as its sponsor and either the larger entity called the "Administration" (which was the case with NSF, OEO, and during a brief few months, for the USOE) as its larger organization or a segment of it called, in this case, the Department of Health, Education and Welfare (DHEW). (The NIMH looks to the National Institutes of Health and the Public Health Service rather than to the larger DHEW.)

As we shall see, these four features have special meaning to the educational R&D story.

The Importance of the Individual Bureaucrat

As noted, the professionalized bureaucrat involved with technocratic politics is a far different person from the stereotypical character who obtained his position in years gone by through being a wardheeler's flunky. He has gained considerable importance among the students of bureaucracy. Consider these comments by Niskanen:

Any theory of the behavior of bureaus that does not incorporate the personal preferences of the bureaucrats, however, will be relevant only in the most rigidly authoritarian environments.
    The individual . . . bureaucrat . . . is assumed to face a set of personal preferences among the outcomes of the possible actions, and to choose the action with the possible set that he most prefers. He is a chooser and a "maximizer" and, in contrast to his part in the characteristic methods of sociology, not just a "role player" in some larger social drama. The larger environment influences the behavior of the individual by constraining his set of possible actions and outcomes, and, to some extent by influencing his person preferences.[9]

Others agree. As Brecht says, "Employees [in bureaucracies] are hired for the purpose of influencing both the making and the execution of laws by their expert knowledge and practical experience,"[10] and Downs describes how most new bureaus are formed by the "zealotry of a few members of an existing bureau."[11] Other authors remind us that as important as any set of individuals may be, they operate within constraints and are influenced by the environment in which they work. So let's examine now some of the more salient characteristics of that environment for the bureaucrats concerned with education R&D programs.

The Socialization of Bureaucrats

It is common knowledge that within any formal structure there are informal social groupings. Where a person fits within that social group depends, in part, on how well he learns its unwritten laws and norms, or how well he is socialized. As Fenno describes this socialization process, "The inexperienced bureaucrat may have to learn those attitudes of respect and those deferential forms of behavior to which the majority of veteran agency officials already subscribe."[12] Others have described the internalized code of ethnics that governs the professional conduct of bureaucrats.[13] Fenno describes socialization as partly a training in perception:

Before members of a group can be expected to observe its norms, they must see and interpret the world around them with reasonably similar results . . . the newcomers' perceptions are brough sufficiently into line with those of the older members to serve as a basis for integration. Radically different perceptions of political reality could promote different sets of expectations and attitudes with seriously disruptive consequences for the group.[14]

That social group for any individual may be composed of many "oldtimers" or in a new bureau may consist predominantly of newcomers. In the OE Bureau of Research, for example, the staff assembled in 1965 and 1966 to launch the regional educational laboratories was composed almost entirely of young persons who were new to the bureaucracy. Dubbed the "kiddie corps," they served as an effective socializing agent for each other and for replacements. Within a relatively short time they had commonly shared beliefs about what constituted a regional laboratory. More importantly, however, they shared implicit norms of behavior toward the staffs in the new laboratories, outside consultants, and fellow bureaucrats. Similar incidents can be found during the early months of NSF and OEO.

Style: A Byproduct of Being Socialized

One of the most important byproducts of the socialization processes is learning acceptable bureaucratic styles of behavior. In other words, doing tasks in ways that will be judged as "correct" in given situations by a high status group, doing what they see is the right thing at the right time. Style is acknowledged as being important in the literature.[15] Fenno talks about it in reference to the way freshman Congressmen are assessed, but he also sees its importance in establishing relationships between bureaucrats and Congressmen. He quotes a bureaucrat:

It took me a long time to learn that they [Congressmen] don't want to be educated in those hearings. They want to size you up as a person. They want to know whether you're on top of your job as an administrator. . . . It's you they want to hear, and your program and your bureau fades into the background.[16]

Style is no replacement for competence or political power but it has importance in its own right—probably in all human endeavors. But it has more importance in federal government than in other, less complex organizations. Congressmen, bureaucrats in the higher echelons, and persons in agencies like the Office and Management and Budget cannot possibly stay abreast of all that is happening within their jurisdictions. The assessment of style offers one of the short cuts to the assessment of the competence of entire bureaus as well as of individuals.

What constitutes "stylishness" in the federal bureaucracy, as anywhere else, is not easy to define. One example will suffice to illustrate this point. During an interview, a former member of the Bureau of the Budget, Richard Emory, compared events and persons in USOE and OCD. This is what he had to say about the Director of OCD in 1972:

We soon discovered that Ed Zigler [then director of OCD] knew what he was talking about; he understood the problems of child development. We would have taken money from other agencies if necessary to give it to him. We had that kind of confidence in him[17]

But Zigler himself, when questioned later about those early months, didn't think that he was on top of his job. "I was pretty naive during those early months," he admits.[18]

The difference in those two comments lies with the two sets of criteria that were used. Zigler, being essentially a scholar, was well aware of how little he knew about the substance of the programs over which he had jurisdiction. Emory was not a psychologist and had little substantive background in the field of child development. He was aware, however, that Zigler had sufficient mastery of the federal bureaucratic style so that his chances of succeeding were quite high.

Stylishness is a subtle blend of substance and sophistication. Frank Keppel and Harold Howe II were the most stylish of persons in USOE and the most widely accepted outside OE among the larger bureaucracy. They brought this with them. Others try to learn to be stylish by using the most current "buzz-words and concepts" (in 1976, for example, using "knowledge-production and utilization" instated of "R&D"), knowing and using the "in-persons" for authorities and consultants (like Jerold Zacharias and Jerome Bruner in the early 1960s), and developing certain speaking and writing characteristics. (These changed drastically from Eisenhower's time to the age of the Kennedy's.) Stylishness is only one of several criteria that are used to win and hold support within the bureaucracy; other factors like outside political support, social relevance, priorities of the president himself or of one of his surrogates like the secretary of a department can be determining factors. But many of the temporary officials of the Bureau of Research in OE who worked long and hard and who found their ideas rejected at the department or Bureau of the Budget (BOB) levels may have been unaware that is was their "lack of style" that doomed them, not necessarily the quality of their ideas.

The Hierarchy of Federal Agencies

Just as there are standards of behavior for individual bureaucrats, there are standards of performance for entire bureaus. Again style is important, but let us move beyond that and look at other factors.

Rourke points out that "agencies which are highly professional in their orientation and employment patterns often occupy a preferred position within the structure of public bureaucracies."[19] This preferred position falls into a more or less well-structured pecking order. Generally speaking, the closer an agency is to the president, the higher it ranks in the pecking order. (There are all kinds of exceptions, the Department of Defense being one of the most notable.) The Course Content Improvement Program (CCIP) of NSF, the program responsible for funding multi-million-dollar curriculum projects over the past two decades has many accomplishments for which it deserves much praise. But CCIP also had considerably smoother sailing because it was imbedded in an agency with considerably more stature than USOE.

This pecking order position of an agency is important if it hopes to make use of the mechanisms for policy formation that go through the president. The lower an agency resides in the order, the more difficulty it typically will encounter in restructuring its policies and in advancing its budget. It must pass through several layers of officials, each of whom are using the stance that the burden of proof for a new position rests with the agency. This is a near-defeating task as USOE officials learned after Lyndon Johnson, the "Education President," left the White House and they again were exposed to their low-status position in the hierarchy. This is what James Gallagher, Deputy Assistant Secretary for Planning, Research, and Evaluation for DHEW referred to when he said:

Outside the Office of Education, at the present time, there are at least five or six major sources of policy review identifiable within the Executive Branch itself. Reviews by the Secretary's Office of Program Planning and Evaluation, by the Department's budgetary analysts, by the staff of the new Secretary, by the Bureau of the Budget, by various parts of the White House staff, etc., lead to many amendments and modifications. The number of these people and their participation in policy decision making appear to be increasing daily: moreover they do not hesitate to exercise veto power over these programs.[20]

Bureaucrats in the lower pecking order agencies must work as hard to educate, must be as responsive to, these higher order officials as they are to key Congressmen and their staffs—that is, they must interact informally to seek and exchange ideas in between formal decision points.

The key agency in many ways in this hierarchy was known during the years of this analysis as the Bureau of the Budget (BOB); in 1972, its name was changed to the Office of Management and Budget (OMB). It had considerable authority, attracted some of the brightest persons in the federal service, and was one of the style setters in government. Not only was it used by the White House to cut and pare budgets, but it served as a staff arm for shaping much new legislation. In Lyndon Johnson's time, all the proposals from task forces were reviewed by BOB staff men. And it was the BOB to whom the task frequently was given by the president to ensure that last year's policies were (1) still in force and (2) reconciled with this year's policies. For example, it was BOB who had the delicate task of seeing that the domestic policies of the Johnson administration were continued even though the Vietnam conflict demanded ever greater sums of money.

Its influence went beyond what it earned from these functions; as Harold Howe says, "BOB was the most stylish agency in the bureaucracy."[21] He and others have noted that in general the quality of the staff is as high as any agency in Washington. Emerson Elliot, a BOB staffer for more than a decade, described how it clearly was his first preference when he applied for government service after completing his graduate work. He knew that it was close to the sources of power in Washington, but it attracted him also because it had a high intellectual reputation. As Howe put it:

They did a good job by and large in thinking in depth about programs, in asking tough questions. And they listened; it was a rational conversation most of the time.[22]

It is no exaggeration to say that the rational conversation involving educational R&D between OE and BOB broke down somewhere toward the end of the Johnson administration and the beginning of the Nixon years. Despairing of being able to influence the R&D programs sufficiently to produce what they and their advisors believed were sensible, intellectually respectable results, BOB concluded that they needed to wipe the slate clean and start again, this time in an agency that was removed from the damaging or stultifying influences of the USOE.

It is ironical that this new agency, NIE, established with such high hopes and given so many advantages that bureaus in USOE could not hope to attain, nevertheless was in considerable difficulty before it reached its third birthday. It attracted top flight administrators, many of whom had successful careers in the BOB and more recognizable and respected scholars than its successors, the Bureau of Research (BR) and the National Center for Educational Research and Development (NCERD), were able to attract. Why, then, it didn't realize its potential is a question that transcends the scope of this analysis. But one of the reasons has to come from the difficulties it encountered with the Congress, where from 1973 on it met with sharp questioning that led to reduced budgets.[23]

This fact leads us to the next ingredient of the bureaucratic-professional complex that needs to be highlighted—the importance of the elected officials and their staffs.

The Place of Congressmen in the B-P Complex

Individual members of Congress, not its committees or blocs, are of most importance in the bureaucratic-professional complex. For example, John Brademas, along with one or two fellow Congressmen like Albert Quie, is credited with salvaging the NIE legislation after the White House seemed unable or unwilling to generate enough support in the Congress. Educating and cultivating an individual Congressman or woman means building informal relationships; for this, a bureaucrat cannot just rely on the formal processes like hearings, as important as these are.[24] Key men on the Joint Atomic Energy Committee turned against the recommendation of the Atomic Energy Commission in 1958 for its Stanford Linear Accelerator (SLAC), when they felt they had not been adequately informed.[25]

In some agencies like the National Science Foundation, contacts between program managers and individual Congressmen are limited; NSF tends to leave the cultivation of congressional support to its top echelons and their liaison assistants. But in four of the other five agencies with which we are concerned—USOE, OEO, NIMH and OCD—there is considerable evidence of frequent staff–congressional interaction. Francis A.J. Ianni, Director of the Cooperative Research Program in OE in the early 1960s, tells of frequent social visits over cocktails with John Fogarty, then chairman of the Sub-Committee on Appropriations for HEW. Leonard Duhl, on the staff of the National Institute of Health, at about the same time recalls similar incidents.[26]

The importance of individual congressmen can be illustrated by the history of John Fogarty's chairmanship of his Appropriations subcommittee. As others have noted,[27] Fogarty consistently favored huge increases in the budget of the National Institute of Health and from 1953 to 1962 increased its appropriations above what the administration itself requested. Medical research was high in public favor during most of that time, but not with everyone in the power structure of the Congress. In the mid-1950s, Congressmen Clarence Cannon and John Taber, alternately chairmen and ranking members of the Appropriations Committee, decided to control Fogarty and the NIH budget. Sometimes they both would show up at subcommittee meetings and executive sessions, and in 1956, Taber appointed himself to the subcommittee.[28] To no avail; Fogarty out maneuvered them both, and the appropriations kept going up.

It is just as important to cultivate the staffs of legislators and their committees. The staff member is more than the eyes and ears of the elected officials for often he or she can, in effect, decide the issue. Senator Wayne Morse, on several occasions publicly credited his former staff assistant, Charles Lee, with devising the scheme that later led to Title I of the Elementary and Secondary Education Act. This was the allocation of federal funds to school systems so as to better equalize educational opportunity throughout the nation.[29] A former member of the USOE congressional liaison staff, Richard Smith describes his work with Lee:

> Morse was struggling with the amendments to Title III of ESEA [Supplementary Centers and Services] in 1967. He knew if he took the Administration's position [to keep it as it was in the original bill and not compromise] that he would get beaten. I was still with OE and Charlie Lee called me. Together we put together a draft, Morse liked it and it became his.[30]

Some observers of the federal scene believe that NIE encountered problems in the Senate because the NIE staff did not take the trouble to cultivate, even to bother with, the little courtesies that bring congressional staffs and agency staffs into effective informal relationships. One staff member discusses the persons with whom he interacts most often:

> If you look at the Congressional staff now working on education you will not find a non-lawyer in a professional position. And we lawyers don't have much respect for academicians. In higher education, for example, the academic community had almost no influence on the higher education bill that was passed last year [1973]. The one person outside our circle who had influence on that bill was Gary Hanna [staff person in OE]. I don't think NIE would have been in the bill if it weren't for Hanna.[31]

This reference to "our circle" brings us to the last point to be made about the characteristics of bureaus and bureaucrats—the way informal social circles form and operate inside the bureaucracy.

Special Interest Circles

One kind of informal social grouping of bureaucrats to which no reference appears in the literature is what can be called "special interest circles" (SICs). I refer to an identifiable number of men and women who increasingly interact with each other because they share a mutual concern and similar views about a major policy or program area. They find each other because they occupy similar statuses in the bureaucracy—that is, they have about the same service ratings and similar amounts of responsibilities and influences and, therefore, frequently rub shoulders at meetings, conferences, and social gatherings.

One example of a SIC that affected policies in educational R&D had its genesis in the Educational Task Force of 1965 chaired by John Gardner. William Cannon, then Chief of the Education, Manpower and Science Division, and his assistant, Emerson Elliott, were the staff for the T/F. They were dedicated, but grew increasingly disappointed with what they viewed as the ineffectual performance of the Bureau of Research in USOE. Over the years, their views were shared and strengthened by several others from other agencies—men like John Mays from the Office of Science and Technology (OST) and Michael O'Keefe from the Office of the Assistant Secretary for Planning, Research and Evaluation (ASPRE) in DHEW—and for a while by some advisors to Commissioner Allen in USOE. It is difficult to accurately delineate everyone who shared their views because there was never a need to count heads. What emerged was described by Roger Levien, one of the planners of NIE, as a "cabal within the government" and what one of the cabal himself referred to as the "Unholy Trinity."[33]

It is difficult to know precisely what policies this circle espoused since, with the exception of Bill Cannon, few of them ever published policy papers, gave speeches, or wrote legislation in the areas of educational R&D.[34] In 1967, members of the SIC were instrumental in establishing a special panel of the President's Science Advisory Committee (PSAC) to review policies in educational research. But the final report of this committee,[35] named for its chairman Frank Westheimer, was not given much attention. This was due in part to when it was submitted, late in the Johnson administration, but also because it was not a very distinguished report. It contained more observations and criticisms than constructive policy alternatives. So the views (and it is more correct to say that they held points of view rather than policies) of this circle must be deduced.

In general, they wanted different and better people running the R&D programs in USOE[36] and in the institutions USOE supported like the regional educational laboratories and the R&D centers. The term "better" most frequently referred to recognizeable scholars from the natural and social sciences. Reaction to specific issues would stem from this position: since there were few good people to be had to conduct educational research, there should be fewer, not more, educational labs and centers. And they probably should be in or connected to prestige institutions. By and large, theirs was a reactive stance,[a] and it frequently was difficult to ascertain on what their reactions were based.

Whatever the cause, the Bureau of Research staff and this circle became adversaries. Early in the ESEA program, the BOB staff attempted to get officials in DHEW to intercede and alter some of the R&D programs, but neither the Secretary of DHEW, John Gardner, nor Commissioner Harold Howe took the necessary action, even though neither of them were particularly enthusiastic about many of the practices of the Bureau. The result was that Cannon, Elliott, Mays, and others had to be content then to move to the sidelines. But so long as they remained on the team they could be sent into the ball game at any time.

When Daniel Moynihan and Edward Morgan of the White House staff organized a task force to shape an educational program for President Nixon in

---

[a]All service agencies like the BOB by their nature are in a reactive stance—that is, they must await policy initiatives from the White House, individual Departments of agencies or from the Congress

1970, several members of the circle were appointed to serve on it. The result was to move the educational R&D programs out from under the protective shield of the Commissioner of Education (and to make it more difficult for the education-ists to interfere if they ever chose to do so) by creating a new agency, NIE.

This SIC in educational R&D virtually disappeared soon thereafter. Elliott, his former assistant Bernard Martin, John Mays, and others eventually appeared on the staff of the Institute. Mike O'Keefe took a position in a university. But even if none of them had changed jobs, the reason for the circle had disappeared, so in all likelihood the circle itself would have dissolved.

There are other examples of SICs from this same time period. Many of the social action programs of the mid-1960s were put together by a group referred to as "young actionists."[37] They included persons like David Hackett, from the Committee on Youth Crime and Juvenile Delinquency, Richard Boone of the White House staff, William Capron from the Council of Economic Advisors, and outsiders like Paul Ylvisaker of the Ford Foundation. Like our circle in educa-tional R&D, they eventually received official sanction and were responsible for putting together program ideas that materialized under Lyndon Johnson as the War on Poverty.

These two examples give the appearance that all SICs are short lived. This may be the case but there also is evidence of informal groupings of bureaucrats outside formal agency settings that persist for long periods of time. As career bureaucrats win recognition for their service beyond their bureau, they can form friendships with their counterparts in other agencies. This process is expedited when they are invited to join a formal organization like the Cosmos Club.[38]

Policies and Growth of Bureaus

Many references have been made so far to the terms policies and policy making—that is, those decisions made in any organization about its goals, their priority ordering, and the delineation of strategies for attaining those goals.[39] Most peo-ple think of federal policies as those enunciated by the president, but they also can be made explicit through decisions of the Supreme Court, from congressional action, or from action of federal agencies. Policies also may be inferred as they evolve out of what Strickland calls the "aggregate of decisions and commitments only indirectly related to one another."[40] Thus:

If nothing else was clear about the national medical research policy in the late 1940s one thing was: it was not going to be established by hard consensus on a grand design. It would be fragmentary and incremental, in short, evolutionary.[41]

Policy processes are messy, take time, and require considerable attention by many persons with many different talents in order to evolve.

In old-time "pork barrel politics," the principal articulator of federal policies were the politicians. But in technocratic politics that task is performed by the bureaucrat. It also rests with the bureaucrat to plot and implement the appropriate strategies and negotiate with whomever is codifying policies.[42] As several authors point out, the people look increasingly these days to the federal government services.

But bureaucratic growth cannot be understood just in terms of the response to citizen demands. As Niskanen also points out, in any particular bureau, public demand is difficult to ascertain, and the bureaucrat frequently is faced with conflicting desires or differing interpretations of demands. These conditions lead many bureaucrats to develop more feasible, operational goals that allow them to get on with their tasks. In fact, it is quite convenient for a bureaucrat to devise operating objectives and procedures that are more related to his life in the bureaucracy than to public concerns. Niskanen calls this "maximizing the budget"—that is, working to obtain more money each year for their bureaus to work with:

A complete statement of the central motivational assumption of this theory is this: bureaucrats maximize the total budget of their bureau during their tenure, subject to the constraint that the budget must be equal to or larger than the minimum total costs of supplying the output expected by the sponsor.[43]

By maximizing his budget over a given period, a bureaucrat gains stature within the bureaucracy through increased staff, larger programs, and, hence, more power. But as Niskanen warns, a bureau must deliver—that is, its promises must live up to the expectations it generates within its sponsor. "A bureau that consistently promises more than it can deliver will be penalized by the discounting of future promises and therefore lower budgets."[44]

Lee Burchinal, formerly a member of the Bureau of Research in USOE and the person credited with founding the Educational Resources Information Center (ERIC), demonstrates that he understood this principle:

One of the rules of the bureaucratic games is that there are upper limits set on any new program or agency. Given reasonalbe consistency of staff some increase can be expected. But there are limits; not hard and fast ones. These are determined in part by the outside appeal of the program, by the internal "efficiency" which usually means how well the staff and manager pay attention to the unwritten as well as written rules of OMB and how well they are perceived by their internal constituents, the administration, congressional staffs, persons like that.
    To get above those limits you must move the program up to a much higher perceived level or get support from a higher level. It depends on the overall budget for the agency what those limits are. In the Bureau of Research any time a program would get above the five million mark, let's say, suddenly it is fair game, targeted for much more examination. In other agencies it might have to be 15 to 20 million. In NSF it is much lower.[45]

What we can deduce from this discussion of maximizing budgets, socialization processes, style, and pecking order among agencies and social circles is that when men and women commit themselves to government service they enter a culture that exerts considerable influence on their lives.[b] Persons outside the government frequently fail to understand the full measure of this influence since there still prevails a stereotype of bureaucrats as paper-pushers who merely pause at their government desks for a few hours each day. The vast majority of bureaucrats, at least the most familiar ones, are conscientious and dedicated. But they can become submerged in their culture, can learn to communicate better among themselves than to outsiders, and can thus find it increasingly difficult to understand what "other" Americans are interested in.

When this author accepted the invitation to work in Washington, D.C., even though it was not a government position, a man who had been induced to try a stint in the government by the Kennedy charisma warned not to stay more than two to three years: "It's an unreal world."

Real or not, it is a world, and it takes persons committed to it to make it work. And outsiders need their "representatives" within the bureaucracy as well as in the legislative branch to protect their interests. The fact that educational R&D has been in trouble in the federal government must be attributed at least in part to the troubles "our" bureaucrats have encountered.

If scientists and scholars don't always understand government, the reverse also is true. So not it is time to turn to the other half of the B-P complex, to highlight what there is about the way the educational R&D community operates that will provide us with additional clues about what happened to educational R&D in the 1960s.

---

[b]I use the term "culture" with reluctance because I agree with Clifford Goertz that the concept has been overused and stretched too thin. I prefer to use the term [of Max Weber that Goertz quotes and endorses] the "sticky web" man weaves for himself. But that will not do in a book like this. See Clifford Goertz, *The Interpretation of Cultures* (New York: Basic Books, Inc., 1973).

2

The Bureaucratic-Professional Complex, Continued: The Outsiders

Beer's use of the term "professional" in describing the complex of persons centrally involved in technocratic politics can be misleading for our purposes. First, there is frequent reference in related literature to the "professional bureaucrat." What is even more bothersome is that we must distinguish educational researchers as a group from the professional educators. So to avoid confusion, the term "outsiders" will be used here to refer to the other portion of the B-P complex, the opposite of the term bureaucrat.

There are many outsider groups to be found in the fifteen-year period that we are examining. Their membership and their influence shifts over time. To help identify who is important for what purposes, we shall use two designations: network and community. The term "constituent"[1] is not included because it has so little relevance in technocratic policies. It is used so frequently by educational researchers, their colleagues in the social and behavioral sciences, and educationists, however, that we must pause to elaborate on that statement.

There can be no denying that the concept of constituencies has significance in understanding the life of the federal government, but in technocratic politics, the currency of exchange is ideas and data more so than votes. A B-P complex, even one composed of thousands of persons, will most likely be spread throughout the country. Few of them will be sufficiently bunched in any given congressional district to form a meaningful voting constituency. Granted, some may be opinion leaders in their respective communities and, as such, influence votes. But, if so, this is an extra bonus. So the use of the term constituencies to describe the groups of researchers or scientists who interact with politicians and bureaucrats can be misleading.

What congressmen and bureaucrats stand to gain from any B-P complex is increased visibility, heightened power, extended contacts with national figures, and, above all, ideas for new policies. Most congressmen want to be part of the informal groupings that form within the legislative branch, the "clubs" as they have been called.[2] There can be a subtle but nevertheless highly important interplay between a congressman's recognition among his peers that enhance his powers within the Congress. The Congress is, after all, another social organization. If a junior member of Congress can gain the reputation as having reliable sources of information and data, he will be more likely to be given choice committee assignments on the assumption that he has other desirable attributes and, therefore, is in a better position to represent his voters.

Becoming integrated into a B-P complex helps congressmen win that recog-

15

nition.[3] The better integrated he or she is in a complex, the more a congressman will be exposed to national leaders, obtain advanced information, and otherwise be on the leading edge of a given policy area. This process is aided by the networks in any complex.

Networks

Merton talks about "networks of personal relations among intellectuals" who are serving an agency—networks that can become self-contained cliques.[4] Marsh and Gortner describe the "compatible and nationwide networks of existing institutions" in education.[5] This term is used to describe the phenomenon of the formation of an interacting informal chain of individuals who want to do something about a given policy; in our case, that is federal policies that affect educational R&D.

Eisenberg and Morey describe this network phenomenon:

The leaders of these attentive groups join with decisionmakers strategically placed within the political system to form a small group we shall describe as the *policy system* . . . . Those who play important roles in policy making have access because they have the skills, expertise, and/or power to participate.[6]

The use of the term "system" may be inappropriate here, because it implies more permanency and durability than networks possess but both terms refer to a circumscribed number of persons who are identifiable because they are interacting with each other for a shared, commonly understood purpose to establish or change given policies.

Networks can be created by persons inside the government; Rourke describes how the Department of State often organized outside groups to support its policies like the Marshall Plan in 1947.[7] But more often they form spontaneously when individuals concerned about government action—or the lack of it—discover others with similar interests.

Networks can form around quite specific policy issues like the Media Research Program of the Office of Education or can be more general (and therefore longer lasting) like agricultural parity programs—or in education, like the network that formed in the late 1950s and persisted until the mid-1960s to obtain federal funding for elementary and secondary education. The research program of the Public Health Service and particularly the National Institutes of Health was well supported for a decade by a network spearheaded by Mary Lasker, her husband, a few other wealthy patrons, some M.D.s, and scientists.[8]

In educational R&D there have been several networks that shaped or helped to shape federal policies. How they operated is described in considerable detail in Chapter 3 of this book, but it is necessary to briefly review their characteristics and some of the activities at this time.

The Foundations-Academic Network

Networks are difficult to label. They are informal, which means they typically involve individuals, not institutions. This gives them a more fluid nature; persons can drift in and out quite readily. Therefore, any label we ascribed to a given network will be as inappropriate as it is accurate.

The network to be described here can be called the Foundation-Academic Network,[a] even though not all the members were employed by foundations and a large number of the members held positions in public school systems, not universities. Nevertheless, the title does cover the professional affiliation of most of the leading members and implies some of the values and the style of operation of the network as a whole.

This network gathered in the late 1950s to improve the quality of education offered in the public schools of the nation. One of the earliest public expressions of this concern appeared in the document that established the Ford Foundation.[9] Two years later this foundation created the Fund for the Advancement of Education. The staff of this subsidiary and several other foundations (like the New World, Russell Sage, and the Carnegie Corporation) and their advisors, principally university professors, corporation executives, and some public school administrators were drawn together during the 1950s. The public school persons tended to be from a different mould than the stereotyped "educationists"; some like Harold Howe II, then Superintendent of Schools in Scarsdale, N.Y., had an Ivy League undergraduate background (his from Yale) and others like James Allen, Jr., Commissioner of Education in New York, completed their graduate work at the Harvard Graduate School of Education (HGSE).

Harvard, in fact, played a key role in this network by contributing both members of its staff as well as many graduates from the HGSE. James B. Conant and Francis Keppel were the best known from the Harvard Community. But not all the academicians came from Harvard by any means. One of the most articulate spokesmen, James I. Goodlad, a graduate of the University of Chicago, was at that time a professor at the University of California at Los Angeles.

How did these men influence R&D policies? One example might suffice. Even before he became Commissioner of Education, Keppel was convinced that there should be a more comprehensive assessment of the state of American education. In conversations with colleagues, he found agreement and support. John Gardner from Carnegie granted the funds to gather together specialists and laymen in several meetings where the ideas for a national assessment were solidified and expanded. The result was the Exploratory Committee for the Assessment of Progress in Education (ECAPE) and eventually the National Assessment of Educational Progress (NAEP).

---

[a]This network had more institutional involvement than most because of the role foundations played.

But there was considerable opposition to any "national testing program" from educational associations and within the Congress. Keppel was able, however, to turn to foundation channels for the necessary financial support and to use significant opinion leaders from the network itself to diffuse opposition, especially from among school administrators (see Chapter 7).

The importance of this network cannot be underestimated for anyone who is trying to understand the way that policies toward education were shaped in Washington during the 1960s. But to fully appreciate how it and other networks functioned, we must digress long enought to review some generalizations about how policy evolves. Think of the process graphically as a parabolic curve. The beginning point for any given policy is very difficult to ascertain, but an idea slowly gathers form as more persons agree with certain beliefs about the way the government should act. Sometimes there are "antecedent events"[10] to federal policies, like foundation programs, White House conferences, or a state or states adopting a given policy. Often congressmen will write bills that they know have no chance of passage but that allow them to air an issue through hearings or simply to get reactions from their fellow congressmen, bureaucrats, and interested outsiders.

The policy process reaches a stage of intense activity usually at the occasion of the policy idea being converted into legislative action. The process does not stop with a bill being signed into law; guidelines are written, and interpretations are made by bureaucrats and later by legal council and the courts themselves. Finally, the persons whom the policy directly affects (i.e., the users of the service) shape the policies by the way they accept the government's programs and the feedback they provide to the bureaucrats and politicians; these networks can influence policies at any place in this process because networks can involve influential people at all levels or at critical places along the paths.

To illustrate this point, let us return to the sample network. Beginning with the Kennedy administration and lasting into the Nixon presidency, persons from the foundations and their colleagues were advisors on major educational policy issues: John Gardner not only chaired a key task force during the Johnson administration but later became Secretary of DHEW. Keppel, in addition to being Commissioner of Education, was a member of the Task Force on Education appointed by President Kennedy. James Allen was appointed commissioner even though new staff entered the White House after Nixon's election. His replacement Sidney Marland, had been included in many of the activities of the Ford Foundation. (The city of which he was superintendent of schools, Pittsburgh, received several large Ford Foundation grants in the 1960s.) Even at some second echelon positions, there were persons who were of, or who used, this network as a reference group—men like David Seeley, a Yale undergraduate and a staff man at HGSE, and Wade Robinson, also a former HGSE staffer.

Policies are affected not only by individuals, however, but more widely by prevailing attitudes that can influence persons not directly involved with the network itself. The foundation-academic network had some very decided opinions about educational research. As might be expected from their backgrounds, they respected scholarship highly. Yet, theirs was a very elitist approach that favored the individual, highly visible scholar. Keppel himself saw the torch of scholarship being passed from individual to individual over the generations with no more than a handful of men at any one time deserving of plaudits.[11] These views were widely shared at Harvard as evidenced by the comments of colleagues or fomer colleagues like Daniel Moynihan, Sheldon White, and Christopher Jencks (see Chapter 8).

Similar ideas were expressed in slightly different form by Ford Foundation officials. The directors of the Fund showed little sympathy for social science in general but educational research in particular.[12] The officials of the Fund, like the larger network, stored its faith in the accumulative effects of better prepared men and women placed in key teaching and administrative positions throughout the educational system of this country.[13]

Between 1952 and 1959 the Fund spent $9.6 million through some sixty colleages and universities to improve teacher selection and education.[14] The majority of these funds went to institutions in the northeastern part of the United States, apparently justifying the charge of some Ford critics that it had an Ivy League bias.[15]

Training was only part of the strategy. The Fund and others in this network (like James Conant in his research for his books) actively sought out the imaginative, the demonstratively more capable administrators already in the educational system; many of these later were recommended for more influential positions. For teachers they were able to use programs like the John Hay Whitney Program (also funded by Ford).

How were these more capable teachers and administrators going to improve the schools? Through new innovations, which really meant inventions. The terms refer to the new ideas in teaching procedures, curricula, administrative practices and organizational arrangements that are devised from knowledge based on experience, not research derived data. The big ideas of the late 1950s and early 1960s that were "favored" by Ford (like team teaching, nongraded schools, educational parks, open schools) had not emerged from solid research evidence, and precious little was gathered from the evaluations.

Those men and women who considered themselves to be educational researchers during those years saw the foundations, particularly Ford, as antiresearch and biased against the midwestern land grant colleges. They saw themselves as being the only group concerned with building a scientific base for educational change. But the men and women who made up this network believed otherwise: they saw themselves as reestablishing standards of excellence, not just for educational scholarship but for the entire educational enterprise. As we shall see, these differing points of view persisted into the 1970s and indeed, continue to exist today.

Other examples could be cited, but the foundation-academic network demonstrates how networks function and how their members can influence federal policies. There is one more point to be made: the significance of overlapping memberships. Most of the men cited in this section are well known to students of modern day history of education. This is because the leaders have been active in many groups influencing federal policies. Francis Keppel, even before he became Commissioner of Education, was one of these as was Gardner and Ralph Tyler. This linking function is extremely important in fashioning common denominator policy ideas through informal processes long before formal bargaining becomes necessary. For example, Keppel and Allen, in discussions with the Gardner Task Force, worked hard to win support for ideas that would strengthen state educational agencies, a position that later was translated into Title V of ESEA, which won considerable support for that bill.[16] Being a member of some networks of educational practitioners, Keppel was aware of what other groups viewed as important.

Many persons who join together in networks do so because of friendships or collegial relationships. For example, Ralph Tyler and Samuel Brownell, Commissioner of Education who fashioned the Cooperative Research Program in 1954, were childhood neighbors and friends. Howe was a roommate at Yale and godfather to one of the children of McGeorge Bundy. It is important, but perhaps obvious, to point out that friendship circles and policy networks are not the same. At the same time there is predisposition or a tendency for policy networks to work and grow through other informal channels,—whether they be friendships or collegial relationships. A clue to why this is so appears in comments by Henry Loomis who served as deputy commissioner under Keppel:

[Keppel and I] knew the same people, we knew the same clubs. We had gone—to the same kind of school. Our way of thinking, although it is quite different on the details, I being more of a management-oriented guy, was similar enough so that we could communicate in shorthand right off the bat.[17]

Networks are only one way that outsiders cluster to influence federal policies. Let us now turn to a different kind of collective influence, a community.

The Public Affairs Subcommunity of Scientists

There has emerged in the scientific fields what Waldo[18] calls a "scientific affairs community." Brooks[19] calls it a "complex of interlocking networks of scientific advisors, and Gilpin[20] sees that the scientific advisory function has become professionalized and shaped into a hierarchy that parallels the hierarchy of the government itself. Some authors[21] estimate that it is comprised of about 200 to 300 critical members.

It is important to understand what is meant by this term "public affairs subcommunity" because it is a key concept in explaining what has happened in educational R&D. To be more exact, a subcommunity of this nature has not materialized. This fact, in turn, explains many of the difficulties the field and the federal government have experienced with each other. So let us examine how these subcommunities have functioned in other fields.

Before World War II, scientific research could be characterized as small and personal. The foundations and the universities, the principal sources of support, operated on laissez-faire principles that granted considerable independence to all mature scientists. This was the world to which most scientists preferred to return after the war—with an added ingredient of federal funding. But they expected these funds to carry little further obligation than had monies from other donors. Scientists saw little need then to mix in much with the political processes of the government.[22] They expected that whatever was needed from government could be arranged by a small handful of their colleagues.

The laissez-faire system, because it was not bound by rigid explicit policies demanded "well-routed practice and customs."[23] There developed what Brooks calls a "connoisseurship" of science advising; those scientists who were interested in these tasks had to be socialized to their job.[24]

But as the government grew and demanded more help from scientists, this behind-the-scenes informal system was found wanting. There were a number of growing criticisms about the abuses of the "in-groups," some of whom had become too tame to criticize the mistakes of the agencies supporting them. As Goodell says, "After less than twenty years, the advisory system was showing signs of old age."[25]

Even more serious was the fact that some scientists had begun to lobby—for example, during the MURA controversy when several laboratories were bidding for the same funds, and when the NSF supported MOHOLE project was under attack in Congress.[26] In both cases, scientists resorted to power politics and lobbying tactics that helped to tarnish the image of science held by many politicians and private citizens.

The informal way of advising also was strained when, during the 1950s, new agencies were created within the federal structure to better develop and implement policies in science. By the 1960s, the NSF, the Atomic Energy Commission, and the National Institutes of Health, to mention just the three most prominent, increasingly involved scientists in their affairs. By then, the higher education system of the nation was inexorably tied to the government funding of research and development. All this demanded more policy-making machinery at a higher level. So new offices like the President's Science Advisor and the Office of Science and Technology (OST) were created and scientific advising became more sophisticated.[27]

What emerged to help manage all this is what is referred to here as a public affairs subcommunity of scientists. It consists of scientists with demonstrated technical credentials who are tapped because of some interest in and competence to operate with public policies. The tapping takes the form of selecting col-

leagues for other purposes—journal editorships, association offices—which unlike those acts is not the sole purview of scientists themselves.

Actually this subcommunity is composed of a mixture of scientists, science administrators (like Harvey Brooks and Don Price, deans at Harvard) and federal bureaucrats. Most of the latter group have had some training in a scientific field— for example, Glenn Bryan, Director of Psychological Sciences Division of the Office of Naval Research, is a trained experimental psychologist; before psychologist Henry Riecken was the vice president and president of the Social Science Research Council, he served as Associate Director of Education in NSF.

How do these subcommunities relate to the networks described in the previous section? Each can be viewed as a pool of manpower from whence emerge members of networks. Remember, networks crystalize to influence specific policies so they almost always include persons outside fields of science, politicians, philanthropists, private citizens, and so forth. One of the purposes of the public affairs subcommunity is to keep scientists informed and abreast of present happenings in government that are of concern to scientific fields. As anyone who has served as advisor to a federal agency can attest, it takes a lot of work to keep abreast with what is happening in Washington and among programs funded by the government. Policies and personnel can change rapidly at times, but even when programs are in a fairly steady state, there are events that require the attention of outsiders: the evaluation of existing programs, planning for future policies, the need to inform and educate other bureaucrats and congressmen, conferences to apprise the state of the art in particular fields, and the advising of government agencies on how to best administer and regulate research programs. Many of these events can have a direct bearing on the work of a scientist. As when BOB, fearful that studies funded by the federal gorvernment would become politically controversial, required all social scientists to submit questionnaires to them for clearance in advance of funding. And policies preventing copyrights for materials produced with government funds has been hotly contested.

The scientists who are on a first-name basis with key bureaucrats are kept abreast of these developments through informal, or gossip, channels as well as formal communication. In turn, they share what they know with their colleagues at their sponsoring institution and those others they meet regularly at meetings and conferences and with whom they interact at regular intervals. From these communications and discussions, they get feedback from their colleagues that help them provide more sensible advice to bureaucrats and politicians.

These interactions also serve another purpose—to give individual advisors greater confidence in advocating his or her policy ideas. Scientists by tradition and training are not accustomed, like many other groups in our society, to devising party lines.[28] Whether it is an issue of expenditures for weaponry, the uses of vitamin C, or the proposed reorganization of a government agency, options of individual scientists will be respected by colleagues since each scientist is presumed to be acting (1) from his conscience and (2) from his best interpretation of what

data are available. Yet, all individuals are limited in the extent to which he or she can stand alone on a given issue; knowing that his or her views are shared by some respected colleagues, even if not by all, provides support.

Most politicians are baffled by the way scientists operate in the policy sphere. The overt and covert bargaining processes of trade, industrial, and labor organization are politically recognizeable; politicians have difficulty comprehending why scientists and scholars don't behave in the same manner. Parenthetically it must be added that many educational researchers also do not understand these differences: how often has been heard the comment that since a consensus cannot (and should not) be obtained on a given issue, no individual researcher should comment on it.[29]

Among the more sophisticated sciences, the subcommunity now operates in elaborate and complex ways. Consider the reaction of the subcommunity of medical researchers to the attempts to create a new national cancer authority in 1971. In July of that year, the Senate passed a bill by a vote of 79 to 1 that created a new cancer cure program and housed it in a newly devised segment of the NIH in ways that gave it virtual autonomy from the management—and the advisory structure—of the Institutes. Working hard for this was what Strickland called the "new cancer lobby" that operated outside the community of scientists.[30] As Strickland goes on to say, they "failed to calculate the difference in size and sophistication of the university-based science community in 1971 from that of the 1950s. The new sophistication included not only much wider awareness of how support programs operate; it included as well a dramatic increase in willingness to try to affect such outcomes and not merely to leave them to 'political forces'."[31] The final result was a dramatic turn-around in the House of Representatives where a different bill was passed by 350 to 5. This one supported the concept of keeping the cancer program within NIH. Says Strickland, "American biomedical science had had their day in the House,"[32] for the bill signed by President Nixon was substantially that approved by the House.

While this story is intended to illustrate how the public affairs subcommunity can operate, it also dramatizes how another network of people might decide an issue if scientists do not take action, and that, unfortunately, is the story of educational R&D in the 1960s. So let us describe how that happened.

The Educational R&D Community—an Undeveloped Public Affairs Subcommunity

Before we can discuss the way public affairs are handled in educational research, we must establish whether or not there is such an entity as a community of researchers and developers in education. To answer the question, in 1967 the American Educational Research Association contracted for several studies, commissioned papers, and finally convened everyone involved for a colloquium, one purpose of which was to determine whether indeed there was a viable community of researchers in education. The conclusion was: yes, educational R&D had the communication structure, the social organization, and identifiable sources of support and was of sufficient size to warrant the definition of a "community."[33] Furthermore, there were indications that expanding career opportunities, new institutional forms, and a growing sense of excitement about new issues were attracting an even larger number of competent scholars from the social and behavioral sciences.[b]

But what kind of community was it? As Bidwell has pointed out, the field of study for which the community was created is not a discipline.[34] And Storer thinks it highly unlikely that educational research "can even be developed in such a way as to enable its adherents to enjoy the advantages that characterize the hard, basic scientific disciplines."[35] There is even some doubt about just where it fits among the social and behavioral sciences. Yet, because the leading educational researchers aspire to be scholars and scientists—that is, men and women who regard themselves "as specializing in the cultivation of knowledge"[36]—they interact with each other and organize themselves like the other fields of science. For example, top priority was given by the governing board of the American Educational Research Association during the decade of the 1960s to expanding and improving the quality of the communication mechanisms that flowed through the Association. A new technical journal was founded in 1964; a new review publication established in 1970; new procedures were added in the 1960s to the annual meeting to make it more selective. Further evidence was the decision in 1967 to break away from the National Education Association, of which AERA had been an affiliate since the 1930s; the leadership decided that it was easier to establish an image as a scholarly society independent from NEA. This example has been cited to support the contention that we can use what has been learned about how scientists interact with each other as a community to help us better understand how educational researchers behave.

How Scientific Communities Function

In all scientific communities the social structure is designed to facilitate the work of individual researchers. As the many sociologists of science point out, a scientist needs colleagues because in the final analysis, it is concensus among the most

[b]There were disagreements on this last point. As Cronbach and Suppes stated in another source, "But it is not at all certain that the full potential of the scholarly community will be realized. There are misconceptions about the nature of scholarly work and its relation to education practice, and these misconceptions divert efforts into unprofitable channels. The course of inquiry is shaped by the ways in which resources are allocated, research institutions administered, and educational innovations adapted." *Research for Tomorrow's Schools,* Lee J. Cronbach and Patrick Suppes (ed.), London, Macmillan Co., 1969, p. 7.

competent men and women that determines what constitutes a body of knowledge.[37] He interacts with a relevant group of colleagues who provide the feedback he needs, and from whom, ultimately, he must seek acceptability for his
findings. So clusters are formed that are called "social circles":

> The social circle is not well instituted compared to the bureaucracy or even to
> less formalized entities such as the tribe or the family. Members of a social circle
> come together on the basis of their interests more often than on the basis of pro-
> pinquity or ascribed status. Members of a research area are brought together by
> their commitment to a particular approach to a set of problems.[38]

Social circles are quite fluid in composition; a person remains a member only so
long as he remains productive, hence current, in his research.

So far we have only described one purpose for the social organization of
scientists; there are other functions. Consider that, as Polanyi describes it, a
scientist must first learn to believe before he can know—that is, to learn how and
what to believe, whom to accept as authorities, and what knowledge to accept as
his base line.[39] And Odegard talks about the morality that science can describe
as its own—a morality that protects the rights of individuals and the processes
used in the search for truth.[40] In other words, young scientists must be socialized and practicing scientists must be "governed."

This government of science has been described as "undisciplined"[41] and an
"amorphous landscape."[42] Yet, there is a governance whose function, according
to Polanyi, "is not to initiate but to grant or to withhold opportunity for research,
publication and teaching, to endorse or discredit contributions put forward by
individuals."[43] The governors" are an elite group, sometimes called an invisible
college, elevated by virtue of their demonstrated competencies through their contributions to the substantive field of study.[44]

These details about the operations of scientific communities are presented
not just because far too few educationists and bureaucrats understand them, but
because it helps further to explain the stance taken by most of the leaders of the
educational research community towards the federal government. It was the same
stance roughly as that adopted by the hard scientists in their early stages of interacting with the government in the early 1950s. Let me explain.

For USOE the first stage in research support occurred roughly from 1956
to 1965. But then matters appeared to change almost overnight. Actually, the
changing began in the early 1960s under the commissionership of Sterling McMurrin, but it took the dynamics of Lyndon Johnson and the Elementary and Secondary Education Act to step up the process. USOE was transformed from a
quiet, stuffy repository for odd, outdated statistics and near-retirement age educational "specialists" to an agency that was expected to become a phalanx in
the battles aginst social and economic ills. The research programs (i.e., the staffs
of bureaus funding research) were expected to do their part. Research was ex-

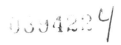

pected to contribute data in support of or that would lead to changes in policies. New advisors were sought out who could help the Office find solutions from research to pressing educational problems. Many of these persons, like Henry Brickell, Elvin Svenson and Roger Levien, were not persons regarded as leaders in the R&D community. This says nothing about their capabilities; most of those tapped by USOE were talented. The point to be made is that the bureaucrats by that time were not interacting with any significant segment, that is, the elite group of the educational R&D community. And while that group by and large disapproved of the policy and personnel shifts in USOE, they failed to take effective action to alter them. One explanation for this is because educational researchers believed, as did the hard scientists at one point, that any form of self-initiated, collective action would compromise their status as scientists.

What many in education were not aware of then (nor now) is that among the scientific communities this latter belief is riddled with doubts. Scientific news journals like *Science* regularly contain articles debating how men and women of science can best spend the taxpayer's dollar and best relate to politicians and bureaucrats—in short, how they can best influence public policies.[45] And they have done more than talk; their associations have become more active in Washington and they have created new mechanisms to deal with policy issues like the Committee on Science and Public Policy of the National Academy of Sciences (COSPUP).[46]

The inability of educational researchers to respond to events in the government transcends prevailing beliefs, however; it reflects the fact the community of researchers did not have its counterpart to the public affairs subcommunities operating in the hard sciences. Moynihan sensed this vacuum when he said:

> . . . there is a need for the development in the field of education policy and of social policy generally, of that rare and wonderous quality of intellect that is to be seen in men such as George Kistiakowsky and Jerome Wiesner which can serve as conduits between the world of the natural sciences and that of public policy.[47]

Moynihan deals in individuals, but there is a larger entity—something greater than the sum of its parts. How this subcommunity might best operate with the government is a subject dealt with in the final chapter, there were many devoted individuals who gave unstintingly of their time and talents—too many to single out here. They struggled to get the best decisions possible out of USOE that would produce the best possible knowledge of how to improve education. But the forces with which they had to contend in the government were too overwhelming, the pace too rapid, and the demands of scholarship in education too great.[48]

The result was that bureaucracy was too much on its own. It had a ready rationale: research in education was not good enough. So they chose to work with too few persons from the outside who were involved in the give-and-take on policy issues with leaders or the larger R&D community. Policies became quite temporary thereby, since each successive director of the research bureau—and there were six between the years 1965 and 1972—was relatively free to select priorities and advisors as he chose. Hence the more persistent and consistent pressures came from inside the government—for example, the planning and budgeting officers in DHEW and BOB. As BR increasingly responded to these pressures, they further alienated itself from external groups and left the staff scrambling to find a "constituency" for support. This isolation made the USOE research program more vulnerable still to the forces that operate within the bureaucracy, specifically to the special interest circle described previously. The reader may now better understand the consequences of a malfunctioning B-P complex: both sides suffer when this occurs, and the need for both to aid and abet the development of the other is underscored.

The relationship must be continuously evolving; outsiders are not needed just in the beginning when policies are being formulated, for as we have demonstrated, the policy process is a continuous one. Original intentions are subjected to conflicting forces and can be ground down into something quite different from what was initiated. Consider this quotation:

The staff who worked on the 1965 ESEA are what I call the second generation of federal aid people. They were the breakthrough people, those who believed, the Charlie Lees and the Sam Halperins. The third generation are the technicians. We concentrate on administrative mechanisms rather than on subject matter. We never ask the question anymore, does Title I (ESEA) work. The more important question is, how do we get it extended, how do we get the money![49]

Summary of the B-P Complex

Let us summarize what has been said in these first two chapters. The increased use of specialized knowledge by the federal government has produced and been produced by a more highly trained bureaucracy. Because professional bureaucrats are socialized into and frequently interact with professional colleagues outside the government they have formed what Beers has labeled a bureaucratic-professional complex.

While there are similarities between these two parts of the complex that come from similar graduate training and have overlapping and mutual goals, there also are many differences. New bureaucrats tend to adopt the values and norms of and tend to seek out informal social and collegial relationships in what is considered by some to be a bureaucratic culture. Within that culture, there is a pecking order of agencies and informal social groups, the membership in which are determined as much by the style of individuals as by their successes with their professional tasks. Success on the job is determined as much by their ability to increase their budgets over the years as by other measures.

The outside professionals relate to the bureaucracy through informal group-ings called networks that form around specific policies or policy areas. In the sciences, a small percentage rise up or are tapped to serve the public affairs inter-ests of the community. As they grow in number over time, they tend to form a subcommunity from which comes most of the advisors to the government and those who join policy networks. This public affairs subcommunity serves to keep a selected group of scientists informed about the activities of the government so that the subcommunity then can better serve the larger interests of scientists. This is important because experience shows that in our pluralistic society many groups usually are interested in shaping any given federal policy; when scientists do not exert their influence, policies will be shaped by others.

The educational R&D complex was not sufficiently formed in the 1960s to be equal to the tasks demanded of it when the federal government increased its funding of and its demands on educational research. Other networks had greater influence on the formulation of these R&D policies. But because the complex had not evolved in the process, the Bureau of Research emerged in an independent position. However, within the government an informal group, called here a special interest circle, that was assembled from several agencies attempted to re-shape the R&D policies, but had little success at first. It remained submerged until Nixon assumed the presidency and then emerged as a dominant group. This special interest circle was largely responsible for creating the NIE.

So much for our summary. Let us get on with a more detailed description of the events from which these generalizations have been drawn.

3   Education and Educational Research, Circa 1960

How did the federal government become involved in educational R&D? Who worked to bring this about? Once involved, how did it attempt to intervene? What ideas from research commanded the most attention of policy makers? How did they expect to use educational research?

To understand the answers to these and related questions it is necessary to understand what was happening to the broader field of education in the late 1950s and early 1960s and the growing interest throughout the federal government in the production of new knowledge. To help organize and highlight the most relevant events from these years, this chapter is divided into three sections. The first will give a general background of what was happening in education that influenced events in educational R&D. The second section describes some of the characteristics of the educational R&D field itself. The third discusses the kinds of interventions into this field by the federal government and foundations. In all three, we shall set the stage for an examination in subsequent chapters of the impact that the federal government had on educational R&D.

The Larger Context of Education

Education never seems to be far below the surface of public interest, but in the 1950s that concern was more intense than at most times. As Woodring put it: "At midcentury the nation was ready for substantial changes in education. It was obvious that the kind and quality of education that had been provided to American children during the first half of the twentieth century would not be adequate for children who would spend a part of their lives in the twenty-first."[1]

Added to these general feelings of discontent were many very concrete matters: there were not enough teachers and far too many were ill prepared. A cause of the shortage and a problem in its own right, was the teacher's economic condition.[2] To the Eisenhower administration, the most pressing problem seemed to be the lack of suitable classrooms.[3] Education was caught in the crunch of years of neglect that stretched back to the 1930s and was aggravated by a continued growth in student population caused by high birth rates in the 1950s and unexpected increases in the numbers who remained in school through grade twelve. Higher education was hit in the late 1950s. There were groans within all segments of the enterprise, and there were gorans outside, too!

Beginning with publications like *Educational Wastelands* by Arthur Bestor published in 1953 and *Quackery in the Public Schools* by Albert Lynd, the dissatisfaction with the schools and those who were running them commanded national, public attention. Many more books followed some of which, like *Why Johnny Can't Read* by Rudolph Flesch, became best sellers. Fortunately, the discontent produced more than rhetoric.

The results lead to a story that is far too complex and lengthy to be adequately treated here. (For an excellent summary the reader is referred to the chapter entitled, "Epilogue" in David Tyack's *The One Best System,* Harvard paperback, 1974). We must select those events that had more implications for the eventual involvement of the Federal Government in educational R&D than others.

One way of selecting is by taking those policies that emerged in educational R&D in the mid 1960s, identifying those groups of people who espoused and influenced relevant policies, and tracing their genesis. We can identify three significant networks of people whose views on education and research are important to our story. (For a definition of networks see Chapter 2). The first of these came out of the national leadership of the business community. The second emerged from among the national scientific leaders. A third was composed of persons from groups concerned about schooling for urban poor children and underpriviledged minorities. We call this group social actionists.

Concern for Education among the National Business Leaders

The national leaders in the business and industrial community did not continue their interest in public education after the World War I years when they unexpectedly joined with labor to support the Smith–Hughes Act,[4] but interest was revived following World War II.

Businessmen began to hear speeches like that given by Frank Abrams, then chairman of the board of Standard Oil of New Jersey, who called upon the business and industrial world to take more interest in and give greater support to public education.[5] More important than the rhetoric were the organizations they created to take action.

One of these can be traced to the efforts of James Conant. Following a series of meetings that had been organized through his efforts, the National Citizens Commission for the Public Schools was founded in 1949. Spearheaded and then chaired by Roy E. Larsen, himself a public school graduate who had won considerable recognition as the head of Time–Life, Inc., the Commission served as a conduit for information and ideas needed to improve schools through action at the state and local level. It served as a model for local groups and as a catalyst for the renewed interest in public education among business and professional men and women.

The Ford Foundation also played an important role. The distinguished committee that advised on programs and policies at the time of its founding in 1949 recommended that education be given a high priority because it had received from its advisors evidence "of an unusual degree of dissatisfaction with educational institutions and influences which now operate in our society."[6] In 1951, the Foundation created the Fund for the Advancement of Education. Although the Fund managed to get itself embroiled in heated political as well as educational controversies, which threatened for awhile to alienate it from the very groups that had created it (and caused the parent foundation to pull it close to its control), it also managed to involve—and educate—some recognized and respected leaders in the business world. In addition to Roy Larsen and Frank Abrams, these included men like Charles Dickey from J.P. Morgan and Co. and Philip Read from General Electric.

To understand the importance of these men and the views they held is to understand the social structure of the American business community at its highest levels. It has been termed the "Establishment"[7] and is a complex structure of many men and women who have risent to prominence, by virtue of individual or family talents, in the economic life of the nation. They are persons who accept and share policy responsibilities not only for the firms with which they were employed but for the economic and political life of this nation. Halberstam's descriptions are helpful. He refers to them as:

That small group of policymakers (who) came from the great banking houses and law firms of New York and Boston. They knew one another, were linked to one another, and they guided America's national security in those years. . . .
They were men linked more to one another, their schools, their own social class and their own concerns than they were linked to the country.[8]

Roby talks about an "elite group" of the corporate establishment.[9] Vannevar Bush describes his host (William Cameron Forbes) during a visit to Maine in the 1920s (at which time he met Herbert Hoover) as "one of the descendants of the Boston men of affairs who molded the nineteenth and much of the twentieth century."[10] Throughout the 1950s, a small but significant number of these men struggled to devise ways to improve the public schools. As difficult as it was for many of them to swallow, they finally recognized that federal funds were needed Consider this statement from a 1959 publication of the Committee for Economic Development, an organization composed mostly of (more liberal) recognized businessmen that served to articulate major issues:

While we regret the necessity for any further expansion of the Federal role, we do find Federal supplementation of state and local funds necessary for the improvement of schools in the poorer states.[11]

By the time John F. Kennedy was elected to the presidency in 1960 there was a discernible network of business leaders and academicians (like Beardsley

Rummel and Theodore Schultz) who were recommending that the federal government adopt a different, more active posture toward the public schools. They communicated these views to and were shaped by a line of advisors from places like Harvard University, Columbia University, and Chicago University. It had become obvious that more than just the educationists and their supporters (like the PTA and the associations for school board members) wanted federal assistance to education.

The form this aid would take and whether or not it would include support for research could not be determined in 1960. But there is evidence that these men were favorably disposed toward educational research. The CED publication referred to above carries this statement:

Methods of determining what is useful and accelerating the adoption of proven ideas may well be the greatest need of all in our educational system.[12]

This sentence was used as the jumping-off place for another CED report produced nine years later, "Innovation in Education: New Directions for the American School," which carried the following recommendation:

We therefore urge the expansion of government and private financing of research in all phases of educational theory, practice and evaluation.[13]

It is not difficult to deduce that these businessmen, most of whom were employed by firms whose present and future health rested on the application of new knowledge would be sympathetic to the need for more, and better, educational R&D.[14] In fact, some of them, as we shall see, already were supporting research in education as defined by a group of scientists. This leads us to a description of the second network of importance.

The Interest among Scientists and Scholars

The second group among whom concern for improving the public schools grew in the 1950s was the scientists and scholars. As early as 1945, in the now legendary Bush report, *Science, the Endless Frontier,* written to answer F.D. Roosevelt's question of how government and science could work together after the war was this comment: ". . . much remains to be done to make our educational system effective in developing the latent talent of the nation by improving the quality of the secondary schools. . . ."[15]

The science community was slow to involve itself. Throughout the period of the late 1940s and early 1950s scientists remained as aloof from the public school scene as they had for the preceeding several decades. The National Science Foundation, the direct outgrowth of the Bush report, served in some ways as a barometer of their interest; it wasn't until 1954 that NSF made any organized attempt to improve teaching below the college level. The first summer institute for high school teachers was funded that year; by 1960, it was supporting 67 institutes in 42 different institutions.[16]

While first priority had been given to the preparation of teachers, the Sixth Annual Report in 1956 indicates a shift in policy by acknowledging the need for up-to-date courses of study. So the Foundation was receptive when approached by Jerold Zacharias, Professor of Physics, M.I.T., in August of 1956 with a proposal to produce a series of teaching films in physics. Anticipating support and moving in his characteristically direct and aggressive fashion, Zacharias convened a group of "first team" scientists and respected administrators before NSF responded formally; his original ideas were expanded considerably and he aimed at producing an entire course.

NSF bought the Zacharias proposal to support the Physical Sciences Study Committee (PSSC) with a grant of almost $450,000 in FY 1957.[17] The Course Content Improvement Program (CCIP) from which this grant was made had been operating since 1954, but the PSSC support marked a noticeable increase in operations; the total expenditures for CCI had been only $18,463 in FY 1956. By 1960, the NSF was spending over $5 million for curriculum development spread among a dozen projects, which included (in addition to the PSSC): the School Mathematics Study Group, chaired by Professor E.G. Begle then at Yale University; the Biological Sciences Curriculum Study, directed by William V. Mayer originally with the American Institute of Biological Sciences; Chemical Education Material Study, chaired by George C. Pimentel, University of California at Berkeley; and Experimental Teaching of Mathematics in the Elementary School, Patrick Suppes, Director, Stanford University. Goodlad, reviewing this movement, was to say, "Clearly a massive reformation of what is to be taught and learned in the schools of the United States of America is underway."[18]

The interest by scientists in public school education also created a network of persons, some of whom were to have much to say about what the federal government was to do in the years to come. Jerold Zacharias became the best known, both in and outside the government. Accustomed to moving among men of influence as well as competence, he drew together outstanding scientists like I.I. Rabi, a Nobel laureate in physics, and administrators like President James Killian of M.I.T., Edwin Land, President of Polaroid Corporation, and others like Jerome Brunner, psychologist from Harvard, to work on problems of instruction in the schools.

While the PSSC group became the most visible and powerful among federal government advisors, each of the other curriculum improvement projects had circles of advisors among mathematicians, biologists, chemists, and eventually even social scientists.[19] It was from this pool that emerged the network that was such an active force on the federal policies in education in the mid and late 1960s.

The Interest among the Social Actionists

The third network of importance actually was a composite of two other networks: those who were interested in the problems of juvenile delinquency and others who were working for urban renewal.[20] In juvenile delinquency, the emphasis shifted from putting more federal funds into old efforts to experimenting with new approaches. This brought the social actionists into a different working relationship with the intellectuals; one of the models became the Mobilization for Youth project in the Harlem district of New York City. The intellectuals most closely identified there were Lloyd Ohlin and Richard Cloward from the Columbia University School of Social Work, but there were many others working on efforts funded by the National Institute of Mental Health or by foundations like the Ford, Markle, Carnegie, and New World.[21]

When John F. Kennedy added the problems of delinquency to his laundry list for governmental action, he assigned to his brother Robert the task of shaping a program. RFK, in turn, brought in an old college friend, David Hackett, who quickly tapped the network operating through the foundation projects. Ohlin, Paul Ylvisaker, from the Public Affairs Division of the Ford Foundation, and others helped him launch the President's Committee on Juvenile Delinquency and Youth Crime.

The second network emerged from the interest in the 1950s in urban renewal—the struggle to save the cities. By the mid 1950s attention had shifted from the physical setting to a more balanced approach that included improvements in social services to humans. Here again were the staff members of several foundations, the most visible being the Public Affairs staff at the Ford Foundation. Ylvisaker and his compatriot David Hunter wanted the renewed sections of urban areas to become the focus for improved living conditions and, as in New Haven, Connecticut, which became the model, the center for community action was to be the school. This led Ylvisaker to work more closely with several large-city superintendents, and in the 1960s he earmarked one-and-one-fourth million dollars for seven projects in seven large-city school districts (in addition to the Mobilization for Youth and New Haven) designed to improve the education for children from the slums. Another grant went to a state, North Carolina, where Terry Sanford was governor. Placed in charge of this project, called the Learning Institute of North Carolina (LINC), was Harold Howe II later to become commissioner of education.

In the early 1960s it was the Ford Foundation and the President's Committee that set the pace and the style for tackling social problems. There were differences in their approach but there were just as many similarities. As Marris and Rein point out, both organizations were drawing from the same fund of ideas. As they explain:

Inspired by a common philosophy, the projects also introduced a similar range of experiment—education innovations, both in and out of the classroom, on the lines

of the earlier great cities schools program; vocational training and employment services for young people; legal aid and community service centers.[22]

These networks were to converge in the mid 1960s to fight President Johnson's "War on Poverty" and to shape the Office of Economic Opportunity. The
approach of that agency showed many differences over that taken by the Com-
mitee and the Ford Foundation, but it included an emphasis on the project approach and on the use of social science knowledge in designing and evaluating
those projects.[23]

Two further comments must be made about the social actionists. They consisted almost exclusively of intellectuals. As Moynihan put it:

The War on Poverty—rather like the War in Vietnam—was preeminently the con-
ception of the liberal, policy-oriented intellectuals, especially those who gathered
in Washington and in a significant sense came to power in the early 1960s under
the Presidency of John F. Kennedy.[24]

Secondly, persons who were involved in the civil rights movement had limited impact on the policies described above. As Moynihan points out, ". . . no
Negro was involved in any significant way at any significant stage in planning the
Economic Opportunity Act of 1964."[25] This is not to say that events and people engaged in those events in the late 1950s the early 1960s that led to the civil
rights legislation of 1957, 1960, and again in 1964 did not have impact on educational policies; quite the reverse is true. (Keppel maintains that the push to improve the life for the minorities, especially the blacks, was one of the major
contributing factors to the passage of the Elementary and Secondary Education
Act of 1964.)[26] But as Sundquist points out, the civil rights movement had
turned away from Washington following the passage of the Civil Rights Act of
1957 to work in the streets of the South.[27]

The Accumulative Effect

One way of assessing the effects of these networks is to identify those persons
who play such prominent roles in this analysis. James Conant, as we already have
shown, was instrumental in helping to stir up and channel interest in education
among the business community; he was also a long-time advisor to the National
Science Foundation and had, in fact, been a member of the so-called Moe Committee that wrote that section of the Bush report, *The Endless Frontier,*[28] that
recommended the need to improve public schools. Finally his book, *Slums and
Suburbs,*[29] published in 1961, spurred on efforts to improve the schools in the
urban centers and improve education for the poor.

John Gardner became increasingly involved in educational issues during
these years. Through the Carnegie Corporation, of which he was president, he

supported several of the curriculum reform projects like the School Mathematics Study Group at the University of Illinois, PSSC, and even helped Zacharias launch his new organization, ESI. Edwin Land, a member of the Board of Trustees of ESI and a charter member of the Board of Directors of PSSC also was on the Research and Policy Committee of the CED. Ralph Tyler was on the National Science Board of the NSF, served as advisor to the CED, and, as we shall see, was chairman of the Research Advisory Committee of the Office of Education. Frank Keppel was influential among key persons in all three networks through collegial relationships at Harvard, and because he was highly respected, he was frequently sought as advisor by the leading foundations. Paul Ylvisaker from the Ford Foundation was one of the most-listened-to advisors for the poverty programs and was active in promoting reforms among big-city school systems.

What does all this mean for educational research? The answers to this question will become more clear as the story unfolds. Each network was formed because of concern about other issues; yet their ideas carried implications for research policies. Businessmen, as we have noted, wanted more innovations in the schools. Some social actionists were hoping to build their social experiments on verifiable research findings and to use scientific procedures to evaluate their projects. And the scientists defined their development of new curricula as educational R&D. While each of these views won adherents within the bureaucracy, the result was differing, and often contradictory, postures toward research and development in education.

A second remarkable feature of these networks is how little they reflected the prevailing views within the educational R&D community, the group that in the final analysis had to be responsible for the quality and the direction of the work to be done. And no wonder. There were very few persons included in the networks who though of themselves as being part of the educational R&D community; not many more were consulted as advisors. Ralph Tyler is the most notable exception.

Why this was so and the reasons for it is the focus of our next section, to which we now turn. It is time to examine what had been happening to the field of educational research during this same time period.[30]

The Condition of Educational Research, Circa 1960

In 1956 Carter Good estimated that the annual output of doctoral dissertations in education exceeded 1,400 and that the grand total of studies in education was "well beyond" 100,000.[31] Bloom claimes that in the years 1940–1965 approximately 70,000 titles were listed in the *Review of Educational Research.*[32] Yet, in spite of this magnitude, there were precious few rave notices. Most of those scholars who questioned what educational research had accomplished came up with cautious responses—for example, John B. Carroll:

. . .there are a number of issues and questions to which we can give definite and useful answers. We know a good deal about how to measure mental abilities, scholastic achievements, and certain aspects of interest, attitude, and even personality. We can describe the course of the child's physical, mental and emotional development and we can give a reasonably satisfactory account of the nature, course, and conditions of learning. We can point to research answers to a good number of specific questions about how we should teach reading, spelling, arithmetic, and other school subjects.

But having mentioned these and a few other topics, we just about reach the limits of our knowledge.[33]

Research, or the scientific study of education as it was referred to in the earlier part of the century, promised much in its earliest years. As Cremin noted, ". . .the professors of education—saw in science the great panacea for their field."[34] But even by the 1930s the enthusiasm had slackened, the expectations lowered.[35]

There were many explanations for the demise. Traxler[36] explained that "we are still in the exploratory and formative stage of a comparatively new science," and Coladarci[37] agreed. Some like Tiedeman and Cohen[38] saw researchers as technically unskilled. Others saw them as retreating into measurement and methodological studies that had the appearance of good research but produced little of substance.[39] In short, according to Cronbach and Suppes,[40] educational research had not kept up with the advances in the social and behavioral sciences. Gage put it succinctly in the preface to the *Handbook of Research on Teaching:* "In recent decades, such research [on teaching] has lost touch with the behavioral sciences. It has not drawn enough nourishment from theoretical and methodological developments in psychology, sociology and anthropology."[41]

Brim[42] and Gross[43] in sociology agreed, as did the distinguished panel of psychologists convened in 1958 by the National Academy of Sciences National Research Council.[44] Acknowledging that it was "upon psychology that education mainly depended for scientific sanction of its principles and for many of its techniques," they found that educational psychologists had not adequately translated the results of other branches of psychology into forms usable in the classroom. But the panel was willing to have psychology accept its share of the blame since it had not been using "language" that was readily applicable to school learning. Findley wasn't concerned with the language so much as the methodologies; he found that the experiment, the most esteemed of all methods among psychologists, was giving fits to the researcher studying conditions in classrooms.[45]

Adding to the confusion in the late 1950s were the action researchers who, it appeared to many, placed greater stress on getting teachers involved in the studies than on the scientific procedures. To most educators, criteria of validity and reliability had little meaning; they tended to see invention as research and vice versa and used terms like "experimentation," and "innovation" interchangeably with research (as an example, see Coombs[46]); even routine social bookkeeping was labeled research.[47]

There appeared to be ample data to support those who were discouraged about the state of the field. Fattu[48] found that of the 94 colleges and universities granting the doctorate in education that he surveyed in 1959, only ten could be said to be making a serious effort to encourage educational research. Lazarsfield and Sieber, in their report concluded:

It is our feeling that at this moment (from data collected in 1963), in contrast to 40 years ago, there does not exist a young generation of scholars within schools of education who are enthusiastic about educational research, who are enlarging its scope, and who are passing on a continuity of problems and techniques to their students.[49]

It is no wonder that Symonds said, "If research in education were to expand significantly, the real bottleneck probably would not be the lack of money but the lack of trained personnel."[50]

The schools of education that did provide research services encountered another set of problems. Research bureaus in most institutions were tied to the concept of service and applied research; the demands from the field for services tended to drain off the resources and limit the contributions that could be made to the generation of new knowledge.[51]

The paradox is that this overattentiveness to service did not bring about corresponding support from school practitioners. The literature of this period is replete with comments ad naseum about the failure of researchers to translate their findings into language understandable to the teachers and administrators or to tackle problems seen to be important to them.[52]

Facing the situation following his tenure as director of the Cooperative Research Program in USOE, David Clark stated:

The devolopment of new knowledge or of new applications for existing knowledge *may* be the "new frontier" for education in the next few years. There is, however, at least as great a likelihood that during the next decade research and researchers in education will continue to inhabit the periphery of the profession, contributing little to the improvement of educational practice.[53]

Percival Symonds had arrived at a similar conclusion six years earlier.[54] Carroll put it another way:

Currently available techniques and findings, however valuable they may be for purposes, do not in my opinion constitute a truly adequate scientific basis for formulating educational policy or for improving the practice of education.[55]

Not everyone was discouraged. Brim[56] saw an "impressive change" in the sociological study of education having occurred since 1950. Gross[57] agreed and cited work that was meritorious: Merton's study of socialization in the medical

schools; the studies of aspirations and social mobility using schools as laboratories by Parsons, Stouffer, and Kluckhohn; and the studies of the adjustment
of social systems to their external influences by Burton R. Clark. Theodore
W. Schultz was opening up education as a respectable area for study by economists.[58] And Gage found "increasing orientation to theory, sophistication in
design, the use of big computers, [and rising expectations for] attracting, selecting, and training the next generation of educational researchers."[59] His comments
are particularly noteworthy because they were made just after he had completed
the editing for the highly touted *Handbook.*

Another of the bright spots was the Cooperative Project in Educational
Administration launched in 1951 and funded by the Kellog Foundation.[60] It
established centers at Columbia, Harvard, Ohio State, and Stanford Universities;
the Universities of Chicago, Oregon, and Texas; and at George Peabody College.
And it supported the work of men like Jacob Getzels, Daniel Griffiths, Roald
Campbell, Lawrence Iannaccone, W.W. Charters, Jr., Andrew Halperin, and others.
These men became a new breed of linkers for education—that is, respectable
scholars in their own right who grounded their work in the disciplines.[61] Yet
they had strong ties to the opinion leaders in educational administration—men
like Walter Cockling, Hollis Caswell, Van Miller, Walter Anderson, and Samuel
Brownell.

The work of B.F. Skinner built around the rediscovery of the "teaching ma-
chine" offered a rich vein for study by 1960. It blended in well with the programmed instruction movement, which was a direct outgrowth and the beneficiary
of the applied work in psychology done for the armed forces during and following
World War II.[62] It was viewed as "a well-disciplined and experimental approach
to instruction. . ."[63] that lent itself to meticulous, controlled studies. And there
was a network of researchers who had worked under men like John Flanagan
and Arthur Melton in the armed forces who were available and eager to pursue
this research.

From the evaluation team assembled by Ralph Tyler for the Ten-Year Study[64]
emerged a handful of persons like Lee Cronbach and Benjamin Bloom who were
having a significant influence both on the direction of the study of education and
the quality of work being done. Tyler had preserved an enclave of excellence in
educational scholarship at Chicago University, and the University of Illinois,
under its President George Stoddard, collected an unusually talented faculty in
the School of Education in the 1950s. Even in the bastion of the educationists,
Teachers College, Columbia University, a small group of scholars like Lawrence
Cremin and Robert Thorndike were reasserting the need for higher quality academic work in education. Several researchers in education were winning recognition by their disciplinary colleagues; the capillary action between education
and those basic disciplines was slowly reforming.[65]

In summary, in spite of a generally dismal picture there was a growing sense of expectation about educational R&D. David Clark, who served as Director of the Cooperative Research Program in the Office of Education in the early 1960s, expressed it this way:

The early 1960s was a period of considerable optimism in regard to research in education. New programs were being passed by Congress, new initiatives were being ventured by the foundation, persons who previously had not participated in educational research and development were becoming involved in the field. A very substantial number of the young scholars involved in educational research at the time felt sincerely that research had substantial possibilities of effecting positively the future of education. In retrospect, I am surprised at the positive feel that seemed to permeate most of the discussions and work that was going on in or about 1960.[66]

For many the reason for encouragement was the funding by the federal government of educational research and curriculum development since the mid-1950s. So it is time that we turn to the federal scene to better understand its effect on R&D.

The Federal Government: Research and Education in the Late 1950s

U.S. Office of Education

If the term research includes the gathering of statistics, the social bookkeeping that Lazarsfeld and Sieber referred to, then the U.S. Office of Education had been involved in research since its inception in 1867. Congress at that time authorized it to collect "such statistics and facts as shall show the condition and progress of education in the several states and territories. . . ."[67] but it wasn't until the mid-1950s that Congress granted it authority to fund extra-mural research.

USOE launched its research support quite undramatically. When asked in 1954 what he would do if he were made Commissioner of Education, by then Secretary of DHEW Oveta Culp Hobby, Samuel D. Brownell reported back within a few days that one of his goals would be to establish a cooperative research program.[68] While there had been some interest expressed for federal funding of education research as early as 1950 in a conference called by then Commissioner Earl McGrath,[69] Brownell's desicsion appeared to be far more one of personal preference and conviction than a response to any organized—or even disorganized—pressure group.

This is borne out by the lack of enthusiasm shown by those who testified for the authorizing legislation. The comments by William G. Carr, Executive Secretary of the National Education Association, are illustrative:

Finally a word on cooperative research. Our association has for years urged adequate support for the United States Office of Education, and we have reason to think that our resolutions adopted at Miami Beach last summer resulted in the reconsideration by Congress of the appropriations with about a 20 percent improvement in the financing going to the Office of Education this current year . . . .

We do desire to see the work of the Office of Education strengthened and we therefore would endorse [this bill].[70]

While Carr can be faulted for his lack of enthusiasm and perhaps even for not understanding the concept of cooperative research, he at least mentioned the act; others like Edgar Fuller, testifying on behalf of the state superintendents organization and Andrew Biemiller from the American Federation of Labor, did not at all.[a]

While Congress approved the legislation (The Cooperative Research Act became P.L. 531) no funds were granted in 1955, even though the Secretary of HEW sought a supplemental appropriation. The cooperative Research Program was viewed by some economy-minded congressmen as another ploy to expand the staff of the Office of Education so the program had to wait another year to get started.[71] In this inconspicuous way, the Cooperative Research Program of the Office of Education was launched.

One might ask, how was it launched at all? What was operating within the federal government, especially within Congress, to pass legislation for which there was so little demand? To find a plausible answer one must recall the exalted place that the concept of research had reached in the 1950s.[72] The success of the sciences during World War II and before that in agriculture, as well as the growing tie between research and industry, had made the support of research popular and safe for politicians. Furthermore, this particular bill was cheap; while it carried no fiscal ceiling restriction, Mrs. Hobby testified that the department intended to seek only $100,000 that first year. (It did and didn't get even that.)

The next few months apparently were well used by Brownell and others; a year later, Congress granted an appropriation of $1,000,000. But there was a hooker: two-thirds of the money was expected by Mr. Fogarty to be spent on research on education of the mentally retarded.[73] The explanation for this priority is that for about two years staff men from the National Institute of Mental Health and the Department of HEW had been talking to Mr. Fogarty about the need for research funds to study and develop new ways of educating the mentally retarded and other handicapped children. But they had received little support from the USOE staff. Brownell's proposal for a Cooperative Research Program was a ready-made solution for them.

After the CRP was funded, the USOE staff saw ways that they could use

---

[a]The Cooperative Research Act was only one of three pieces of legislation before Congress; the other two were to create a National Advisory Committee and to authorize the White House Conference on Education

research money. To them the term extra-mural research meant that they would be able to contract for the kind of questionnaire surveys that would assist them in their work. The professional staff at that time consisted largely of subject-matter specialists who advised educators, through writings and personal consultation, on the latest trends and events in American education.[74] Brownell, supported by the Research Advisory Committee, a group of distinguished researchers led by Ralph Tyler, held the staff back. After Brownell left in 1958 and during the interim period of a few weeks before the next Commissioner, Lawrence Derthick, arrived, the RAC had to defend the program virtually by itself. Staff appeared before the Research Advisory Committee and proposed that authority for screening and recommending projects be transferred to them.[75] The RAC refused its support, and later when Derthick indicated that he was solidly behind the Committee, the CRP continued for several more years with the highest priority given to unsolicited, field-initiated projects. But not without attemps being made from time to time to divert the funds for use by the staff.

The CRP encountered other problems in these early years; $1 million turned out to be a lot of money to dispense when there was only one staff person operating the machinery for soliciting and screening proposals. Partly out of necessity and partly out of conviction, Alice Scates, employed as the staff for the program, relied heavily on the advice and the experience of the National Institute of Mental Health and used outsiders to screen and recommend which proposals to fund.[76]

In spite of many administrative difficulties, the program soon sprouted wings. The appropriations increased each year in the late 1950s, to $2,300,000 in FY 1958 and $2,700,000 in FY 1959.[77] By 1959, the staff had been increased to four and was being directed by Roy M. Hall, who had been employed specifically to head up the research program.

Hall was an interesting and fortunate choice for several reasons. Among those from whom Brownell had sought advice (and who himself was considered for the position) was a former student at Yale, Daniel Griffiths. Griffiths among others put him onto Hall who at that time was directing a CPEA project at the University of Texas. Hall checked out through the advisory committee as someone who, while not a respected researcher in his own right, was a good administrator who understood and valued research. Furthermore, Hall's Georgia and Texas background made it more likely that he would be accepted by the existing staff that was seen to have a southern and rural orientation.[78]

Staff acceptance was very important at that time. At mid-century, the Office was segmented into nearly autonomous fief doms of professional specialists or administrators of programs that held high congressional interest like the impacted aid to schools (P.L. 874) and vocational education. As Bailey and Mosher described it:

Real power was lodged in the guilds of professionals who ran the operating sub-units of the major bureaus: library consultants; vocational education experts;

reading and curricular specialists; experts on education of the handicapped; specialists in home economics; agricultural education; counseling and guidance—each with a scattering of friends in appropriate groups at the regional, state and local level.[79]

The tie at the national level was particularly strong with organizations like the National Education Association, the Vocational Education Association, and the Council for Exceptional Children.

As important, however, were the ties that specific specialists had with individual congressmen. Chairman and ranking members of Senate and House Committees had seen four commissioners serve in the 1950s. Men like Wayne Reed who joined the Office in 1951 and Ralph Flynt who joined in 1934 were often seen to be better informed and certainly were better known.[b] These were the realities Hall and his staff had to confront to make Coop a success. That they did redounds to their everlasting credit.

The Cooperative Research Program was only in its second operating year when USOE unexpectedly was given authority for two more research support programs. In October 1957, the country was stunned by the headlines announcing that the USSR had launched its first sattelite, Sputnik I. Congress finally was ignited to do something about perceived weaknesses in the educational system. The National Defense Education Act was drafted and submitted two-and-a-half months later!

It consisted of ten titles, two of which authorized funds for studies and research: Title VI empowered the U.S. Commissioner of Education "directly or by contract, to make studies and surveys to determine the need for increased or improved instruction in modern foreign languages and other fields needed to provide a full understanding of the areas, regions, or countries in which such languages are commonly used, to conduct research for more effective methods of teaching such languages and in such other fields, and to develop specialized materials for use in such training, or in training teachers of such languages or in such fields."[80]

Title VII consisted of two parts: Part A authorized the commissioner through grants and contracts to conduct, assist, and foster research and experimentation (1) on a variety of audio-visual aids, (2) for training teachers to use these aids, and (3) for presenting academic subject matter through such media; Part B authorized the commissioner to disseminate information about new technologies and the research about them by (1) studies and surveys to determine need, (2) catalogs, reviews, bibliographies, abstracts, analyses of research and experimentation to encourage more effective use, and (3) advising, counseling, and demonstrating to state and local educational agencies and institutions of higher education.[81]

---

[b]These ties persisted into the late 1960s and account for, in the words of Michael Kirst, why USOE always was though of as having more leaks to Congress than a sieve (from interview, April 2, 1974).

Title VII did not appear in this form in the original draft of the bill but was written at the last minute by the congressional staff from materials prepared by Henry Ruark and Donald White, then officers of the National Audio-Visual Association, Inc., the lobbyists for the audio-visual industry.[82] Not a single researcher or scholar from the educational research community testified in its behalf; neither Secretary Folsom nor Commissioner Derthick mentioned research in their testimonies. We see another instance of a research support program of education launched by a small handful of persons without widespread support in or outside the Office of Education.

The National Defense Education Act itself encountered some tough sledding in the Congress,[83] but was passed and signed into law on September 2, 1958. It authorized $3 million in FY 1959 for Title VII, but increased this to $5 million for each of the next three fiscal years. Studies under Title VI received an authorization of $1 million each year.[84]

The Media Research Program from its inception tended to attract researchers with different specialties than those who responded to the Cooperative Research Program. The staff in USOE also was more conscious of whose "interests" were being served.[85] Of the three original staff members, Kenneth Norberg was viewed as being from the audio-visual types (those who saw the Department of Audio-Visual Instruction [DAVI] of the NEA as their principal association); Clarence W. (Walter) Stone, a professor of library sciences from the University of Illinois at Urbana, was highly regarded by librarians and the "TV interests," and Calvin Stordahl, an educational psychologist and formerly a research administrator with the Department of Defense, was more highly regarded by the researchers. The National Advisory Committee on New Educational Media was structured in the Act to include, in addition to the commissioner as chairman, a representative of the National Science Foundation, and three persons from each of the following constituencies: (1) individuals identified with the sciences, liberal arts, or modern foreign languages institutions of higher education; (2) individuals engaged in teaching or supervison of teaching in elementary or secondary schools; (3) individuals of demonstrated ability in the utilization or adaptation of (instructional) media; and (4) individual representatives of the lay public who have demonstrated interests in the problems of communication media.[86]

While it encountered all of the problems of staffing and establishing new procedures faced by the CRP, the Title VII program was able to spend or commit almost $1,600,000 that first year; the staff processed roughly 250 proposals of which 45 were approved.[87] The Fly 1959 budget included a request for $3 million.

So by FY 1960 and in just four year's time, USOE was spending more than $10,000,000 for research and dissemination. By some standards, particularly within the federal government, this was not a large amount, but for educational research and even for some of the other social sciences, it was an unexpectedly huge figure. The Office of Naval Research during this same time period was spending from $2 to $4 million annually for its entire behavioral sciences research effort.[88] Still, far less was being spent to study educational issues than was being spent for research in industry and agriculture, a fact frequently cited in budget hearings and public addresses.

Other Federal Agencies

National Institute of Mental Health. "We were supporting more educational research than the Office of Education in the early 1960s." says Eli Bower, formerly a program officer in NIMH.

We were interested in testing out different approaches to training emotionally disturbed children. This led us to an interest in teacher training and we gave grants to institutions like San Francisco State, the University of Texas, Wisconsin University and Bank Street College.[89]

The National Institute of Mental Health had the funds and the freedom in those years to move in many directions.[90] Established in 1946 (but not funded until FY 1948), the organization grew at a nominal pace for its first several years. In FY 1956, for example, it awarded 223 grants for a total outlay of $23,990,649.[91] Beginning in 1951, the Professional Services Branch of NIMH was authorized to stimulate research in areas in which few proposals were being received; one area in which they encouraged research was on the study of mental health in the schools.

Beginning in the 1950s, the Institute shared in the overall fortunes of the parent organization, the National Institutes of Health. Congress followed the leadership of Congressman James Fogarty of Rhode Island, Chairman of the Subcommittee on Appropriations for DHEW of the Committee on Appropriations of the House of Representatives and Senator Carl T. Elliot, Chairman of the Committee on Education and Labor. Together these gentlemen almost annually for more than a decade gave the Institutes more funds to spend than that recommended by the president in his budget.[92] In 1962, the research appropriations in NIMH alone passed $50 million, almost one-half of the total budget figure for the parent agency.

The problems of mental health were only of marginal interest to the typical educational researcher. Men like Nicholas Hobbs of Peabody College, George Kelley of Ohio State, George Kirk at the University of Illinois, who were recipients of grants and oft-used consultants to NIMH, were respected names across many fields. But within schools of education, interest in NIMH programs usually was limited to those in special education; the typical education researcher—the bulk of the field—found little encouragement for his work from this government agency.

National Science Foundation. The NSF was established in 1950 after a gruelling struggle over political and organizational issues. From the beginning its interest in the social and behavioral sciences was extremely limited. After much debate and some political maneuvering, the proponents of NSF agreed that it was not mandatory that NSF support the social sciences, but it would be permitted to "explore the possibility" for supporting it.[93] In its earliest years, NSF chose to do very little exploring.

It was interested in improving the teaching of the sciences, however, and in 1954, established a program called Special Projects in Science Education (SPISE). It concentrated on teacher training institutes, first at the college level and later for high school teachers, but largely through the efforts of Richard Paulson, an NSF staff member, SPISE was expanded to include work in curricula. The result was the Course Content Improvement Program. By 1960, $6,302,000 was allocated for curriculum work.[94]

But NSF was not receptive to educational research as defined by USOE or to the work of educational researchers. As Mike Atkin put it:

NSF people were then (and still are for the most part) contemptuous of educational scholarship including educational evaluation. I was the first educationist to get a grant from them but without my co-director, an astronomer, I probably wouldn't have gotten it.[95]

In sum, these three institutions permit a study in contrast in styles and objectives. The National Science Foundation had clear objectives in funding their curriculum projects: to improve the instruction in the sciences so as to ensure a steady flow of the best minds into the sciences. As one of the present-day NSF staff member puts it:

Interest in improving science education has abated. Scientists seem to be satisfied that the career lines are solid and it turns out that the rest of the population doesn't really care about improving science education.[96]

It was a sharply defined focus that commanded support from the leadership of scientific fields. The NSF staff could and did capitalize on this support and worked with and through the existing scientific communities, quietly and largely informally.

NIMH almost from its inception had several mission objectives for which there was less consensus and support among intellectual communities. Frequently NIMH would adopt a policy and only then attempt to elicit the support of visible researchers. But like other government agencies, the NIMH staff would compromise by seeking out researchers whose on-going work was close to the adopted missions and then trying to find areas of mutual concern.

The USOE, through the Cooperative Research Program, committed itself to a long-range effort of expanding and improving an existing research and development field. This policy was best articulated in an off-the-cuff statement by Ralph Tyler as chairman of the USOE Research Advisory Committee in 1959:

. . .my basic assumption is that the limitations now are more personnel than any-thing else, that what's going to stop you from spending "X" million dollars is that you don't have that many good people yet ready to carry on; so the first thing to see is that every competent research person working on problems that you would consider relevant has the funds to carry on significant research and to help to train some other people.[97]

The best way to attract and support these good people, they concluded, was to keep the Bureau of Research responsive to the ideas from the field, whether large or small. The typical project in those days was estimated to be about $30,000[98] (two multi-million dollar projects—Project Talent and the Internation-al Association for the Evaluation of Educational Achievement (the IEA study)— probably were not computed in determining this average), so the staff of the Bureau of Research was encouraged to interact formally with a wide range of scholars from education and the disciplines. They could seize every possible op-portunity while visiting project investigators on-site to meet with psychologists, sociologists, and others, individually and in small groups.

It was not easy to maintain this priority for the staff, and the RAC were well aware that USOE had many constituencies. And some of them had other expectations for the CRP. For example, here is an excerpt from a letter written by the executive secretary of the Chief State School Officers, dated December, 13, 1956, to Lawrence Derthick, newly arived in Washington as Commissioner of Education:

Enclosed is a copy of a resolution adopted at the Council's annual meeting in San Francisco on Nobember 19, 1956. The chief state school officers are quite concerned about the way the cooperative research program has begun. With some exceptions, it has seemed to be as miscellaneous as a list of dissertation titles, with pure research rules interpreted in ways that appear to exclude fruitful at-tacks on current and important problems in education. Some of us do not believe it was intended that the Office should operate its cooperative research program more or less on a foundation-like project grant basis at all, but rather on the basis of truly cooperative work with colleges, universities and state departments of education on problems of mutual concern.[99]

"Problems of mutual concern" to most administrators were like those listed by Herold Hunt, then Superintendent of the Chicago Public Schools, in a *Phi Delta Kappan* article:

Should departmentalized instruction be continued in this school? How can we make certain that children's emotional needs are being cared for adequately? How should we present controversial issues at the various academic levels? How can we provide counseling services for all students? How can we make the recording and reporting of pupil achievement more reliable? How can we recruit better candidates for teaching?[100]

So from the beginning, the USOE staff, and the men who advised them, were faced with dilemmas: to produce sound research, more established research-ers of higher quality needed to be enticed into examining issues that fell within the purview of USOE's interests. The long-term strategies that would most likely reach this objective were founded on granting maximum freedom to the inves-tigators and keeping the agency responsive to their interests. Yet, any long-term strategy demanded the support of the other audiences that shaped policies for the Office—the administrators, teacher trainers, and other practitioners. They expected to receive some results from the research that would make their tasks more manageable, which meant that they needed to see some ordering of expect-ations (i.e., priorities).

In the early years, progress was maintained toward this delicate task of satis-fying mutually unsatisfiable demands because (1) the research program was of such low order of magnitude in the federal scene that it didn't attract much pol-itical attention (i.e., flak); (2) the demands being made on USOE, hence on the bureaucrats, were relatively modest and manageable; and (3) an effective relation-ship was forged between a competent staff and representatives of the intellectual communities with whom they were working. There appeared to be a mutually shared set of assumptions about the goals of the staff and the needs of the field as well as a shared respect for the procedures needed to reach those goals.

Unfortunately, by 1960, there already were clearly discernible forces and personalities in the wings of the federal scene that would change all of this. The Office of Education was about to become the center of political action that would no longer permit any research staff to engage in such quiet and delicate long-range tasks. It now is time to turn to those years and those events to better under-stand the changes that were made in the R&D funding policies.

4 Research and the Breakthrough in Federal Aid for Schools

Dramatic events and time have clouded the feelings produced by the election of John F. Kennedy to the presidency. In retrospect, it was a time of cautious hope; his youth and uninspiring public record in the Senate seemed to contradict many of his promises and calls for action. His political successes overshadowed his substantive convictions; his boyish charm and casual public style contrasted with the tales of his political strong-arm methods. His narrow victory was less a hesitation by the American people to get the country moving again than doubts about whether this young, wealthy, Irish Catholic was the man to lead them.

Educators reflected this ambivalence. There was little doubt which party they favored:[1] Nixon had stayed with Eisenhower's begruding approach to federal aid—for new school construction only. The Democrats called for federal funding as general aid to schools—for teachers' salaries as well as classroom construction—and Kennedy demonstrated far more interest in education and had devoted an entire speech to the subject on November 2, 1960, in Los Angeles. Yet, the educational associations, particularly the National Education Association and its affiliates, also were adamant in their opposition to federal support for nonpublic schools. While Kennedy was clearly on record as supporting the Constitutional guarantees for the separation of church and state (see his speech of September 12, 1960, to the Greater Houston Ministerial Association), some educators still were unsure of what action he would take once elected to the presidency.[2]

They remained cautious into his first year. He carried through with his promises by requesting additional funds for education in an amendment to the Eisenhower budget of 1961 and submitted educational legislation early in 1961 that asked for unprecedented amounts for the construction of public elementary and secondary classrooms, for boosting teachers' salaries, for higher education facilities, and for student scholarships and construction loans. (The fact that none of these bills passed must be attributed to the disarray among the educational interest groups as much as to the ineptitude of the Kennedy team.[3]) Yet there remained a distance between this administration and the leading educational associations.

This was due in part to whom Kennedy was turning for advice and leadership on educational matters. Even before he assumed office, he had put together a task force on education chaired by Keith Hovde, President of Purdue University. Prominent in this group was Francis Keppel, Dean of the Graduate School of Education, Harvard University, and a recognized leader among the noneduca-

49

tionists. It is to Keppel that the comment is attributed that later became something of a watchword for so many: "Education is too important to be left solely to the educators." Within the White House were several persons involved in planning new legislation and new strategies for federal involvement in education. One of these was Jerome B. Wiesner who had left his post as Dean of the Massachusetts Institute of Technology to become the Special Assistant to the President for Science and Technology and Chairman of the President's Science Advisory Committee (PSAC). While at MIT, he had been involved in Professor Zacharias' efforts to improve the teaching of physics in American high schools and was a charter member of the Board of Directors of Educational Services Incorporated, the organization created by Zacharias to house the Physical Sciences Study Committee and other curriculum improvement projects.

One of Wiesner's early tasks was to create a special panel on Educational Research and Development and appoint Zacharias as its chairman. Zacharias was no stranger to PSAC activities, having been one of the original Truman appointees in 1951; his term had just expired in 1959. But now this extraordinarily energetic scientist qua educational reformer had a platform and a new conduit for shaping federal policies on education.

Zacharias left no doubts about his biases and one of these was that he found USOE personnel by and large incompetent and of little use to him;[4] his funding had come from the National Science Foundation (and private sources), and it was with them that he preferred to interact and channel his ideas. The appointments to his panel showed his preferences for scientists, scholars, and persons with wider intellectual recognition than he found among the typical educationists. This explains why the NEA central staff was not represented on the panel; Dr. Benjamin C. Willis, General Superintendent of Schools from Chicago, was the only NEA "regular" from among seventeen members, and his contribution was described as "minimal" by Dr. Zacharias.

Who were important members of the panel? Persons like Jerome Bruner, Harvard University, whose research and writings were a major contribution in altering the decades' old notions of learning readiness; Frederick Burkardt, President of the American Council of Learned Societies, who was urging scholars to improve the curriculum in high schools as Zacharias was doing with the scientists; John H. Fischer, part of the reform movement in Teachers College, Columbia University; and Patrick Suppes, a philosopher and mathematician, who was seeking new ways to use the computer for instruction.

It was a distinguished group, and they took their tasks seriously. They met often and regularly, as much as once a month for two days at a time from September 1962 through April 1963. Seminars and special meetings were held at universities around the country on such diverse topics as music education, nongraded schools, and the education of the deprived and segregated. The list of participants and invited guests is strikingly diverse, but prestigious, and bureaucrats from the federal government were brought into contact with persons and ideas outside government in ways that the Office of Education was not doing then.

With what consequences? In retrospect, the PSAC panel seems to have accomplished little. The planning for new educational legislation went forward outside its channels, but it gave the Kennedy administration access to some of the best thinkers and doers in education at that time and to their ideas.

Of course it made life in the NEA—and the USOE—more difficult. As Bailey and Mosher point out, the USOE was ill prepared to respond to the demands of the Kennedy administration. "Over the decades, Congress had virtually ignored USOE—financially it was starved; administratively it was victimized."[5] The bulk of its roughly 1,300 persons in 1962 were traditional bureaucrats. Robinson described it by saying, "Its authority is circumscribed, its salaries limited, its functions divided among many agencies. It is buffeted by gusts of criticism. . . ."[6] To be useful to the dynamic White House in 1961, it needed a special kind of commissioner. After several reported refusals, it got a man distinguished mostly by being unknown to almost all the audiences who mattered.

Sterling McMurrin came to Washington from the University of Utah where he had been the academic vice president and a professor of philosophy. By his own admission, he was not a member of the NEA and was not well acquainted with the activities of the agency he came to head. It is always difficult to retain how any candidate gets on any list in Washington, but in retrospect, reasons for the McMurrin appointment have become obscured. Many believe that Abraham Ribicoff, the newly appointed Secretary of DHEW, found him through New York City foundation channels.

After a brief year-and-a-half he resigned the commissionership, some said because of his frustration in not being able to break into the White House circles. The rumor at that time was that when President Kennedy read of his resignation in the morning paper, he asked McGeorge Bundy who McMurrin was and what the trouble was. Bundy's response reportedly was, "Mr. President, that's exactly the trouble; you never heard of the fellow."

So by the end of Kennedy's first year in office, educators had a right to be discouraged. As Bailey and Mosher put it, ". . .the successful forces against the [1961 Omnibus Education] bill were so powerful and pervasive as to make thoughtful analysts predict that no breakthrough in substantial Federal aid to elementary and secondary education would likely occur for years or even decades."[7] The educational interests were bickering among themselves and felt increasingly alienated from those in the federal government who were interested in making changes in American education. The picture was indeed gloomy by the fall of 1962; Sundquist reports that "years of frustration had produced a pervading pessimism."[8]

The Beginning: Preparing for Effective Battle

McMurrin's major contribution in Washington at that time may have been his resignation, effective August 1962. Now the White House had to do something.

They turned for help this time, as they had done so frequently, to Harvard and asked the urbane, cagey Dean of the Graduate School of Education to take the commissionship. He was well-known in the White House; he had served on the President's Task Force on Education and often had been an advisor to USOE.[a]

Keppel was a logical choice for the job. As a former Assistant Dean at Harvard College and then as Dean of the Graduate School of Education, he was highly regarded by a large number of leaders within the Harvard community (including James B. Conant who appointed him to both deanships) and the foundation networks. After receiving a personal telephone call from the president, Keppel accepted. He was officially appointed on December 10, 1962. It was to be a bellweather event for the administration's changes in education. As Bailey and Mosher put it, "No one understood the political preconditions of new Federal aid to education better than Francis Keppel."[9]

His reception among the educational establishment, however, was mixed. He was highly regarded personally, but here was the second Kennedy appointment outside the educational establishment. As Parker said, "The appointment of Francis Keppel. . . . planted the new guard's flag in education's cubicle within the Department of Health, Education and Welfare."[10]

Keppel was faced with two monstrous tasks: shaping legislation and steering it through the many conflicting interests in education, and building a more effective, better-respected Office of Education. He got right to work on both.

Legislation

Keppel became known in Washington as a "tireless broker, negotiator, and salesman."[11] He seemed to have a sixth sense for who was important in situations and cultivated them no matter how powerful or junior they were.[b] It was a personal approach to collective action in an atmosphere supposedly triggered more by protocol and precedent.[c] Yet he remained aloof, even from his closest associates and could be bitingly sardonic; a "Brahmin rotarian," some labeled him.

---

[a]At one of their early meetings the president remembered that his brother Joseph had run against a Keppel for the elected position of Class Marshall. He inquired whether Frank were that Keppel. When it was confirmed, JFK asked who won. "Joe did," replied Keppel. "Good" came the emphatic reply. A Washington rumour confirmed by Francis Keppel.

[b]Charles Lee, who at that time was staff to the Senate Subcommittee on Education says, "It was ego flattering to a staff man to have a commissioner phone asking you to have lunch, asking to be educated" (from his interview, March 14, 1974).

[c]This style also was demanding. When asked how much time he devoted to legislation during his term, he replied, "I spent 60 percent of my time thinking about it, at least, maybe 70 percent thinking about the bills. As to how much time up there, I don't know. It just seemed to me that I lived up there [meaning the Capitol]." Transcript, Francis Keppel Oral History Interview, April 21, 1969, LBJ Library, p. 4

In a matter of weeks, his political acuman was tested. He was given a complex, all-encompassing bill, the Omnibus Education Act that contained something for almost everybody in education. His task was to hammer out a pact that would keep each of the educational interests from picking out just its favorite section and attacking the rest. It worked even though Congress eventually split up the bill and gave priority to the Higher Education Facilities Act of 1963; other interests supported this tactic and waited their turn. This time the NEA did not flood the Congress with opposing telegrams as they had done the year before; the remainder of the bill was receiving favorable attention in committees; the stage was set for unified action among the educational interests on federal support for schools.

Progress toward the second objective, improving the Office of Education, was not so apparent. But to understand why this was so we must first review the conditions and state of USOE in 1962 when Keppel became commissioner.

USOE in 1962

The Office of Education in 1962 could be cited as an outstanding example of the French axiom, *"plus ca change è plus c'est la meme chose."* The total budget for OE had increased from $233,212,892 in 1955 to $602,590,455 in FY 1962.[12] The number of authorized positions had increased to 1,143 by 1962, more than doubled in five years.[13] Robinson in 1962 was able to list sixteen major tasks of USOE that took it "beyond the routines imposed by grants for land-grant collegs under the Morrill Act and for vocational education under the Smith–Hughes and George–Barden Acts":

1. Administered graduate fellowships and loans for college students under the National Defense Education Act (NDEA).
2. Provided foreign language institutes for elementary and secondary school language teachers.
3. Established area study centers for work in rare modern languages.
4. Administered grants to states and loans to private schools to purchase equipment for science, math, and foreign language instruction and for improved state supervision of these programs.
5. Made grants to states to strengthen guidance, counseling, and testing in secondary schools.
6. Provided for research and experimentation in more effective use of modern communications media in education.
7. Made grants to the states for vocational education related to national defense.
8. Aided school construction and maintenance in areas effected by federal activities.
9. Assisted in retraining of unemployed workers.

10. Began vocational training under the 1962 Manpower Development and Training Act, which will retrain up to 100,000 unemployed workers a year.
11. Administered grants and fellowships to improve programs for the mentally retarded.
12. Extended library services for rural areas.
13. Recruited education technicians to work abroad.
14. Administered international teacher exchange and technical assistance programs.
15. Made studies of foreign education.
16. Cooperated with international agencies in projects and publications.[14]

In 1962, the Office of Education launched programs to improve the teaching of English and committed over $2 million to 26 projects;[15] almost $5 million was made available for research and demonstration projects in educational media.

There were other evidences of growth and change. Fenno shows that from an examination of the fiscal history of government bureaus, the U.S. Office of Education ranked first over a sixteen-year period among all agencies in the percentage increase over previous year's appropriations.[16] Furthermore, it ranked eleventh among 36 agencies in the percentage of appropriation requests granted for that same time period. This rank reflects the fact that USOE's budget in 1947 was very low ($29,052,956),[17] and Congressman Fogarty, who was Chairman of the DHEW Subcommittee on Appropriations from 1949 to 1967 (except for the Republican years of 1953 and 1954) was favorably inclined toward education. Nevertheless, it also showed that the federal government was increasing its responsibility for public education.

The pace was too slow, however, to satisfy the enormously expanded demands and expectations of the Kennedy Administration and most of those outside the government who were now turning to the federal government to change American education. Keppel was well aware that one of his first tasks had to be strengthening USOE, which meant bringing in different kinds of people. But until there were new programs, a different kind of organization (that would theoretically realign relationships internally) and more higher salaried positions, he knew he couldn't do much.

The top bureaucratic positions were filled by oldtimers like Wayne Reed, who served as acting commissioner between McMurrin and Keppel; Ralph C.M. Flynt; and Arthur L. Harris, associate commissioners whose total years of service in USOE exceed fifty years. Their power had been solidified by the reorganization announced in February of that year by Commissioner McMurrin, but Keppel could and did fill some of the junior posts, and these now formed what one staff person at that time called a "shadow group,"[18] a collection of the younger staff who helped in the search for talent and who supported each other. The best known of this group included Samuel Halperin, who came to the Office of Education Legislative Bureau in 1961 after serving as an intern both on the House and Senate staffs; David Seeley, a Yale Law School graduate who had come to

Keppel's attention as a graduate student at Harvard and who was brought down to be one of his special assistants; Francis A.J. Ianni, who became director of the Bureau of Research and Development; Peter Muirhead in higher education; and John Naisbitt, Keppel's assistant for public information. These five were able to establish and maintain influence with the real locus of control on educational matters in the White House, the Office of Science and Technology, the Bureau of the Budget, and in Congress. Seeley became best known to the social actionists and eventually was appointed Assistant Commissioner of Education for Equal Educational Opportunities. Halperin moved up the ladder by being appointed assistant commissioner for legislation and eventually deputy assistant secretary for legislation in DHEW.

"Fritz" Ianni was hired in 1961 by David Clark, then the Director of the Cooperative Research Branch, from the staff of the Department of Sociology, Russell Sage College, where as an anthropologist he had been studying the reactions of parents and children in the depressed neighborhoods of Troy, N.Y., to the administering of the Salk vaccine. He was brought in to help spread the Cooperative Research Program among the disciplines. When Clark resigned the directorship, he recommended Ianni as his replacement, but Flynt was cautious; he saw Fritz as part of what he called the "Northeastern" group—or the Ivy Leaguers as others would call them.[19] But Fritz' willingness to work fifty to seventy hours a week and his ability to favorably represent the program and the Office in Congress and in DHEW eventually won Flynt over.

Ianni began to appear more often than any other staff person from USOE on the committees and at the meetings called by the PSAC panel, and he took the initiative to seek out from among the scholars those most interested in education in universities throughout the country and on foundations. In the course, he made significant changes to the Cooperative Research Program. But to understand those changes it is necessary to digress to discuss how the Cooperative Research Program had been developing.

The Cooperative Research Program

After a few lackluster years, the Cooperative Research Program in the 1960s began to look good. Lazarsfeld and Sieber[20] show that proposals received from scholars in the disciplines increased fourfold in the first seven years of the program while those from professional educators remained about the same. In April 1961, Congressmen John Fogarty commented, "This [program] is so popular with the deans of all the schools that I have been hearing from that I wonder if the Coop Research Program shouldn't be set out as a separate appropriation."[21] Keppel, who had misgivings about a lot that passed for educational research said ". . . educational research is now making significant new beginnings. . . ."[22]

This satisfaction was reflected in the increases in appropriations: Cooperative Research was authorized $3,200,000 in 1960; by FY 1964, this figure had jumped to $11,500,000.[23] Yet these increases also produced strains on and controversies among the staff.

The objectives of the CRP had remained remarkably steady after Ralph Tyler and the Research Advisory Committee in 1957 beat back the attempts of the staff to capture the program and its funds for staff support studies. Lawrence Derthick as commissioner gave the program his full support so that it could concentrate on the task of creating a new community of scholars from a mix of the educational researchers (primarily those who had been produced in schools of education) with their counterparts in the basic disciplines. This meant that the CRP staff had to play according to the rules of scientific and scholarly communities if they were to make the program attractive to these audiences.

If a lengthy list of recognizeable scholars who were willing to serve on advisory committees and working panels are any indication, the CRP staff was succeeding. By 1963, the list was impressive and included men like Lee Cronbach, Harry Levin, Patrick Suppes, Albert Marckwardt, Orville Brim, and Lawrence Cremin. The list of persons whose research was being supported also contained some highly visible, well-recognized scholars—persons like James S. Coleman, J.P. Guilford, Ronald Lippitt, Richard Alpert, Carl R. Rogers, Paul Lazarsfeld, and Jerome Bruner.

But building a more sound research community is not very politically appealing, especially to an administration that is seeking ways to respond to widespread dissatisfaction with the schools of the nation—even more so when that program does not have an active or influential constituency.[24] It was quite likely that the new commissioner appointed by the Kennedy administration would want to do something more dramatic with the CRP discretionary funds.

In fact, the CRP staff was fearful that McMurrin would want to eliminate altogether the competitive projects approach to research funding so they put before him their plan to concentrate research funding in four broad areas, indicating priorities: The Learner; Curriculum Content and Methods; Environment; and Social Control.[25] To help them quietly influence the networks of researchers, they created four panels.[d] But they found that McMurrin had still other interests.

He favored the kinds of projects funded and priorities held by the foundations and the National Science Foundation. So the CRP staff, now led by the resourceful David Clark, devised Project English and Project Social Studies, two curriculum improvement areas not likely to be covered by the NSF. Funding for

---

[d]These panels also were given the task of screening research proposals, thereby relieving the Research Advisory Committee of what had become an impossible load. In USOE in those days the RAC read and acted on all proposals, USOE staff discretion was quite limited. As an indication of the volume, the February 8 and 9, 1961 meeting of the RAC, they acted on 157 proposals.

these projects was requested over and above that needed to keep the competitive projects going. They also initiated Project Literacy and seized the chance to initiative the Developmental Program, which brought the CRP closer to direct intervention in the education system.

The objective of building a research community was not abandoned, however. For example, as early as 1960, the staff was considering improvements to the kind of institutional support that educational researchers needed.[26] By 1962, two studies supported jointly by the CRP and Title VII, NDEA funds, were underway to examine the feasibility and the necessary characteristics of research and development centers.[27] By 1963, Paul Lazarsfeld and Sam Sieber had been funded to investigate the organization of educational research, which study was to underscore the need for different kinds of logistical and organizational support than that provided by the typical school of education.

In summary, Ianni took over at a time when solid groundwork had been done by the CRP staff among the educational research community and with their counterparts in the disciplines. Yet there was increasing pressure to use the R&D processes and results more directly in improving the schools. The USOE response was to try to straddle the dilemma, to do both in ways that limited their effectiveness in both directions. These limitations produced criticisms with which, as it turned out, Ianni was both sensitive and in sympathy.

The Ianni Years

Fritz Ianni became a somewhat controversial character during his more than four years in Washington. Tireless, almost a whirlwind, he was a master in the art of keeping many balls in the air at the same time. He was infectiously enthusiastic about his work, but he was accused of encouraging persons to seek from the CRP more than he or the program could realistically support. He also was accused of being a poor administrator. For good or ill, he inherited the leadership of the CRP and eventually the entire USOE R&D effort. In Keppel, the White House had a leader in which they had confidence; this opened up possibilities for any resourceful, ambitious person on the OE staff.

Ianni was well aware of this. And he knew who to stay in touch with to make his branch, later his bureau, well thought of, persons like Joseph Terner, staff man to the PSAC panel for the Office of Science and Technology; Henry Riecken, Program Director, Social Science Research in the National Science Foundation; and Zacharias himself. And he spent what he remembers were endless hours with John Fogarty and his staff.[28] To what end? Two results were seen.

The staff itself became more influential in setting policies and the R&D program of the Office of Education moved into a higher gear. Ironically, when Ianni first took over, the influence of the field increased. By 1963 there were seven panels, later expanded to nine,[e] consisting of 64 outsiders in addition to the Research Advisory Council (changed from Committee in 1963). Some of the principal advisors in retrospect view those years as the times when they felt most at home in USOE.[29]

One decided improvement was the change in the primary function of the RAC away from reviewing and recommending to the commissioner which proposals to fund; the Office of Education up to 1964 was only one of four federal agencies of 22 surveyed that relied completely on advisory committees to recommend which projects to fund, with the staff merely concurring in that decision.[30] The fact that it served at all as a channel for policy advising was due more to the informal relationships between staff and committee members. For example, Commissioner Derthick had served as chairman of the Cooperative Program for Educational Administration funded by the Kellog Foundation prior to coming to USOE which helped him become acquainted with some of the better-known researchers. This was not the case with McMurrin, but by Ianni's time there were too many programs involving too many persons in the field to have a small handful of informal relationships with RAC members provide the advice and the information needed by the staff. Hence the use of panels.

Ianni had other plans. It was as if he wanted more of everything—applied research, demonstration, and dissemination—in his own helter-skelter sort of way. He paid a lot of attention to organization and institution building, like the demonstration and curriculum study centers in Project English and Project Social Studies,[31] but his biggest plans were reserved for the Research and Development centers (R&D centers).

R&D centers were being discussed, Ianni maintains, when he joined the CRP staff in 1961.[32] One input came from Harvard where the staff of the School and University Program for Research and Development (SUPRAD) was seeking a source of funds to replace the expiring Ford Foundation grant; Keppel sent a memorandum to McMurrin that eventually brought Ianni together with Wade Robinson, Director of SUPRAD. In another quarter, John Flanagan, President of the American Institutes for Research, with Robert Glaser, drafted and submitted a trial run proposal for an R&D institution in 1962. Slowly the plans for institutional support gathered momentum in USOE.

In 1962, Commissioner McMurrin appointed an ad hoc advisory committee of 27 scholars who made a series of recommendations for ways the Office might proceed. A year later an advisory panel was appointed with Ralph Tyler as its chairman. He was assisted by an august group; Alan Pifer, Vice President then of the Carnegie Corporation; Thomas Eliot, Chancellor, Washington University at St. Louis; William Robinson, Commissioner of Education, Rhode Island; and Benjamin S. Bloom, Professor, University of Chicago. With their guidance, the

---

[e]The nine panels were: Arts and Humanities; Basic Reading; English; Environment; Curriculum Improvement; Demonstration; Educational Processes; Research and Development Centers; Psychological Processes.

staff produced the first set of guidelines, solicited proposals, and set up the first site visits.

The R&D centers were expected to do many things; consider this description by Ward Mason and Howard Hjelm in 1965:

The Research and Development Center Program was devised for the purposes of concentrating human and financial resources on significant educational problems over an extended period of time in order to improve our understanding of these problems and to develop and disseminate specific innovations. Each works along the entire continuum from basic research to action programs.[33]

So the centers were really expected to be R, D, D and D organizations—that is, to deal also with the development of new products and procedures, demonstrate these to the pracitioners in schools, and disseminate the results of research as widely as possible.[34]

These expectations, as unrealistic as they may appear in retrospect, were compatible with the existing belief in those days that research could be passed along in assembly line fashion, the final step (if all were engineered well) being adoption. Consider this statement by Ianni:

These steps of basic research, field testing, demonstration, and diffusion form, along with continuous research planning and development and the training of research personnel, the basic steps in a program of research which leads to innovation. Unless these additional steps are carried out, the results of educational research are simply not going to have any immediate payoff in practice.[35]

This approach became known as the linear R&D model or the "Guba and Clark" model, after the two men, Egon Guba and David Clark, who wrote most frequently and lucidly about it.[36]

It is questionable, however, whether the founders of those early centers really expected to undertake all of those functions. The Learning Research and Development Center (LRDC) at the University of Pittsburgh, one of the first two centers funded and one of the most successful of the entire program, concentrated its attention and resources on research and product evaluation and was quite uncertain at the onset how it would meet the requirements of demonstration and diffusion.[37] Nevertheless, the Office of Education by 1964 was building a new kind of institution. The Center for Advanced Study of Educational Administration at the University of Oregon, Eugene, was the other center funded in that fiscal year. In the fall of 1964, two more centers were created: The Center for Research and Development for Learning and Reeducation at the University of Wisconsin at Madison; and the Center for Research and Development on Educational Differences at Harvard University. A sum of $500,000 each was committed to these institutions annually through a five-year cost reimbursement contract.

Ianni was not satisfied to stop here. The R&D center idea offered great hope to overcome the two most common criticisms of the USOE R&D program to date: that it fostered small-scale, inconsequential studies and had still failed to attract the best thinkers in sufficient quantity to develop ideas that made a difference to school people. As Keppel put it:

Our principal faults from the past are these: The most common form of educational research has been and is still the small, easily-managed project which focuses on miniature, obscure and non-controversial issues, which are seldom taken seriously by administrators or teachers. Education research has been and is still short of the best minds needed for the best possible results. Without the best of researchers, we have yet to show an innovative, creative vigor matching our counterparts in medicine, science, agriculture and industry.[38]

Certainly, four centers wouldn't turn the trick. How many would? When questioned by Fogarty during the 1965 budget hearings about the eventual goal for the R&D center program Ralph Flynt responded: "I would say every state should have a center. . . ."[39] But while eventually ten centers were created, neither the advisory panel nor Keppel was this ambitious.

The centers were not greeted enthusiastically by everyone. Keppel showed some ambivalence. He gave the idea his full support for budgetary purposes and felt that the centers were "a good idea," but in retrospect did not see them as one of his major accomplishments as commissioner.[40] There was even less enthusiasm in the Bureau of the Budget and within the PSAC panel.[41] To understand why, we must stop to examine some of the prevailing views of this group about educational R&D at that time.

The articles and documents produced by members of this panel contained statements about the ills of educational research and ways to correct them that are remarkably similar to what the USOE staff were saying. One of the stated goals of the panel was ". . . to create a climate favorable to educational research and development. . . ." and they wanted to "enlist the services of many people already busy doing other things—outstanding scholars or practitioners at the frontiers of their art or science and outstanding teachers."[42] Where the two agencies differed was how to accomplish these goals and particularly WHO should be carrying the ball.

Jerrold Zacharias, for many, became the prototype of the caliber of person who should be involved in the new curricular efforts. He had been a clearly recognized and respected physicist since the days in the mid 1940s with the Los Alamos Laboratory and was as well a protege of the Nobel prize winner, I.I. Rabi. He reached a spending level unprecedented in curriculum-making history, and NSF had the foresight and the tenacity to back him: they budgeted $445,000 in Fy 1957, $505,750 in 1958, and $1,800,100 in 1959.[43] PSSC set the level of magnitude for the NSF curriculum program by producing printed materials, apparatus, films, paperback books, and teachers' materials and by recognizing that teachers had to be trained to use all this as part of the developmental process.

There were other reasons for Zacharias' appeal in the late 1950s. Remember the controversial state of public education. As Conant described it, there was a struggle between the educational practitioners and their allies in schools of education on the one hand and the scholars, scientists, and alumni of colleges and the news media on the other for the control of what would be taught in the schools and who would do the teaching.[44] Zacharias demonstrated his ability to organize on the scale that promised to bring "sweeping changes" to the schools of the nation, as one critic viewed it.[45]

Zacharias devised and launched his own research organization Educational Services, Incorporated (ESI), in 1960. As he explains it, he never intended that his employing institution, MIT, get into the curriculum building business; he foresaw administrative difficulties as his plans for curriculum improvement grew. He was not content simply to revise the teaching of physics in high schools; eventually he hoped to reshape or influence the teaching of every subject in every grade. ESI would become an administrative and logistical service to these curriculum makers. That is how it was described in an NSF publication:

ESI was established as a nonprofit organization to assist those groups who wished its help in acting as the grantee organization, providing required administrative management services and certain facilities and persons such as file studies, cameramen, shops and craftsmen. ESI is, therefore, the grantee organization for a number of activities supported by the Foundation, other Government agencies, and private organizations. ESI itself does not maintain a large staff of professional employees. The work administered by the organization is carried on largely by consortia of professional scientists organized for the accomplishment of a particular project.[46]

An irony in the differences in approach between many of those supported by NSF and some of those supported by USOE is that they both were trying to improve education from outside the establishment and viewed educationists as their foe. Robert Glaser, Director of the LRDC at the University of Pittsburgh, purposely structured the center so that it was outside the School of Education. Glaser, a psychologist who had won his recognition for work done for the Air Force in the early 1950s, was interested in using some of the principles of operant conditioning in designing more individualized programs of instruction in elementary schools. This was the work for competent behavioral scientists, not the traditional educational curriculum designer.

Other education researchers at that time also were fighting to extricate themselves from the research establishment that they saw as being dominated by school administrators and teacher trainers in schools of education. The battles over the Cooperative Research Program in the 1950s was a battle to keep control over research funding in the hands of the researchers and way from the practitioners who almost inevitably demanded service on immediate problems at the expense of building basic knowledge.

To those who were impatient with the entire educational establishment, however, the R&D center program was not far enough removed from the educationists. As William Cannon from BOB said, "We didn't see the R&D centers as being good enough. We were thinking of other kinds of institutions even before the Gardner Task Force.[47] In fact, by that fall of 1963, there were a lot of ideas being advocated for changing American education through the federal government. Typical of the American style, there were competing groups strung out along several dimensions; some were in opposition, others in temporary collusion. But the supporters were beginning to crystallize; in August the Higher Education Facilities Act passed the House by 287–113, and other legislation was being favorably received and viewed in both House and Senate committees.[48] The forces that would support the breakthrough in federal support for elementary and secondary education were growing more hopeful and confident; among them were many who supported more funds for research.

LBJ Takes Over

The persons who were in Washington that fateful day when President Kennedy was assassinated have little difficulty recalling where they were and what they were doing when they first received the news. Moynihan gives a vivid description of his sense of loss and bewilderment:

I was in the White House when the word came that President Kennedy was dead. There were perhaps a dozen of us gathered in Ralph Dungan's office in the southeast corner of the west wing, waiting. The knowledge came silently. Somehow in the same instant everyone in the room knew. Hubert Humphrey arrived. A strong, good man. He opened his arms, embraced Dungan, eyes blazing and wet, and exclaimed: "What have they done to us?"[49]

So much was underway, so many had been making preparations for the years ahead; so much spade work had been accomplished. And now, to what purpose?

Lyndon Baines Johnson gave answers far more quickly than anyone expected. As Halberstam described it:

Lyndon Johnson seemed in those first few months to be always in motion, running, doing, persuading; if later much of the nation, bitter over its seemingly unscheduled and unchartered journey into Southeast Asia, turned on him and remembered his years with distaste, it was grateful for him then, with good reason. His mandate seemed to be to hold the country together, to continue to exhort from those around him their best, to heal wounds and divisions.[50]

In a mood of grief, the Congress was spurred on to action in education as in so many other areas in which President Kennedy had expressed an interest. The Higher Education Facilities Act of 1963 was passed on December 16; then the

Vocational Education Act, that authorized 10 percent of all furture appropriations be set aside for research and development, was passed two days later.

Congress matched Johnson's deep interest in education in 1964. Carl Perkins, Chairman of the Committee on Labor and Education of the House of Representatives submitted the Elementary and Secondary Education Improvement Act of 1964 that provided $1 billion per year to be distributed to the states. In the Senate, Senator Wayne Morse produced the Morse-Dent bill that had a new twist to how federal funds might be distributed under a definition of "impaction."[51] The administration was caught off balance with Morse's bill, but found much to study in it.[52] And they needed to stall, for the administration's legislative package was in the process of being put together by a special task force.

The Gardner Task Force

On May 22, 1964, at the University of Michigan, President Johnson announced that he was assembling a series of working groups to help him design the Great Society. One of these was to become the Task Force on Education, chaired by John Gardner, then President of the Carnegie Corporation. Gardner, a psychologist before becoming a foundation executive, had shown an interest in improving education for many years. He supported the Commission on Mathematics in 1955; funded the James Conant studies of the American high school, junior high school, and teacher education. A life-long Republican, he had drafted the chapter on national education goals for President Eisenhower's Commission on National Goals.

Joining Gardner's Task Force were twelve other members:

James E. Allen, Jr., Commissioner of Education, N.Y. State Department of Education;

Hedley W. Donovan, Editor in Chief, *Time;*

Harold B. Gores, President, Educational Facilities Laboratories, Inc.;

Clark Kerr, President, University of California;

Edwin H. Land, President, Polaroid Corporation;

Sidney P. Marland, Superintendent of Schools, Pittsburgh;

David Riesman, Henry Ford II, Professor of the Social Sciences, Harvard;

The Reverend Paul C. Reinert, President, St. Louis University;

Mayor Raymond R. Tucker, St. Louis, Missouri;

Ralph W. Tyler, Director, Center for Advanced Study in the Behavioral Sciences;

Stephen J. Wright, President, Fisk University;

Jerrold R. Zacharias, Professor of Physics, Massachusetts Institute of Technology.

Staff to this committee was William Cannon from BOB.

This task force, like the other thirteen recruited at the time, were instructed to operate secretly; neither names nor final reports were made public during the Johnson presidency. This style would enable each group to concentrate on finding new ideas and new approaches to the problems faced by American society, Johnson reasoned.[53] Many working papers were prepared by members of the Task Force and staff; these were circulated and reviewed with dispatch. Gardner himself set the pace and the standards for the group so that by Labor Day, 1964, the major ideas had emerged.[54]

The importance of this Task Force has been debated. Ianni thinks that the major ideas, particularly in research, came from other sources, and Keppel himself does not now believe that it had as much impact as others like to believe.[55] His reaction comes in part because the legislative program was being put together at the same time the Task Force was writing its report. But while Johnson wanted this like all his groups to leave the political matters to him and his assistants, the Gardner Task Force was acutely aware of the political realities of educational legislation and the need for breakthroughs in educational ideas in Congress.[56]

The Gardner Task Force served three important functions: (1) it helped to crystallize some important new ideas about how to improve American education, (2) it dared to think big and thereby helped to legitimate an effort in public education at a level hereto unknown, and (3) it served as something like a grand privy council for the several networks that had been trying to improve education. In many ways, the Gardner Task Force was the high water mark for a distinguished group of persons whose influence on federal policy in education had been growing in the late 1950s and early 1960s (see Chapter 3).

What did Gardner believe about American schools? "Education," he was to write in 1965, "needs to be better than it is—not just somewhat better but a great deal better."[57] In the Task Force report, he had written, "We must overhaul American education."[58] And to him money was not the only answer, but new ideas; "innovation" became the watch word of the task force. "We are not going to succeed. . . in solving the major problems facing us without substantial innovation."[59] And in the report, "We now know, beyond all doubt, that educationally speaking, the old ways of doing things will not solve our problems. We are going to have to shed outworn educational practices, dismantle outmoded educational facilities, and create [a] new and better learning environment."[60]

The problems were of such magnitude and were so complex that the Task Force recognized that "in this era of rapid change, we cannot depend on a single burst of innovation. We need a system designed to accomplish its own continuous renewal."[61] And in another place in the report, "Curriculum improvement today is hampered by the fact that we have very inadequate institutional arrangements for innovation . . . ."[62]

Throughout the report is the assumption, both stated and tacit, that the new ideas must be based on sound research. And as Tyler said, "The view that educational research would make a difference, that if you brought knowledge to bear on social problems it would improve them, dominated the Gardner Task Force."[63] Gardner himself admitted that he believed in 1964 that research in the social and behavioral science had produced a fund of ideas that needed to be applied to education.[64] Furthermore, the entire task force was viewed as believing that "not only was more research needed but that there *should* be more research."[65]

But research alone wouldn't produce the changes that were needed in education. New mechanisms were needed to encourage the use of research in the system. Thus, the Task Force concentrated on the processes needed for change and the institutions that were needed rather than on the substantive issues.[f]

What were these new institutions? Two terms appear in the main body of the report: educational laboratories and supplementary educational centers. Educational laboratories are labeled "national" on page iii of the report, and it was the intention of the Task Force in the beginning to make them analogous to national science laboratories, like the Argonne lab outside Chicago and the Brookhaven Lab on Long Island:

As we conceive them, the laboratories would be more closely akin to the great national laboratories of the Atomic Energy Commission and should share many of their features.[66]

But while "ample" attention should be paid to research, "the central focus of the laboratories will be on the development and dissemination of educational innovations."[67] The report acknowledges that the Office of Education already has created new institutions for this purpose, called R&D centers, but sees the labs as going extensively beyond them in three respects:

(a) considerably greater emphasis on development and upon the dissemination of innovation, (b) the use of experimental schools and extensive pilot programs in the regular schools and (c) provision for teacher training as an integral part of the program.[68]

To Zacharias, this statement described his ESI. But not to Ralph Tyler, an author of another position paper. He wanted institutions that would help extend the

---

[f]The report does also deal in substantive issues. For example it has reference to the nongraded school throughout and discusses the need for curriculum reform in some detail. But I agree with William Cannon that they concentrated on how to bring about reform in American education more than what reforms they saw as needed. Interview with William Cannon, September 30, 1974.

knowledge base and produce new instructional, or learning systems, and would not just imitate book publishing houses. As he said, "I wanted institutions that were alerted to the needs of schools but aware of the research literature in what they designed to meet those needs. We wanted them to be able to use what the labs produced with slight modification."[69]

The supplementary education centers were viewed by some members of the Task Force as a way to get massive federal funding to schools by avoiding the church–state issue and at the same time avoiding the pitfalls of formula-type aid. Some saw the centers as a way of loosening up the existing system, to make it more innovative. Others saw them as establishing a parallel school system or as a way of taking some of the pressure off parochial schools. To the total Task Force, it was a way of making available to children ". . . the full range of the community's educational and cultural resources."[70] While the centers might be housed in existing schools, they also could be located in museums or libraries. Several options were provided for funding this program: through the states, local communities, local school districts, or through nonprofit, private groups. But whatever agency was selected, the Task Force intended that it seek the funds through application to a federal authority.

The final report was submitted to the president on November 14, 1964,[g] and soon thereafter an internal group was called together to incorporate the recommendations into legislation. Its principal members were Cannon (who with Gardner had prepared the final copy for the report), Douglas Cater from the White House staff, Wilbur Cohen, Assistant Secretary for Legislation in HEW, and Keppel. Each had a vital role to play in shaping and supporting the Elementary and Secondary Education Act of 1965. Cater represented the president who played a very active role in lining up support. Wilbur Cohen was well known and respected by the Congress for his previous work in the fields of health and welfare. Keppel worked well with and through him on the Hill but was his own man with the interest groups outside government.

ESEA was written with artistry; Titles I, II, III and V provided a delicate balance in what they provided for whom.[h] Title I, assistance for the education of children of low-income families, satisfied a large bulk of the public school people who wanted massive federal aid; Title II, funds for school library resources and instructional materials, gave something both to public and parochial schools; Title III Promised help to parochial schools and pleased those who were looking for educational improvement; Title V strengthened the state agencies, thereby pleasing powerful forces in the educational establishment. No wonder that the admin-

---

[g]Copies of the report were marked "For your eyes only," and each person to whom it was sent was instructed not to distribute it to staff members. The report was made public only after the opening of the Lyndon B. Johnson Library in 1973.

[h]Title IV of the Act was viewed primarily as an amendment to the Cooperative Research Act, and while it was worthwhile, it was not essential to building the balance needed to get the bill passed.

istration was able to extract pledges from both the educational lobbyists and the Congress to pass the bill intact, without amendments until ESEA became law.[71]

A few weeks after Johnson had been overwhelmingly returned to the White House, he called together all those responsible for major bills to hear a progress report and to urge them on to quick action. "Look," Keppel reports him as saying, "get this done as fast as you can—we came in here with a very large majority, but we may lose it at the rate of a million votes a month. Get those hearings. Get this done. Get that coonskin up on the wall."[72]

The result is well-known history. With almost unprecedented haste, the Congress passed the Elementary and Secondary Education Act, in the House by a margin of 263 to 153 and in the Senate by 73 to 18. President Johnson signed the bill into law (P.L. 89–10) on April 11, 1965, in his own one-room schoolhouse in Texas. The next day, the White House was filled with invited supporters of education who heard him say: "I think Congress has passed the most significant education bill in the history of Congress."[73]

The federal government had taken on a new responsibility in the support of public education. And while there had been talk of creating a new agency to handle this responsibility (the Gardner Task Force report discussed the creation of an independent Office of Education at the presidential level, like the Office of Economic Opportunity, and/or the creation of a new cabinet-level Department of Education at that time), there was only the Office of Education available. It would have to do. Besides, it had Frank Keppel, whose star still appeared to many on the outside as rising because of the ESEA victory. The prospects were that a new day might be dawning for USOE and its supporters.

Educational research could only benefit from all this, or so it also seemed at the time. Title IV, ESEA, broadened the authority of the Office of Education under the original Cooperative Research Act. It authorized grant as well as contract procedures and extended these privileges to private, profit-making research organizations in addition to the nonprofit agencies previously covered. It also authorized funds for the training of researchers and those in research-related activities. And it gave impetus to the creation of the educational laboratories by authorizing funds for the construction of laboratory facilities.

Research also was aided in several indirect ways. As cited previously, the Gardner Task Force believed that educational research would make a difference. As Sam Halperin put it, "We saw researchers to be the good guys."[74] It was the personnel in the research bureau that continued to interact most frequently with those who were writing ESEA and who enjoyed the closest relationships with the experts whom the White House consulted. Members of that bureau had many reasons to expect that they would lead the way in carving out the new leadership role for the USOE in American education. That they were not to do so is the story of how ESEA and the ideas of the Gardner Task Force were implemented.

5 Gearing Up to Go

Will Washington, D.C., ever again be as exciting for educators as it was in the 1960s? Money from Congress at unthinkable levels sparked ideas, zany and sound together, but with an aura of hope. As Moynihan said, ". . .in the early 1960s in Washington we thought we could do anything. . . ."[1]

President Johnson set the tone by believing that the federal government could remake the American society, not just cure some of its fundamental problems as it had done under Franklin Roosevelt. The Great Society would be a better world, and its benefactor would be the institutions of government in Washington, D.C.

That he was the leader there could be little doubt. He grabbed hold of the reins early and unmistakingly held them as long as the American people let him. "He was a relentless man," says Halberstan, "who pushed himself and all others with the same severity. He expected the bureaucracy to touch and move the country as he touched and moved them. He sensed his opportunities, particularly after his big win in 1964. He knew that when you wind that big, you can have almost anything you want for a while."[2]

And education was right in the middle of Johnson's domestic policies. Education, he announced is ". . . central to the purposes of this Administration, and at the core of all of our hopes for a Great Society."[3] In his educational message to Congress, he stated:

Every child must be encouraged to get as much education as he has the ability to take. We must demand that our schools increase not only the quantity but the quality of American education.[4]

Whatever other way those around him came to view Johnson toward the end of his career, few doubted his sincerity about the value of education.[5]

How did this priority affect educators? Read again these words by Frank Keppel written at the end of 1965:

A wonderful thing happened to 1965 on its way into history. It became a year to remember: as the year the nation fully recognized it can reach its potential only through education;—as the year a citizenry, expressing its will through elected leadership, called on education to take the lead in charting our nation's course.
Quite suddenly—or so it seems—the educator is a captain in a nationwide crusade to improve the quality of life; goals that seemed unreachable have become practical and close at hand.[6]

More important than words were the appropriations voted by the Congress; in the 1964 fiscal year the federal government spent $896,956,000 for public elementary and secondary schools, or 4.4 percent of the total revenue receipts. In the next fiscal year, this had increased to $2,015,000,000, 7.9 percent of the total revenue receipts.[7] For Title I of the Elementary and Secondary Education Act alone, Congress appropriated nearly $1 billion in FY 1966. The budget request for the entire bill that year was over $1.33 billion.[8] Looking back, those figures may seem paltry for the hopes of the time (we have become far more knowledgeable about what it takes to change our schools) but to a generation accustomed to far more limited resources, they fed the fires of hope and excitement.

The Office of Education, the ancient regime as some termed it, became infected with the new spirit. Visitors could not help but notice day after day the new furniture being moved in and around FOB #6 (the inauspicious designation for the structure in which USOE was housed) or the many workmen constructing new partitions and installing seemingly unlimited numbers of telephones. Most obvious was the increased hustle among employees as they shuttled in and out of cubicles; the Office of Education, which had become increasingly more animated after the passage of the National Defense Education Act, reached a pace that was reminiscent of military agencies during World War II.

Reorganizing USOE

The problem was that the Office of Education wasn't up to it; growth accentuated many lingering problems. In September 1965, it had 2,071 employees, an increase of 577 in one year.[9] For the next fiscal year, it was given an additional 634 positions.[10] It was faced with "complex problems of design, priority-setting, and consent-building,"[11] all within a heightened and intensified political climate. The Office was caught in a double crunch of launching massive new spending programs in new ways that demanded innovative, yet untried and untested mechanisms.

Keppel was well aware of the inadequacies of his agency, but the task of designing a legislative package that would win the necessary support inside and outside the government kept him from dealing effectively with the management problems. Besides he did not see himself particularly as an effective manager. He needed some high-powered administrative help. But the shortage of supergrade positions (GS 16 through 18) in USOE made this difficult; his own salary in 1964 was only $20,000,[12] which was less than most of the school superintendents in the D.C. area.

Nevertheless, he had been quietly working through men like Kermit Gordon, Director, Bureau of the Budget; John Gardner; and John Macy of the Civil Service Commission who was one of the president's advisors on these matters. During the winter of 1963, Keppel was pointed toward Henry Loomis, at that time Director of the Voice of America.

Loomis thought of himself as a career civil servant who worked in the government by choice after launching a successful career outside it; earlier he had been an assistant to Karl Compton and then to his successor, James R. Killian, Jr., presidents of the Massachusetts Institute of Technology. Before going to the Voice of America, he had served in important positions in the Department of Defense, the National Security Council, and the Office of Science and Technology.

Loomis refused Keppel's first offer, but by March 1965, he was experiencing difficulties in running the Voice of America so that he was more receptive when Keppel again contacted him.[13] But after checking more closely into the Office of Education, he was not encouraged by what he saw. By then, as he put it, the question was whether to leave government and say, "To hell with it," or, to try to straighten out USOE. After thinking it over he decided that it sounded like "pretty good fun."[14] In March 1964, he accepted the offer to become the deputy commissioner for USOE.

All hell broke loose in the White House when the president found out.[15] Apparently Johnson had known about Loomis (who was, after all, an admirer of Eisenhower and kept his photograph on his office wall) for some time, but word got to LBJ that his farewell address at the Voice of America, as reported in a local Washington newspaper was critical of the president's policies. Keppel tells that while he was on the phone to a Southern governor, the operator broke in announcing that the president was on the phone—to tell him that Loomis was impossible and to rescind the appointment.[16] Johnson saw Loomis as being disloyal and loyalty to the president as a person, not abstract loyalty to an issue or a cause, was demanded of his appointees "above all other qualities."[17]

Keppel stood his ground and won that battle, but his relationship to the president was impaired from that point on. For example, all new supergrades for USOE had to be cleared personally by Marvin Watson in the White House, thereby adding "another hurdle to an already cumbersome process of personnel recruitment."[18]

Loomis found the Office in even worse shape than he had imagined. He describes how he had been in his job only a few minutes when a Deputy Commissioner came to him with some tax rebate papers to sign; USOE staff were accustomed to taking every little thing to the top.[19] That was only one of the several problems that plagued the agency. Bailey lists six: (1) the atomization and specialization of departments; (2) superannuated personnel and antiquated personnel systems; (3) archaic financial and management information systems; (4) an unrationalized bureau and field structure; (5) anomie with the executive branch; (6) fear of the charge of federal control.[20]

Loomis prepared himself to do battle by bringing some of his staff with him, the best known of whom became Walter Mylecrain, called by some the "Terrible Turk," who even Loomis admitted was "ruthless."[21] Considering that Loomis himself was considered as being "tough," this team presented a formidable image. But that is precisely what some thought was needed, for the Office was in for a shakeup of unparalleled proportions.

The president's victory statement made at the signing of the ESEA at Stonewall, Texas, announced that he was preparing the Office of Education for the big job it would have to do by appointing a task force to assist the Secretary of HEW in the next sixty days to work out organizational and personnel problems. Loomis and Keppel agreed with Bill Cannon and others outside of USOE that sweeping changes were called for; the Office had to be drastically revised and that meant assistance from the highest levels of the government. On April 16, 1965, Douglas Cater announced to Secretary Calebrezze that three men were being assigned full-time for from thirty to sixty days to reorganize the Office of Education.[22] The chairman was Dwight A. Ink from the Atomic Energy Commission. They were encouraged to go fast and hard and with a "meat ax."[23]

One of the crunch issues became the number of supergrade positions that the Civil Service Commission would authorize. The Task Force and the Keppel–Loomis team agreed to ask for fifty. For this, they needed help from the White House, but Cater balked at first. Loomis went after him:

I said, "I don't give a god damn how many there are in the government, and you know it. You know you can't make it otherwise; you want this thing to fall? You want the President to be discredited? You're going to tell me, sitting here, that you can't get fifty? That's absurd"–that was done deliberately to be a shocker, to say that this wasn't business as usual.[24]

Eventually they settled for an increase of fifteen to twenty, but a point had been made and an order of magnitude for the impending changes established.

There were many problems like this. It was generally believed the new programs required persons who knew the bureaucracy rather than those who were just educational specialists. But there were almost 2,000 existing employees, many of whom were not considered to be proficient bureaucrats, for whom jobs had to be found. New job descriptions were put together by cutting and pasting from the new and the old.[25] As a result, many persons ended up being program "specialists" who were responsible for overseeing projects for which they had had little, if any, preparation.[26]

Then there was the issue of how to organize the existing and traditional thirty-six units of USOE in more functional relationships, given the new authority granted by the 88th and 89th Congresses. They settled on a plan that recognized the major constituencies of the Office but that dispersed the duties among four bureaus (Elementary and Secondary; Adult and Vocational; Higher Education; and Research) and a number of staff offices for administration, legislation, information, and the like.[27] Two centers also were created, one of which was for educational statistics. The report was submitted to the president on June 15, and in less than two weeks the reorganization was acted upon.

Bailey describes the results:

The anguish can only be imagined. The ensuing, if temporary, administrative chaos was shattering. For days and weeks, people could not find each other's offices—sometimes not even their own. Telephone extensions connected appropriate parties only by coincidence. A large number of key positions in the new order were vacant or were occupied by acting directors who were frequently demoralized by status loss. Those who could not live with the status loss resigned. And all of this came at a time of maximum workload.[28]

More than two-thirds of the bureaus were changed, and seventeen of the twenty-five supergrade officers were assigned new roles or functions. As Loomis describes it, the Ink Report "violated every sacred cow in the pasture, of which there were a great many."[29] And total authorized positions in USOE were increased to 2,400, which, given the number of vacancies caused by resignations and unfilled positions, meant that 800 new persons were being sought.

Recruiting went into high gear. An executive staffing group and a special supergrade examining board for USOE were set up in the Civil Service Commission to expedite processing. Keppel sent out special letters to foundations and universities and other letters went out to civil service regional directors. More than 1,000 names in White House files were reexamined. New faces appeared at all levels. And they were noticeably different on the whole from the "oldtimers"; they were viewed as younger on the average and were "lawyer-manager types or academicians from the disciplines or from the "better" schools of education.[30]

Therein lay probably the principal dilemma for the recruiters. The largest pool of interested persons, the educationists, were precisely the category that wasn't wanted and there was a shortage of those who were desired.[31] The shortage of personnel became a constant complaint during the Keppel and Howe years in USOE and became intensified as Congress continued to pass new legislation like the Higher Education Act of 1965 that launched the National Teacher Corps and the Education Professions Development Act.

Did the Ink Commission report and the cateclismic reorganization help or hinder the work of the Office of Education? The "oldtimers" saw that it went too far, too fast and the implementors as being unnecessarily ruthless. And there is some doubt that the results were lasting; Loomis was not there long enough and the career men then set about "putting it back properly the way it was in 1962."[32] Nevertheless Bailey sees many improvements: the commissioner's office was strengthened; a new personnel system and more modern financial and management systems were installed; and a more rational bureau and field structure were implemented.[33]

It was within this framework that the research programs of the Office were reexamined and recast and it is to them that we now turn our attention.

The Bureau of Research

The reorganization recognized research as one of the major functions of the office by creating a bureau for it, but it had been a touch-and-go issue. Loomis called it the toughest issue of the reorganization since there were strong feelings that research should be a part of all the other bureaus; in the end, the "tipping argument" was that USOE needed another bureau chief.[34] Ianni describes how this issue was decided "on the last day" of the Commission's study.[35]

The reorganization gave to the Bureau of Research the responsibility for administering all of the Office of Education's extramural research. It was to be an attempt to "produce the necessary total approach to educational improvement,"[36] for the focus of educational research had shifted in the Office "to the solution of emerging problems and the development of new and better ways for education to fulfill its changing responsibilities."[37] A single bureau could better coordinate, plan, and administer the several funding programs.[a]

There had been sound arguments on the other side, however—the side that wanted research kept within, and therefore closer to, the other operating bureaus. Research results would more likely be used, it was argued, and could more quickly be translated into action. Also the needs of the practitioners could be communicated more effectively to the researchers. To counter these arguments, the new Bureau of Research was organized into divisions drawn along lines that reflected the larger structure of the Office. So there was created a Division of Elementary and Secondary Research; Adult and Vocational Research; and Higher Education Research. For those programs that didn't fall into those categories, two more divisions were established: a Division of Laboratories (which became the Division of Laboratories and Research Development) and a Division of Research Training and Dissemination.

Who would fill the new position of Associate Commissioner for the Bureau of Research? Ralph Flynt, who had served as the assistant commissioner and head of the Bureau of Educational Research and Development, was moved to an associate commissionership for International Education. Ianni was given the deputy associate commissionership. The search was on for a new, more highly powered figure—but from the industrial world, not academia. For Keppel himself saw the need "for closer relations with the private sector."[38]

The 1960s was the time when the business and industrial world was showing a heightened interest in public education as a market place.[39] New subsidiaries were created like General Learning Corporation, and many major firms acquired textbook publishing companies like Silver Burdett and D.C. Heath. With public

---

[a]In 1965, there were eight separate legislative authroizations providing support for programs administered by the Bureau of Research: The Cooperative Research Act, P.L. 83–531 amended by ESEA, P.L. 89–10; The Vocational Education Act of 1963; Handicapped Children and Youth Research and Demonstration; Title VII of NDEA; Title VI of NDEA; P.L. 480, the counterpart funds; Captioned films for the deaf; and Library Research, Title II of the Higher Education Act of 1965.

expenditures for education at the $50 billion level,[40] exceeded only by defense spending (that appeared to be peaking in the mid 1960s), it is not surprising that education had market appeal. A *Saturday Review* editorial said in reviewing the scene:

Education has suddenly become the nation's major growth industry, offering a commercial market that is expanding with astonishing speed as new funds, in large amounts, become available.[41]

Keppel was seen as wanting to fill one of the new posts with a person experienced in, and knowledgeable about, the new industries; the most logical spot was the Bureau of Research rather than one of the bureaus that operated more closely with the state agencies and school men.[b] He was wise to be careful because many educators were bothered by these developments and suspicious that industry would become too influential.[42]

The two highest men on the list for the job were from IBM and Westinghouse Electric Corporation; eventually R. Louis Bright, Director of Educational Technology from Westinghouse, was selected, and he assumed his responsibilities in January 1966.

Bright had some impressive credentials. He received his doctorate in electrical engineering from Carnegie Institute of Technology, where he then taught for seven years. He shifted to Westinghouse where, as an engineer, he moved steadily up the ladder to his directorship. In 1955, he was awarded the Alfred Nobel prize for the best paper published in any of the professional engineering journals. And he was no stranger to the political life of Washington. The interchange that took place during the budget hearings on February 7, 1966, may have surprised some of the USOE staff about this quiet, unobtrusive new associate commissioner:

Fogarty: I too notice you have Mr. Bright over there in the back who I met a year or two ago when he was with industry developing some of his equipment.[43]

As Bright explains it, he was one of the executives Westinghouse relied upon to keep the corporation informed of what was happening within the federal government.[44]

Bright needed all that experience, both political and administrative, for he inherited a federal agency that in some ways could be described as an Oklahoma-style land rush, and one in which persons outside USOE were in danger of being bowled over. To help explain all the changes, the Bureau of Research toward the end of 1965 scheduled two meetings, one each in San Francisco and Washington,

---

[b]He also turned outside academia for the assistant commissioner to head the National Center for Educational Statistics, Alexander M. Mood—formerly, with the CEIR Corporation and head of the General Analysis Corporation.

D.C., to which more than 1,000 persons were invited. The five new divisions each described their new initiatives and procedures. The field was told about the new laboratory program, the nine new R&D centers that had been funded, the developing Educational Research Information Center (ERIC), and the new program in research training. Emerging efforts in vocational and adult education were discussed, and new curriculum studies and comparative research programs in higher education were presented. Basic research was encouraged, along with applied studies and development projects. To fund all this, the Office in fiscal year 1966 had slightly over $100 million.[45]

To run all of this sensibly, the research bureau may have needed new blood, but it also needed some continuity. As it turned out, the three sources of leadership, the commissioner, the director of the Bureau and the Advisory Committee, were changed, and there became a sharp break with the past.

Keppel Leaves; Howe Enters

It was an accepted fact of political life in Washington in the 1960s that Commissioners of Education had limited tenure. In the ninety-five years of its existence at the time Keppel arrived, the Office had seen fifteen commissioners; in the decade 1953–1963, there had been four. In many ways, it was amazing that Keppel lasted three years, for he had become controversial in Congress and had been assigned responsibilities for which the office of commissioner provided little real backup authority. So long as there was support of the White House, he was protected, but by 1965, he had skated far out onto thin political ice.

He had lost most of his political maneuvrability because of the very active role he had sought (and been granted) for the Office of Education in the civil rights struggle. Title VI of the Civil Rights Act of 1964 (P.L. 88–352) required that all federal agencies withhold federal funds from any state program that did not meet the requirements for desegregating facilities. But it had special meaning to USOE, which was given primary responsibility for determining compliance of all educational institutions.[46]

President Johnson in 1965 wanted to see the 5,000 school districts of the South desegregated as rapidly as possible. During the summer of 1965, he called almost daily for reports from the Commissioner. In other ways, Johnson maintained a more discreet distance. Keppel explained that when it came to drawing up the guidelines on desegregation, for example, ". . . the President played no part in this personally";[47] neither did the Justice Department nor the Department of HEW.[48] As the Commissioner saw it, ". . . [Secretary] Celebrezze was for the Civil rights Act but he sure as hell didn't want to get into political trouble with it. . . ." Keppel, however, was willing to take this responsibility and is proud of it:

Here I will take some credit, if I may. I had pushed the Office of Education from being a southern oriented bureaucracy to being a leader in desegregation within HEW. We were well ahead of the Public Health Service and the other services. We were sort of the front runners.[50]

As sticky as the struggle in the South was, matters became stickier when the attention shifted to desegregating northern school districts as well. And it was here that Keppel eventually foundered.

The story of how he withheld funds from the Chicago school system is well known.[51] Mayor Daley got to the president who ordered Keppel to back off and the commissioner knew his days were numbered. Actually he had already had discussions with key aides and friends about how long he should remain, and he was seen as suffering from "battle fatigue" by some of his associates.[52]

In December 1965, Keppel resigned as commissioner but was then appointed Assistant Secretary for Education in the Department of Health, Education and Welfare. Given Lyndon Johnson's habit of discarding employees for whom he had no further use,[53] it was symbolic of how esteemed Keppel was that his colleagues were able to bring about this kind of transfer and in such an affable manner.

His passing produced remarkably few ripples outside the government. An editorial in the *Saturday Review*, which had only tepid praise, used phrases like: ". . . he has discharged his responsibilities with great distinction, though not with unmitigated success."[54] Yet he left a remarkable record, particularly when it is remembered all that happened in the Office of Education during his three years there and with, as Michael Kirst puts it, "a very slim staff."[55]

Thus, before the new research efforts of the Office were really launched, the man who had presided over so many of the discussions and who had influenced or made so many critical decisions, was gone.

Ianni Leaves; Bright Enters

Ianni's influence on the research program of the Office was discussed in Chapter 4. Most of his colleagues from those days are certain he wanted to be the new associate commissioner for research. In many ways the very growth that Ianni worked to produce is what prevented him from getting the appointment. He was seen primarily as a "super salesman," particularly with congressional staffs and committee members. Salvatore Rinaldi, one of his assistants, describes his approach:

Whenever he met with Congressmen or their assistants he would deal in specific examples, using projects that were popular like the Bank Street School Project. It showed that he did his homework in advance, he could talk to committee members about what research was going on in their districts. He would meet with them in their offices, for lunches, in the evening—with members of both sides (Republicans or Democrats). He would meet with Herman Downy, the staff director then of the Senate Subcommittee every couple of weeks. Ralph Flynt would cover for us.[56]

But the time for salesmanship had passed. New talent was demanded now of the top man, and with the commissioner wrapped up with issues of desegregation and other "hot items," all bureau heads in USOE had to handle many more of their own administrative and programmatic problems. Ianni was not seen as that kind of man.

His departure also went largely unnoticed. Only a brief comment about his resignation appeared in the official newsletter of the American Educational Research Association, for example.[57] In private conversations, his resignation was discussed—but with an ambivalence that reflected the growing separation between the people in the field who produced the research and the agency that was supporting them. It was as if they wanted someone in Washington they knew, even if they weren't quite certain that he was on their side. As one observer put it:

Clark worked hard so that he could pass the cudgel to Ianni, believing that Fritz would continue his and Roy Hall's efforts to expand the field. That he did. But Clark also thought Fritz would protect the molecular field and he got fooled.[58]

Ianni's replacement reflected a far greater break with that strategy of the 1950s and early 1960s. Richard Louis Bright was an industrial engineer; they and academic scholars have a history of difficulties in appreciating each other's accomplishments.[59] But Bright saw even more differences. To him educational researchers were not up to what was now demanded of them; he once referred to most of the papers read at the 1966 AERA Annual Meeting as "second rate dissertations."[60]

Ianni may have shared this view privately, but his solution was to involve and to keep uppermost more highly respected scholars and school men. Bright's response was to turn to his staff, to emphasize staff planning and resource allocation, and to contract for specific assignments thereby with capable, recognized research organizations. As a result, within a few months, many researchers who for years had been consulted by USOE officials felt left out.

There was yet the third support link to the field—the Research and Advisory Committee. Here, too, continuity was disrupted.

The Research Advisory Council. Public Law 531 originally specified that the commissioner must obtain the advice and recommendations of educational research specialists who were competent to evaluate proposals. Commissioner Brownell created a nine-member advisory committee for this purpose in 1956. In 1962 the name was changed to the Research Advisory Council (RAC), and in

1963 seven panels were created to assist the RAC by providing technical review and evaluation of proposals.[61] In 1965, these panels were disbanded and a new system using field readers and consultants substituted. The Council was expanded to twelve members and its function more broadly defined to advise the commissioner on matters of policy.

In the early years, the appointments to the Council tended to come from the fraternity of educational researchers. In 1957, for example, seven of the nine members were persons well known in the educational research literature who had high elected or appointed positions in the American Educational Research Association.[c] Ianni saw the Council in those days as representing a small circle of friends,[62] but by the 1960s, this number of "fraternity members" had dropped to three, a reflection both of the attempts of the Office staff to push outward from what they saw as a narrow base of researchers[63] and of the spreading interest among other fields of research in the extramural program of USOE.

Keppel's appointments to all of his advisory committees reflected his well-publicized attempts to disengage the Office of Education from the cozy relationship that had built up with the well-known educational associations. Yet he was as concerned with extending the involvement in policy advising to more individuals and groups than simply shutting others out. As one staff member reports, "Keppel wanted more people involved in OE affairs in those days. We consulted widely with organizations like the Chamber of Commerce, the American Medical Association, labor unions, and the like."[64] And in some ways Keppel had no other choice. For by the end of 1965 the responsibility of the Bureau of Research had expanded so widely that it was receiving proposals for activities as diverse as requests for support for an international conference to extend the concerns of American art education to other nations and ways to explore the potential role of vocational education in pre-service and in-service training for occupations in state and local governments.[65]

The 1966 RAC reflected another of Keppel's concerns—for high quality appointments. There has never been a more distinguished group of advisors on educational research in a federal agency. Yet whatever hopes Keppel had for this group, little materialized. In fact, the Council never seems to have understood what their function was. The Chairman, Fred C. Cole, admitted at the April 29, 1966, meeting that he did not understand the status of this Council or its responsibilities.[66] Various attempts were made verbally and in writing to clarify its functions. For example, at the October 7, 1966, meeting, R. Louis Bright described four duties of the RAC:

1.   To advise on programs;
2.   To identify larger research gaps and priorities;

---

[c]These members were Ralph Tyler, Chester Harris, Frank Hubbard, Erick Lindman, J. Cayce Morrison, Willard Olson, and H.H. Remers.

3. To serve as a link between the Bureau of Research and the research com-
    munity;
4. Where appropriate, to sit as a review group on major programs or contracts.[67]

But the difficulty did not lie with the inability of the staff to express *desir-able* functions so much as their inability to find and hold to a working relation-ship with an outside group during a time when events were moving so rapidly. The Advisory Council had no direct responsibility in the budget-building process, the legislative process, nor in communicating with vital influencials within or out-side the government. In the early years, when the RAC members were recognized members of what was then a fairly cohesive research community, the USOE staff knew that the Council members were opinion leaders. Their reactions to events and personalities in the Office would form the images and responses of the men and women in the field. But by the mid-1960s the community had become so diverse and amorphous that individual RAC members at best could communicate effectively with only a small segment of it. And some members had no linkages at all to research producers. The chairman was Fred Cole, President of Washing-ton and Lee University; both he and his institution were virtually unknown to educational researchers and other social scientists.

The importance given to "prestige appointments"—that is, selecting men and women who were highly visible academicians or administrators, reflected the mistaken notion that political support from the constituencies of the Office of Education would be forthcoming if a few of their leaders could be "involved" in the activities of the Bureau of Research. The differing functions and responsibili-ties of research communities as opposed to political constituencies[68] was seldom understood or appreciated among the bureaucrats in the Bureau of Research.

On the other hand, the educational research community in the mid-1960s was not easy to plat. Recognizing this, the American Educational Research Asso-ciation in 1967 went in search of its membership universe, to see what had hap-pened to it after ten years of federal government funding. The result was a series of studies and commissioned papers that were reported on at a colloquium held in October, 1968. One of the studies, which examined the way scientific infor-mation is exchanged in educational research, found that AERA members were less familiar with the work of their colleagues than researchers represented in nine other scientific or engineering associations.[69] The investigators (William Garvey, Carnot Nelson, and Nan Lin) found that the 256 educational researchers cited 67 different journals to which they planned to submit technical papers, the largest number of journals cited in any other study. The communications net-works in educational research had become diffused. These data also lead the in-vestigators to state that they saw no evidence of an invisible college in educational research—that inner, elite core of the most respected scholars or scientists in any field of study that gave so much coherency to a field.[70]

The best way the AERA colloquium could view the educational research community in 1968 was to consider it as an emerging field or as a field in transition. But however it could be described, educational research was not in the best condition to set up the kind of controls of the federal research support program that was characteristic of most of the other fields of research. As Kash said:

By the 1960s a highly decentralized but nonetheless well-established and smoothly functioning set of mechanisms existed for the management of the politics-research linkages. Much of the decision making and operation of federal research policy was handled by the research system itself.[71]

Even if the education R&D community had these mechanisms, however, the RAC probably would have had difficulties functioning well. Cronin and Thomas discovered in their study of education councils and committees in HEW that operated between 1966 and 1969 that most of the 26 did not have "a clear understanding of what they are accepting in terms of the definition of their assignment, the work load, and the results expected of them."[72]

Whatever the reason, by the mid-1960s the Research Advisory Council had slipped into a not-too-significant role. Chairman Cole summarized what he saw as its role when he said, ". . . I think what is going to be our function is to try to raise questions, to give advice, and probably hold up things until we can be convinced."[73] David Krathwohl, who served two terms on the RAC states: "By 1965 most RAC members felt that the staff–Council lines were set and that the staff was looking mostly for legitimation."[74]

With new men in key management positions, a pocketful of money and increased authority, heady expectations, a field that was preoccupied with taking advantage of unexpected resources, and little restraint operating through the formal advisory system, the Bureau of Research of USOE, like a flock of fluttering fledglings, was taking off in many directions all at the same time.

Some Bureaucrats and How They Fared: The Division of Educational Laboratories

What was the staff of this newly created Bureau of Research like? How did they function as a group? What were their hopes and aspirations for educational research? And to what forces and events did they respond during these crucial several months in 1966 and 1967?

It would be helpful to answer the first question—what were they like?—if a systematic study had been made of the staff in those days. But events were moving too swiftly and the staff changed too rapidly. Like most agencies, they were composed of leftovers and newcomers—persons with competency in education (or the social sciences) and career officers.

Those staff hired during the Keppel and Ianni years were different from those hired prior to that time. As noted in Chapters 4 and 5, the early staff were mostly persons from the educational enterprise who were sympathetic to academic research and knowledgeable about who was doing what and where. Alice Scates, the first full-time administrator of the CRP, was hired away from the American Council on Education where she was involved in a research project funded by the Office of Naval Research. J. William Asher, another staff assistant, had completed his graduate work in statistics and research design from Purdue University. Howard Hjelm was employed in 1959 after completing his doctoral studies at Peabody College in psychometrics. David Clark, who served as Director of the Cooperative Research Branch in the early 1960s had gained research experience through the Cooperative Program in Educational Administration, a Kellogg Foundation–funded training program aimed at increasing the research sophistication of school practitioners.

Clark, who aspired to become a professor of educational administration, saw the offer to work with the Cooperative Research Program as a real opportunity. He says:

I didn't know much about the literature in educational psychology then and saw the job offer in OE as a way to become more familiar with it. I wanted to learn more about the substance and methodology of inquiry broadly conceived. I saw it as a post-doctoral experience that would give me visibility. I never doubted that to me this was THE major development in education in the federal government.[1]

In the 1960s, recruiting reflected the attempts to broaden the interest in education among the disciplines. Francis A.J. Ianni left the Department of Sociology at Russel Sage College to come to USOE. His promotion to head the Cooperative Research Branch in 1962 gave impetus to that policy. But growth was so slow in those years before ESEA that there were not many key positions to fill; there were only eighteen persons in the Office administering all the R&D programs in 1964.[2] The total appropriations for research administered by USOE in FY 1963 was $13,785,000, up only $3,500,000 since FY 1960.[3]

Beginning in FY 1964, however, appropriations increased appreciably to $19,300,000; they made an even more startling jump the next two years, up to $36,863,000 in 1965 and $100,500,000 a year following that.[4] The Bureau of Research (or the Bureau of Research and Development—BERD as it was called after the reorganization of 1961) increasingly needed new people during those years.

Where did they turn? From outside, Ianni found men like Hendrik Gideonse, a bright 28 year old Harvard Graduate School of Education product who was teaching at Bowdoin College; his specialty was the social sciences curriculum. From inside, he located Lee Burchinal, a credentialed rural, social system sociologist who left teaching at Iowa State to work first with the Department of Agriculture and then with the Vocational Rehabilitation Program in HEW. But these two capable men were exceptions to the rule; recruiting did not go well for the Bureau of Research. As Keppel himself admits, "We didn't bring in the best people there."[5]

Ianni knew where to look for competent researchers in the social and behavioral sciences but not many were interested. The Office of Education was not viewed as an attractive place for bright young people to work, and professors and foundation officials were reluctant to steer their proteges there. But wasn't the work important enough? The response so frequently was "yes" and "no." Take Frank Keppel as an example. He believed in scholarship and he supported the Cooperative Research Program, both as dean at Harvard and later as commissioner. Yet he had reservations. "If you want to find the most meaningful research in the past two decades," he remonstrates, "look at the ideas and the people supported by the foundations, not by the Office of Education."[6]

Keppel's ambivalence was a reflection of a view that was prevalent among many persons from East Coast institutions in those days that the Cooperative Research Program was a captive of a group variously described as "educational psychologists," "midwestern university types," or "teachers college types." These terms—all rather vague and stereotypic—meant to them that the "wrong" group was in control.

In the early Kennedy years, Jerome Wiesner and Sterling McMurrin tried to make the research program something different. Wiesner was viewed as believing that the Course Content Improvement Program of the National Science Foundation provided a better model that attracted better people. McMurrin described Project English, begun during his tenure as commissioner as "patterned after the work done under the auspices of the National Science Foundation in physics, chemistry, mathematics and biology."[7] But McMurrin discovered, as did Keppel after him, that policies and precedent made it very difficult to alter the character and direction of the R&D programs. The National Media Advisory Committee had statutory authority to review all proposals by the commissioner to enter into contracts under Title VII of the NDEA and to review all applications for grants-in-aid under Part A and to certify approval. The Cooperative Research Act specified that no grant or contract could be made by the commissioner until he had obtained the advice and recommendation of outside specialists. Change was to be slow until large increases in expenditures could produce new programs, new people, and new procedures.

This is exactly what happened following the passage of the Elementary and Secondary Education Act. The Ink Commission Reorganization Plan authorized forty positions for the new Bureau of Research.[8] Bodies of all kinds, professional and bureaucratic, were needed immediately. By the fall of 1965, researchers in the field were looking at an array of unknown names as the staff of the Bureau of Research.

At two meetings at which several hundred researchers were invited Walter Mylecraine, Assistant Deputy Commissioner, informed them, "We are no longer a series of professional forces ensconced in the Federal structure; we are Federal administrators." He announced that the staff would "use their professional competencies as a stepping stone for educational change."[9] And indeed they did, as we shall see.

But what did this add up to? Kirst sees that the Bureau of Research evolved into a kind of separatist culture with the Office. "They were off on their own and guarded their money jealously," he reports. This was inspired in part because Ianni had the attitude, as Kirst and many of his colleagues in the Bureau of Elementary and Secondary Education saw it, that the other bureaus were staffed by "dumbells."[10]

This same separatist tendency—a mixture of independence and hautiness—carried over in the relationship of the Bureau of Research to the field. Some of the junior staff, persons with little or no research experience, frequently expressed disdain for most of what happened in research before they were on the scene in the Office.

Bright at times seemed to encourage this attitude. So when he moved to strengthen the power of his staff, it appeared to many to underscore the attitude of "we know best." As one outsider put it, "The bureaucrats in OE ran that program [in the Bureau of Research] with a very heavy hand."[11]

After Ianni left, the Bureau also lost rapport with the Office of Science and Technology and the Bureau of the Budget. This may have been due in part to the change in staff in OST; Joseph Terner left and was replaced by John Mays, a chemist who had been an Associate Program Director in the Course Content Improvement Section of the National Science Foundation. Bright tried to maintain open communication with Emerson Elliot in BOB and with Mays, but increasingly, the Bureau of Research from 1966 was on a divergent course from the views of educational R&D held by the service agencies of the executive branch.

To understand fully how the staff functioned under Bright, we must examine in more detail what they did about specific ideas and how they administered specific programs. We shall concentrate on four: The Regional Educational Laboratories; the R&D Centers; the Educational Research (later Resources) Information Center; and the ES '70 Program. This chapter focuses on the first of these programs.

The Regional Educational Laboratories: Planning Issues

It is a pattern with the federal government that the persons who initiate new programs frequently are not the ones who carry them out. This certainly was to be the case with the educational laboratories. At first there were many links between the Gardner Task Force (T/F) and the USOE staff. Gardner saw that the T/F had "total communication with members of HEW."[12] There were frequent discussions among Ralph Tyler, Keppel, Ianni, and other USOE staff.[a] Nevertheless, Keppel's testimony and later decisions differed from what key members of the T/F later recall were their aspirations for the laboratories.

Two issues surfaced early: whether the labs were intended to be nationally or regionally oriented, and how many of them there should be. Depending on where someone stood on these two issues, the labs could be viewed as quite different entities.

William Cannon, the staff assistant to the T/F from BOB who prepared most of the drafts of the report, remembers that the educational labs were meant to be fashioned after the Argonne and the Brookhaven labs—that is, nationally focused and few in number. The report itself states: ". . .the laboratories would be more closely akin to the great national laboratories of the Atomic Energy Commission."[13] They are specifically labeled "National Educational Laboratories" and expected to work through a "nationwide network to test the feasibility of new methods."[14] So where did the idea of regionality come from?

In Keppel's testimony in January 1965, the "national" label is replaced by "regional." When Arthur Singer, then of the Carnegie Corporation but serving as a consultant to USOE, appealed to the commissioner to hold to the national concept and designation, he reports Keppel responded that he could not:

He explained to me that he couldn't abandon the regional concept. "Title IV labs are going to be porkbarrel," he said; "every Congressman is going to want one in his region."[15]

HEW officials were well aware that Congress was increasing its pressure on

---

[a]Some of the USOE staff did manage surreptiously to obtain a copy of the Task Force report in spite of the demand for confidentiality by the president himself.

most agencies to spread its research and development money around more widely and equitably throughout the academic world. As Greenberg notes, the goegraphical issue in research allocations had come to a boil in 1963 because of the decision to kill the Midwestern Universities Research Association (MURA, the high intensity FFAG accelerator.)[16]

Congress also continued to be concerned about federal control of education. As William Cannon admits, "the concept of the national labs ran into difficulties because it raised the spectre of federal control. So we called them regional."[17] But what is a region?

Everyone had difficulty finding a satisfactory answer—the staff, consultants, and the Research Advisory Council. The Council thought that the staff was giving too much consideration to geography. Alfred Dent, one of the RAC members, urged them to look for commonness of problems and concerns, and Fred Cole raised the question as to whether there were regions defined by the flow of teachers to and from key teacher-preparing institutions; his analogue was the region that formed around medical colleges. Anthony Wallace was dubious of the approach that the staff was taking. As he put it:

I have a feeling that, you know, there has been an announcement that there is money and that some people say, well, okay, we've got to get some of it, and we have to define a region, so let's call up our buddies and we'll get together and make a proposal![18]

There also was the issue of the number of laboratories. While it obviously was related to whether labs were viewed primarily as national or regional, it was debated as a separate question. Ralph Tyler originally wanted five or seven.[19] Ianni claims to have preferred no more than six originally.[20] But others wanted more. Keppel in his testimony for ESEA called for ten to fifteen in one place,[21] but upped that to fifteen to twenty later during questioning.[22] There was even talk on the staff of putting one in each state.

Part of the difficulty on both issues was that the ideas that appeared in the Task Force report were based more on speculation than on hard data. Some of the members believed that there were three or four "centers of excellence" in the United States that only needed a new institutional form to produce worthwhile educational innovations. After all, this is what was happening in the Boston area with ESI. Why couldn't it happen in the Chicago and San Francisco areas where there were outstanding universities and public schools? But persons in those areas had other interests.

This was the state of thinking about laboratories in the Spring of 1965 as ESEA passed into law. What the labs should look like and how many there should be at what level of funding[23] were unresolved questions that now passed to the staff of the Bureau of Research to wrestle with.

The Staff Gets the Task

One of Ianni's first acts was to contract with a team of consultants—made up of Arthur Singer of the Carnegie Corporation; Charles Brown Superintendent of the Newton, Massachusetts, schools; and Albert Boucher, Chancellor, City University of New York—to locate and stimulate persons and institutions in the United States to organize educational laboratories. They began by literally shadowing some of the staff of the Ford Foundation Education Division when they visited sites in which their projects were located. They also sought out and discussed the lab idea with recognized professors like James Coleman and Robert Havighurst in Chicago and Patrick Suppes at Stanford. But while seeking advice, they also were viewed as quietly encouraging "favored" places and people to organize a laboratory before official announcements were made. "At that time most of us in OE assumed we wouldn't get many proposals from other places," relates "Skip" McCann, then a USOE staff person.[24]

The consultants returned to Washington in the summer to help draft the first guidelines, but the scene was beginning to shape up much more differently then had been expected. Many of the leading universities were not taking the leadership in forming labs. This was due in part because several of them (Stanford, Harvard, and Wisconsin) already had committed themselves to R&D centers. Others were wary of the independent nature of the laboratories.

But if the prestigious universities didn't respond, many other groups did; the staff were unprepared for the number of inquiries they received. In the July monthly report of the Bureau of Research, we find:

So many groups have expressed interest in educational laboratory programs that the primary task of the Laboratory Branch is to coordinate the efforts of interested parties and to broaden their thinking so that laboratories will be truly regional.[25]

Events were now moving at a dizzy pace. Guidelines had to be prepared that would encourage fair, politically sound judgments about who were to be funded. New panels of experts were created, and the reorganization within USOE complicated administrative matters. As Gideonse put it, "It never was clear in those days who were making the decisions about the labs."[26]

Throughout all this hung the two critical issues: regionality versus national scope—a few centers of excellence versus blanketing the nation? What could the staff do? They hedged. In July, they prepared draft guidelines for both regional and national labs.[27] The final draft was written on July 14 only for regional laboratories, but a separate set of guidelines were prepared on July 29 for "A National Program of Educational Laboratories."[28]

These guidelines for regional labs were mailed out in August carrying an October deadline for submitting proposals. Four panels of five to seven persons each screened all prospecti and letters of intent; each panel was assigned a region of the country and instructed to visit on-site with those groups that seemed to have the most promise. USOE provided one staff person for each team. An executive panel was formed of the chairman of each regional panel to recommend to the commissioner which prospecti to fund; its chairperson was Lawrence Cremin of Teachers College, Columbia University.

The pace became dizzier in the fall. By the end of October, USOE had received 28 prospecti and "about 50" letters of intent.[29] The staff was spread thin writing additional guidelines, visiting sites, meeting with panels, trying to operate within the new organization, being introduced to new staff, and losing key people at critical junctures; by the fall it was known that Ianni would not be the new associate commissioner and probably would be leaving. Keppel was busy with more pressing political matters so that a lot of authority fell to Henry Loomis his deputy who chose, in turn, to delegate matters to Walter Mylecrain, who was assistant deputy commissioner, who had no previous experience in educational research nor any previous exposure to the laboratory concept.

Bright's Influence

This was where matters stood when Bright arrived on the scene. To Bright, the primary purpose of the labs was to "implement beneficial change in the schools in its territory. The laboratory will identify what it believes are the one or two major educational problems in a region and mount a program to solve the problems."[30] He took the concept of regionality seriously, in the view of some—much more so than a lot of the planners intended.[31] To him, school districts throughout the country now had large sums of federal money provided by Titles I and III of ESEA to spend on innovations, new ideas, and products. So "one of the major functions of the regional laboratories is to provide guidance to local school districts in the effective use of Title I and Title III funds," which meant the pressure was on USOE to get the labs moving. "The schools cannot wait," as Bright saw it.[32]

This meant to him to move out from the discussions among the advisory groups and the groups in the field and get the staff to work. After the April panel meeting, when the Cremin panel resigned,[33] the staff was directed to play a more active role and to help the groups in the field to better understand that the goal of USOE was to create a regional network. "We were told to 'shape their behavior'," said one former USOE staffer, but "toward what we weren't quite sure."[34]

What Bright and most of his young, inexperienced staff were insensitive to is that the hurry-up attitude meant that educational groups had to talk about and use the concepts of educational R&D that they best understood. As Svenson saw it, the creators of the lab ideas were anxious to build "new institutions which, once launched, would perform functions neglected by the educational system and thus hasten the process of quality educational change,"[35] but under the pressure from Washington groups in the field focused instead on relationships. "Thus," as Svenson explains it, "without adequate consideration of the reasons for creating a 'new mix', the purposes it would serve or, once forged, the work it would pursue, many developing laboratory groups began to enunciate 'relationship' as one of their primary functions. Operationalized, 'relationship' became service—and service would be their mission and program."[36]

What of the National Laboratory Idea?

In the meantime the concept of the national laboratories was kept alive by Ianni. Acting independently of the rest of the staff, he contacted John Goodlad, then professor of education at UCLA and tried to lure him to Washington to assume a directorship in Washington of a National Laboratory for Early Childhood Education. As bait, he talked to Goodlad about at least $30 million over a five-year period of time.[37]

While Goodlad was not interested in the directorship, he did agree to help organize the laboratory. On December 9 and 10, 1965, he assembled six consultants in Los Angeles, including Ralph Tyler, Susan Gray from George Peabody University, and Robert Hess, then from the University of Chicago. They considered the feasibility, desirability, and the possibile organization of a national system of laboratories focused on the education of young children. A second meeting of this group was held a month later with nine additional consultants including persons like Sheldon White of Harvard, Pauline Sears of Stanford, and Samuel Kirk of the University of Illinois. A third meeting held in February included yet another group of well-known scholars. The result was a series of recommendations for creating a "multi-disciplinary and multi-functional nationwide system of laboratories and institutions focused on early childhood education."[38] They called for diversity of programs to be conducted by several constituent offices but with national coordinating center. But the center was not intended to direct the program, rather to facilitate communication and to make wise use of resources and ideas. This was yet a new approach, a new kind of institution, a meld of ideas from the Gardner Task Force and from other sources.

All would have been well and good—except that Ianni and Keppel left and Bright arrived. As Goodlad reports:

I received a rather frantic telephone call from Lou Bright. He said, more of less, "We were sitting around a table making final decisions on the budget for next year and somebody asked about what was to be done with John Goodlad's project." There was immediate consternation and a good deal of questioning. Following the meeting, Lou called to ask what all this was about. He had gathered some vague information about my being charged to set up this laboratory with 30 million dollars.[39]

Ianni had carried the idea of the Early Childhood Lab around in his head. As one colleague reports, "No one on the staff knew what he was up to."[40] But Bright honored the commitment and pledged to find as much money as he could. Given the pressures building up from the Vietnam War, he concluded that $1.5 million was a more realistic figure. Proposals were solicited, and in June 1966, nine proposals and two letters of intent were received. Representatives from some institutions were invited to a general meeting in July. An advisory council of twelve persons were appointed and a directorship created.

Before he left, Ianni had started the wheels moving for a second national distributive laboratory that would be focused on using computers in instruction. During the fall and winter, a staff assistant visited prospective applicants and an ad hoc panel with Lawrence Cremin as chairman was created. But when they reported out to Bright that they did not recommend that a national lab be established for this purpose, he concurred. Some of those persons who had been contacted by the staff, like Patrick Suppes at Stanford and John Flanagan from the American Institute for Research, eventually submitted a proposal and a site visit was held, but the idea was never funded.

By the fall of 1966, the idea of creating any other distributive national laboratories was dead. An October memo from Hendrik Gideonse provided a rationale.[41] But probably it was the momentum and the demands of the regional lab effort that carried the most convincing arguments.

The Rush toward Creating Twenty Regional Labs

The eleven grants made in February 1966 authorized a 75-day developmental period (which was extended first by 30 days and then again for 15 days); this was referred to by the staff as the "75-day orgy." In June, six-month contracts were granted to those eleven, and eight more groups were given developmental grants. (See Appendix B for the list of laboratories). These first contracts were announced from the White House and were compared in importance to the "large-scale laboratories of the Defense or Atomic Energy establishments."[42] In September, one more planning grant was made, bringing the total number of labs to twenty.

This rapid turn of events, while it may have been pleasing to the White House, was becoming increasingly bothersome in other quarters. In the budget review by the BOB staff in the late spring of 1966, Emerson Elliot attempted to reinject the ideas of the Gardner Task Force as he understood them. He pressed to have the major part of the laboratory budgets be concerned with demonstration and dissemination,[43] and questioned the need for so many.[44]

BOB officials and others also became bothered about who was advising the USOE staff. After the Cremin panel resigned, the Research Advisory Committee requested Bright to present a plan at the next meeting of how a new advisory committee could be formed.[45] The minutes of that meeting indicate considerable discussion of the issue in the presence of Commissioner Howe.

Howe was conscious of growing dissatisfaction of the way the lab program was going:

I was aware of a rising controversy within the government as to how fast the lab program ought to move, how many there ought to be, and whether they were good enough. Bright and his people did some good thinking but there was a lot of questioning, especially from the Bureau of the Budget and the President's Science Advisor.[46]

Outsiders shared his concern. Frank Chase saw "devastating criticism" from university people and state department people."[47] And Art Singer, now the Director of ESI in Boston, got word back to his former boss, Gardner, that he and several mutual friends viewed those now connected with the lab program, by and large, as "pedestrian" and the USOE staff as administratively inept.[48]

Gardner finally took action. He called in Francis S. Chase, Dean of the School of Education and Chairman of the Department of Education, University of Chicago, in whom both Howe and Cannon had confidence and asked Chase to undertake an independent investigation of the program. Four days later, on November 15, the Secretary placed a thirty-day freeze on the renegotiations of the twenty laboratory contracts scheduled to take effect on December 1.[b] Some of the USOE staff and many men in the field remember how devastated they were by this announcement.[49]

Chase set out across the country to interview former Gardner Task Force members, former advisors, and those who were planning specific laboratories. He found a wide range of expectations and ideas. About the former Gardner Task Force members, he states:

Each was clear about what the report said but anyone reading the report would doubt that they were all that clear.[50]

About the labs themselves:

They were going in all directions—service-oriented, research-oriented, giving grants to people who couldn't have gotten them in national competition, some behaving like state departments of education, others behaving like weak schools of education. A lot of trial and error.[51]

---

[b]Gideonse is certain that the freeze was pressed on Gardner by Cannon and Elliott in BOB, his interview, March 29, 1974.

Within two months, Chase had formed some opinions and made these public at a meeting of the Laboratory Directors in New Orleans on January 15, 1967:

I would say that considering the short lapse of time since the laboratories have been funded and the presence of conditions which interfere seriously with orderly processes of planning and staffing, it is little short of remarkable that so many of the laboratories (1) have achieved a defensible definition of functions and goals, (2) have built the nuclei of staffs of considerable promise, and (3) are demonstrating that they can make contributions which may enable all parts of the educational enterprise to perform more effectively. I am also inclined to think that several laboratories are engaging in dubious activities and have become the prisioners of mistaken concepts of regionality, of self-defeating attempts to address themselves to everyone's perceptions of needs, and of "entangling alliances" of various kinds.[52]

Earlier, he had reported something similar to Gardner. His confidence that matters could be corrected as well as the appointment by Howe of a blue ribbon advisory committee behind Chase (who was appointed chairman), kept Gardner from renewing the freeze. Later, Chase wrote a report[53] of his views and observations, but his more lasting accomplishments came from his interactions at several levels—from the secretarial level in HEW down to talks with individual board members of specific laboratories. Over the next several years, Frank Chase became a kind of itinerant preacher instructing all who would listen on what these new institutions could do for education. In incapsulated form, this is what he told them:

What is missing in education is systematic development, the notion of R&D as a systematic approach to identifying problems and creating processes and products that would assist with the solution of those problems. Universities never have been good at development nor have state departments or local districts. You need new kinds of institutions.[54]

Chase reiterated (and refined over time) several messages: the labs must concentrate on the processes that have been missing in education and that have prevented the "systematic adaption of knowledge and technology to educational use through a set of closely related processes ranging from the design of models and prototypes through the successive modification of materials, technologies, strategies, and systems for the achievement of specified effects."[55] They must view research and development as "a closely integrated system for producing specified changes in educational institutions and processes."[56] The end products of laboratories must be the "development of tested products, operable systems, or other demonstrably useful contributions to the improvement of educational institutions and processes."[57]

Back in Washington, some persons were disappointed and skeptical of Chase's opinions. The OST staff were not satisfied and went ahead with their plans to have a second, newly created Panel on Educational Research and Development of the President's Science Advisory Committee conduct a separate investigation of the labs and the R&D centers. The new chairman was Frank H. Westheimer, a professor of chemistry from Harvard, who only recently had gained considerable notoriety for directing a study sponsored by the National Academy of Sciences that assessed the quality and organizational structure of chemical research in the United States. Like Chase, Westheimer soon was touring the country and talking to people about the labs, centers, and educational research in general.

Anyone who expected the Westheimer study to turn around the lab and R&D center program had to be disappointed. The panel was loaded with talent like Herbert A. Simon, Department of Industrial Administration, Carnegie-Mellon University; Neil J. Smelser, Department of Sociology, University of California (Berkeley); and George A. Miller, Department of Psychology, Rockefeller University. But the initial impetus for the study seemed to fizzle out; the report itself was not submitted until October of 1968. Some explain this delay to the fact that the issues surrounding the labs and centers were more complex than Westheimer originally foresaw and demanded more time and attention than he or other members of the panel were willing to give. Another explanation is that no dramatic move was possible in 1967 and 1968; education's time had come and gone in the White House. The president was more and more preoccupied with other issues.

The PSAC panel had impact, however. Staff within DHEW and particularly USOE were aware that there was a watchdog group reporting to the executive branch. More important still, the panel provided justification for continuing to assign one OST staff man, John Mays, to educational research.

Mays didn't like much of what he saw of educational R&D in those years. He admits to finding much in the Chase report with which he agreed and that he recognized some positive accomplishments like the Library of Toys at the Far West Lab and the use of TV feedback in training teachers. But the labs and centers in general were particularly bothersome to him. He found them relying too much on what he termed the "curriculum people" from the field of education and being too far removed from the intellectual community. He was not dissuaded (by Chase) in his belief that there were too many labs and centers.[58]

Even though the critics in OST and BOB were not satisfied, Chase is viewed as having had a settling influence on the laboratory program.[59] Beginning in late 1966, the signals from the USOE to the labs became relatively more coherent; service to a region was downplayed and product development was emphasized.

There were other signs of stabilization. In February 1967, the National Advisory Committee for the Educational Laboratories had its first meeting and recommended that "no sudden change is required in policy or directives for the educational laboratories at this time."[60] In March, contracts were negotiated with twenty laboratories to continue their funding through a nine-month period. Later in the spring, the Bureau of the Budget approved a request to Congress for $27,000,000, or almost $10 million over the request of the previous fiscal year.[61] In November 1967, full-year contracts were negotiated with all twenty labs. By the end of the summer, Chase had helped to locate Norman Boyan, a professor of education at Stanford, who agreed to head up the Laboratory Division of the Bureau of Research.

Boyan's appointment was critical because by 1967 the program needed a stronger hand. Bright was serving both as Assistant Commissioner and as acting head of the lab program. Too much was happening with too few staff available to keep up. Events were straining Bright's administrative style that was viewed as low key. There had been criticism of his work from the Bureau of the Budget and DHEW. Many people did not believe that he had a firm enough hand but instead that he had delegated too much to the young bureaucrats. As one lab director said:

He was in control in the beginning but circumstances rendered that difficult to maintain. A core of persons at lower levels, a group of nice 27-year-old kids, persons with no experience in R&D or politics, with their evaluators, took over. It was a strange mystery.[62]

Neither was Bright adept at galvanizing support in the field, from the practitioners or the researchers.[63] When this issue was discussed by the RAC, Bright was ready to attribute the coolness of researchers to the fact that they could get money from a variety of sources to do their research and therefore didn't need the labs.[64] But he was aware that there were other explanations and toward the end of his tenure he called into Washington a number of leaders from the field to seek their counsel. They gave him advice but without a noticeable increase in support.

Boyan, whose field was educational administration, was not noted for his scholarship but he carried a respectable academic career as a student at Harvard and on the faculties at Wisconsin and Stanford. Both administratively and as a link to the field, he promised stability, and he listened to and agreed with Chase.

Difficulties with Congress

Where Frank Chase's influence was not felt was with the Congress. Here there were forces operating with such strength that neither he nor any single person could prevent a dimming of enthusiasm for the laboratory program in a relatively short period of time. These factors were (1) the death of John Fogarty; (2) Edith Green's opposition; (3) the growing disenchantment with science and scientific research; and (4) the growing rift with the White House over expenditures both for domestic programs and the Vietnam conflict. Each of these four factors is discussed in more detail in the following sections.

1. John Fogarty, Democrat from Rhode Island, had been chairman of the Subcommittee for the Department of HEW of the Committee on Appropriations for all but two years since 1949. During that time, expenditures for research in several programs multiplied, the most dramatic being those for medical research. In FY 1957, the National Institute of Health's appropriation was $213 million. In 1959, it jumped to $324 and by 1961 had reached $750 million![65] As Fenno said of him, "John Fogarty has an obsession about the value of medical research. And he's become a real leader in the field."[66]

His interests spilled over into education, and often he favored granting more money than the official administration budgets requested. Dave Clark remembers how "delightful" it was to testify before him and how upset Fogarty was in private when the Kennedy administration didn't give more support to educational research.[67] Had Fogarty not died in 1968, the labs most likely would have had more lead time to get established. Fogarty's successor, Daniel Flood from Pennsylvania, wasn't opposed to the labs or to educational research; it was simply that he wasn't willing to "give up any blue chips to support it."[68]

2. Congresswoman Edith Green materialized as an opponent of the laboratories. From August through December 1966, in her capacity as chairperson of the Special Subcommittee to Study the Office of Education, she held a series of hearings across the country. Congress took little action as a result of the study, but the issues that were raised remained bothersome for some time. For example, there was the matter of salaries for lab staff. She discovered and made public that:

. . . One half or 10 of the regional laboratory directors had salaries which exceeded that of the U.S. Commissioner of Education;

. . . 95 percent of the lab directors received $20,000 or more per year as compared with 45 percent of the chief state school officers.[69]

She also found "widespread confusion and uncertainty even among the personnel in the laboratories about their missions and the respective roles and responsibilities of the labs, the Research and Development Centers, and the Title III supplemental centers."[70]

In the summer of 1967, Mrs. Green continued her interest in the labs by asking Leon P. Minear, State Superintendent of Education for the State of Oregon, to study the relationships between the labs and the state departments of education. And in spite of the fact that neither of these two studies, or any of the others she was to undertake, led to any drastic alterations, Edith Green became an unwavering opponent to the program, to education R&D and, later, to NIE.

3. A pervasive influence operating in Congress at the time that helped to sour the members against the labs was the growing discontent with the way

science was handling its affairs and the public's money. No longer were they willing to buy such statements as the one made by Alan T. Waterman in his 1963 Annual Report of the National Science Foundation:

Basic research is a highly specialized activity; it is not one where the judgment of laymen has validity. Consequently, planning for basic research and such evaluation of its performance as is needed for the continuation of existing programs must be left in the hands of competent and experienced scientists.[71]

Science had become too expensive to allow that kind of freedom from congressional scrutiny. And when they did begin to scrutinize, they didn't like all that they found.

Two very basic criticisms emerged. First, basic research was not as important as they once thought as a source of new knowledge on which national social programs should be based. Second, the applied research funded by governmental agencies was not focused on the problems of most concern to Congress.[72]

So Congress through investigations, like that of the so-called Elliot Committee established in 1964 (The Select Committee on Government Research), began to set new guidelines for the relationship of the government to the world of science. From the mid-1960s on, congressional committees were expected to probe more deeply into why various research funds were requested, how they would be spent, and what were the assurances of successful consequences. Even NSF, the most hallowed of scientific agencies, felt the difference. It sought a $267 million increase in its budget for FY 1964 but got only $30 million![73] As Greenberg put it, "All along the line, Congress, after seeing funds for research and development triple in a period of seven or eight years, was in a sour mood about this incomprehensible, burgeoning monster . . . ."[74]

4. By 1967 Congress also had turned sour about Johnson's requests for funds both for new domestic programs and for expanding U.S. involvement in the Vietnam conflict. As Rivlin reports, ". . . Heavy military spending for the escallating war in Vietnam and accelerating inflation had completely altered the outlook for additional domestic programs. Strenuous efforts were made to hold down domestic spending."[75]

With all these obstacles, it is a wonder that the labs were supported as well as they were; in FY 1968, $22,926 million was obligated, or more than $5 million over FY 1967.[76] Part of the explanation is that while the labs may not have been held in such high esteem, nor was the Office of Education through which they were supported, educational R&D was still viewed by many high in the bureaucracy as worthy of support. Evidence of this were the reports of four task forces convened during the years 1966 through 1968. The first two of these, the so-called Friday Task Force (for its chairman William C. Friday, then president of the University of North Carolina) and an internal task force chaired by secretary of DHEW, John Gardner, called for increasing federal support for educational research and development.[77] The Gardner Task Force called for a 50 percent increase in R&D funds.

Another task force, convened in 1967 and chaired by an assistant secretary, William Gorham, devoted much attention to strengthening R&D in DHEW. A 1968 task force, this one headed by then Secretary of DHEW, Wilbur Cohen, called for increased funding of educational R&D and for new types of research institutions specifically focused on problems of higher education.

But R&D had other sources of strength in Washington. Commissioner Howe remained a perennial supporter, and since he maintained good rapport with Secretary Gardner and the White House throughout his term that support counted. And as a seasoned government advisor once commented, the labs and centers as organizations had latent political power.

"Remember," warned RAC and PSAC panel member, Jacob Getzels, "a potential constituency in Washington can be stronger than an actual one."[78]

Thus, there were factors supporting the labs and centers as well as factors in opposition. Who would carry the day?

Congress Acts

The crunch came for the labs in 1968. USOE had convinced HEW and the White House to request a 50 percent increase in funds for FY 1969. Boyan describes how the lab directors "were jubilant" when they heard the president's budget message during a meeting in January 1968. Then he went on:

But the money never materialized. Gardner and Howe could influence the White House but not key Congressmen like Wilbur Mills. It turns out that this was the high water mark.[79]

In July, the House of Representatives voted to freeze the funds for labs at the 1968 level of $22.6 million. Eventually this was raised in the final budget bill to $23.6 million, but the lab program clearly had lost momentum. USOE policies toward the labs now would have to change: either all twenty would have to be scaled down, or some would have to be closed to allow others to grow.

During late summer and the fall of 1968, the staff and their consultants agonized. Finally the decision was reached and recommended to Gardner: cut out five labs. He bought it but resigned before action could be taken. Wilbur Cohen inherited that task along with the Secretariat.

The five labs were given notice that their institutional support would be phased out, which meant their imminent demise. These were the Central Atlantic Regional Educational Laboratory, based in Washington, D.C.; the Cooperative Educational Research Laboratory in the Chicago area; the Michigan–Ohio Regional Educational Laboratory located in Detroit; the Rockey Mountain Educational

Laboratory in Colorado; and the South Central Regional Educational Laboratory Corporation in Little Rock, Arkansas.

Gone henceforth were the discussions about how to "fill the map" of the United States with laboratories. The cutback to fifteen also dampened what remained of the arguments about keeping labs focused on their regions. But surprisingly few other changes resulted from the cutback. The plans of the staff and their consultants were still hopeful. FY 1969 was viewed by some as only a temporary setback for the program. They now saw an opportunity to increase support for the better labs. The updated Five-Year Plan produced in 1969 projected a sum of $161.8 million in FY 1974.[80]

How could this be so? Why didn't the staff see what Boyan, in retrospect, describes as "clearly the end of the first phase" of the laboratory program?[81] Inevitably, as one former BOB staffer points out, decision making in a bureaucracy slips to the second echelon; the top level staff are forced by the peculiar cycle of the budget-making processes to be concerned with newer issues. Last year's ideas slip to those below them.[82] And the staff administering the regional laboratories became increasingly isolated and independent. "You must remember," Bailey cautions, "that at the federal level there were only three or four persons in OE and a handful of consultants who parachuted in from time to time, men like Elwin Svenson and "Mitch" Brickell, who were vitally interested in the labs. Howe gave it considerable support but he was tied up on other matters."[83]

As an illustration of this point, consider the case of the relationship between the Educational Development Center, Inc. (EDC) and the Laboratory Branch in USOE. As noted previously (see Chapter 2), EDC was an outgrowth of ESI, Inc., which was founded in 1959 by Jerold Zacharias and his associates to house the work of the Physical Sciences Study Committee. ESI became a symbol of the laboratory idea for some of those on, or associated with members of, the Gardner Task Force of 1964. Keppel and Ianni were well aware of the political importance of ESI, and its supporters also were convinced that it was one of the viable models for the lab program.

In 1965, however, ESI's expectations about receiving USOE support ran into difficulties. USOE staff had received communication from another New England group, this one linked to the majority of the chief state school officers. The lab staff in USOE knew that they couldn't justify having two laboratories in New England, and they knew that they had to go with ESI.[c] So they initiated delicate negotiations in an attempt to have ESI alter some of its views about how it wanted to operate. Getting the other group headed by the State Superin-

---

[c]For a time ESI was considered to be a national distributive lab (letter from Frank Patterson to Arthur Singer, October 5, 1965, Administrative File IV–III G Folder, National Institute of Education). When the Bureau dropped plans for national labs, ESI had only one direction to go and became a competitor to the Second New England group.

tendent of Public Instruction in Vermont, William Holden, to merge with ESI was equally as delicate. What complicated matters is that the chairman of the Northeast Advisory Panel, Arthur Singer, was a former consultant to ESI and was clearly biased in favor of the way it had operated before Holden's group and USOE came into the picture.[d]

ESI eventually was selected as one of the regional labs in the second round in the spring of 1966, but only after lengthy and tortuous negotiations, topped by a meeting involving Secretary Gardner; Jerome Wiesner, the President's Science Advisor; Commissioner Howe; and Jerold Zacharias, among others.

Difficulties continued even after the Educational Development Center, as it was now called, was chosen to become one of the twenty labs. The staff of the lab division saw EDC as having weak management, little control from its board of directors, and essentially still a one-man show (the man being Jerold Zacharias). Since these were features that prevented other groups from being selected in the first place, the staff pressed for changes. They were supported by the report of the review team in the spring of 1966.[e]

Singer, now the director of EDC, appealed for relief through his friends in Washington in BOB, OST, and the Department of HEW. Their concern led the staff to arrange for a second and special review in August. But this field report was no more complimentary than the first. EDC's rating in USOE kept it mired among the weak labs even though by then its budget topped $10,000,000, and it was producing a variety of widely used products.[84]

What this illustrates is how a second-echelon staff was able to resolve what was essentially a policy issue through administrative devices. The laboratory staff of USOE did the job for which they were charged—that is, they developed criteria and procedures for selecting the better proposals for laboratories and attempted to apply these as equitably and uniformly as they could. In this task, they were supported by outside consultants who were essentially honest and unbiased, but since the consultants themselves were unsure of what these new institutions should look like, they tended to support the staff.

The foolishness was that the criteria were challengeable; the policy issues on which they should have rested had not been resolved. The laboratory staff acted as if they, and their superiors in USOE, knew what a "real" educational laboratory was. They didn't. In retrospect, the decisions that continually gave EDC low grades, and that foreordained the cutoff of USOE funds in 1971, helped to turn a group of EDC supporters within the bureaucracy into critics of USOE. Had EDC remained as one of the regional labs, this group probably

---

[d]Singer eventually became president of ESI

[e]The USOE staff members who were interviewed remember that the materials received from EDC were among the poorest prepared by any group aspiring to form a laboratory. As a member of one of the review teams for EDC, the author can testify personally to the disdain with which some of the principal members of the EDC staff regarded the procedures used by USOE to evaluate proposals.

would have had to temper its expectations and criticisms of all labs. USOE, on the other hand, would have had a politically attractive alternative.

PPBS: A Contributing Factor

The administrative power of the laboratory staff was enhanced in another way— that is, through the initiation of some new management techniques that, ironically, were designed to help straighten out the kind of policy confusion that existed in USOE in the mid 1960s. The USOE staff were put through elaborate, detailed exercises, one of the purposes of which was to clarify the objectives of all programs.

There were several new planning and evaluation procedures: Program Planning and Budgeting System (PPBS); Program Evaluation and Review Techniques (PERT); and a variety of plans to make activities more cost accountable.[85]

On August 25, 1965, President Johnson issued a directive that ordered all federal agencies to apply the PPBS techniques to their operations. At the DHEW level, this task fell to the newly established Assistant Secretary for Program Evaluation William Gorham, and to Deputy Assistant Secretary Alice Rivlin. In the Office of Education, several new offices were created by the Ink Commission for, as Bailey said, "PPBS was in the air at the time of ESEA's drafting and passage."[86]

The lab program was affected in a variety of ways. Lab staffs were required to learn how to use these new techniques, like PERT charting and new cost-accounting procedures. New techniques for long-range planning were devised and great stress was placed on establishing a management information system.

How did the lab staffs respond? One lab director sees that USOE got what they asked for: "We saw them more concerned with how we would organize and operate the lab than what we would do with it, what the program would be like."[87] Lou Bright is seen as supporting this approach. "Bright made us all very conscious of the cost dimension of our operation. He put the Bureau of Research in a management mode of operation."[88] So it appears in retrospect that the procedures that were being pushed throughout government as ways of clarifying goals and coordinating programs emphasized management procedures and consciousness and probably helped thereby to postpone the clarification of the substantive goals for the laboratory program. Bailey gives an explanation of why this was so:

The labs were caught in a dilemma because there was little agreement on their purpose. The NEA people, the chief state school officers, the researchers—all had different expectations for them.[89]

Bailey was correct; there were essentially three sets of expectations (goals) for the labs in the mid 1960s. Two were present at their outset, and a third materialized early in their history. The first two were part of the debates that took place within and around the Gardner Task Force. The "reformers from Cambridge," as some called Zacharias, Jerome Wiesner, and their colleagues, saw the labs as part of a new structure through which better ideas would flow from sources outside the old educational establishment. But for many persons who had devoted years of their careers to improving education through systematic study viewed the labs in a different way. As Frank Chase put it:

The ideas in the Gardner Task Force represented the general feeling that many of us had for years that something like [the laboratories] ought to happen. Tyler talked about them for years. There must have been hundreds who were thinking that we needed more development and research.[90]

As the laboratory program was inserted into the federal structure, it was subjected to yet a third set of expectations. This was given expression in a report written in November 1968 by the staff for Alice Rivlin, the Assistant Secretary for Planning and Evaluation, DHEW. It states:

Being an integral part of the total R&D effort, the programs of the laboratories clearly must be considered along with and not separately from other in the Bureau. Having the laboratories compete for program support (as opposed to operational support which would be regularly provided when the laboratory had proved itself) would therfore be appropriate.[91]

If the ultimate test of policy is where an agency puts its money, the Office of Education had two primary missions in the mid 1960s: to desegregate American schools and to improve the education offered to children of the poor. Was the laboratory branch or the entire bureau being responsive to the priorities of the federal government in education? As Alice Rivlin put it:

The Bureau [of Research] seems to be ambivalent about program direction. On the one hand, it views its proper role as focusing the research and development effort, on the other it appears reluctant to do so. There is a fine balance to be struck in this connection which the Bureau as manager of the research and development effort must find. There clearly must be a well-considered, thoroughly coordinated attack on the major educational problems which have been identified—the extent to which leaving the choice of its projects to the Regional Laboratories is compatible with this end is unknown.[92]

Essentially, USOE was operating a program for which there were at least three differing sets of objectives; the program and the staff was being judged by three different groups. *How successfully or how poorly the labs were doing depended to a large extent in those days (and still today) on which of the three groups was doing the judging.*

This is not an uncommon state of affairs in government, as Stephen Bailey points out:

In the actual political world legislation and guidelines are the result of compromise among many, often conflicting goals that have to be papered over. Therefore, not all the goals of an agency can be stated precisely, and they shouldn't be for political reasons.[93]

Keeping a program moving so that multiple groups with differing expectations are satisfied is the art of management—in the private world as well as the public. That art was at a low state as concerns the laboratory program. This statement is not made to condemn the leadership in the Office of Education even though they are open to criticism. It is done more to establish a principle: all programs must have payoff, either politically or professionally (and preferably both) for the principal bureaucrats and legislators who support them. That payoff must be commensurate with the time and attention demanded of the program. The laboratory program was sufficiently politically visible and expensive to command a great deal of attention from the beginning in BOB, the Congress, and even in the White House. Incidents like the EDC controversy increased the amount of attention that was needed, and the ante increased accordingly. There were too few political and professional payoffs to win widespread and loyal followers outside the laboratory staff of USOE and, accordingly, this program has been perched from the beginning on a very unstable political base within the federal government.

7

Other USOE R & D Efforts In and Outside the Bureau of Research

The Regional Educational Laboratories were, of course, only one of several educational R&D programs operated by the Office of Education in the mid 1960s. Since the purpose of this and the previous chapter is to explain how the Bureau of Research operated, we need to look at some of its other programs. The other three that have been selected are the Research and Development (R&D) Center Program; the Educational Resources Information Center (ERIC); and the ES '70 Program. In addition there are two other important research projects that we shall examine that were not run by the Bureau: The Equality of Educational Opportunity Survey and the National Assessment of Student Progress. These provide insights into how the Bureau was viewed by the commissioner in those days and what was involved in major policy research at the federal level.

Research and Development Centers

In the flury and bustle of the early ESEA days in USOE, the R&D Center Program stands out for its administrative evenness and quietude. The centers also escaped from many of the criticisms leveled at the laboratories.

From the beginning the centers were somewhat better integrated into the R&D communities than the labs. This was due in part to the fact that the centers tended to draw upon and use researchers whose work was known. They were urged to extend work already in progress.[1] Many leading researchers and scholars also responded to invitations to serve as advisors and consultants. In a report submitted following a review of the centers made by a panel of the President's Science Advisory Committee (see page 94), there was the comment that "the advisory committees for the R&D centers appear to be of high quality and active. . . ."[2] But their acceptance also was due to the strong position assumed from 1963 through 1965 by the advisory panel, chaired by Ralph Tyler, that screened all proposals, visited the sites, and recommended action to the commissioner.[a] The work of the Tyler panel ended with the selection of ten centers (see Appendix C for listing of centers), but ad hoc groups of outsiders

---

[a]Membership of this panel changed over time. In addition to well recognized scholars like Benjamin Bloom, Wayne Holtzman, and Paul Lazarsfeld, the panel included Leon Minear, Superintendent of Public Instruction for Oregon; Byron Hansford, Commissioner of Education, Colorado; Alan Pifer, Carnegie Corporation.

convened annually to review the progress of each center and recommend which programs should be funded.

The USOE staff itself were helpful in integrating these new institutions into the academic community. While there never were more than three professionals responsible for administering this program (even though the budget reached $12.4 million), persons like Howard Hjelm and Ward Mason worked well with outside groups. Mason, who took over in 1965, was familiar with the norms and vagaries of the academic world and carried a respectable research reputation as a result of his work with Samuel Stouffer and Neal Gross at Harvard.[3] He was frequently viewed by personnel in the centers as not being aggressive enough in representing them in the in-fighting of the agency, but they also saw him as being sensible, competent, and sympathetic to researchers.

By 1968, those who were reviewing the R&D centers were cautiously nodding approval. Samuel Brownell, for example, the former commissioner who had launched the Cooperative Research Program, stated that he was "optimistic."[4] Bloom found the reports of the research at the centers to be of "first order quality."[5] He credits the centers with expanding the base of scholarship within the educational enterprise:

In the period from 1935 through, say, 1965, you were unlikely to find people in schools of education concerned with the scholarly treatment of ideas. But now I must turn to people at Pittsburgh, UCLA, places other than where there is a tradition of scholarship like at Chicago and Stanford, where they formerly concentrated pretty much just on producing teachers; now they are producing ideas that must be considered.[6]

This optimism was shared within USOE. The first two centers were created at the University of Pittsburgh and the University of Oregon in 1963. Two more at Harvard University and the University of Wisconsin were approved that same year out of FY 1965 funds. In fiscal 1966, six more centers were begun; one of these, the Center for Urban Education (CUE) eventually shifted to become a laboratory. But one more at Johns Hopkins brought the total number of centers by 1967 to ten. In the five-year plan completed in May of 1966, USOE proposed to increase the number of centers to twenty-five by the end of 1971; the estimated cost of operating these was to be $40 million by 1972.

If the centers did become more productive more quickly than the laboratories, it was because they did not need to devote as much attention and resources to administrative and organizational matters. While the centers legally could have been sponsored by state departments of education and profit and nonprofit organizations (after the amendments to the Cooperative Research Act were passed as part of the Title IV, ESEA), all were located within university complexes. They were required to make direct and indirect financial contributions, a requirement that was met largely through granting long-range commitments to tenured faculty members.[7] But this relationship accounted in no small part for the relative administrative evenness mentioned earlier; USOE had to account for the years of experience and the structure of universities that was devised to deal with federal research support procedures. That USOE did not do so as well as many other agencies is the subject of almost an endless number of anecdotes that are exchanged whenever center directors meet. Nevertheless, the centers did have recourse to university channels of authority and experience to help them organize and develop stability earlier than the laboratories.

Not that there weren't problems in this program, too. As pointed out in Chapter 4, the R&D centers as an idea did not attract much enthusiasm from men like William Cannon and others in the Bureau of the Budget and the Office of Science and Technology. And many of their views were shared by the Westheimer PSAC Task Group whose report raised "fundamental questions" about what the centers were and what they should be.[8] Westheimer had doubts about the quality of the work that was being produced and expressed disappointment that the centers were not supporting the work of more recognized scholars. The Task Group finally questioned whether or not the centers could be abandoned. There was similar criticism from the Office of the Assistant Secretary for Planning and Evaluation in DHEW.

This accounts in part for the loss of appropriations for the program. Support for the centers reached a high of $12.4 million in FY 1968 and dropped steadily over the next three years to $7.2 million.[9] By that time, it was decided to phase out the Harvard Center (institutional support was terminated in 1968, but program support continued for two more years) and not to grant a second five-year commitment to the Georgia Center. No plans materialized to replace these with new centers.

By this time, the centers were facing another set of problems: they were losing their identity and blurring in with the labs. "Labs and Centers became one word too early," says Mason.[10]

This blurring was hastened by the fact that the center program was housed within the Division of Educational Laboratories and in 1968 the National Advisory Committee on Educational Laboratories was given additional duties of overseeing the center program. In spite of continued efforts during the latter 1960s to separate out the two institutions, it was inevitable, in retrospect, that the two categories would not hold. And so individual labs and centers ended up ranging along a continuum of functions, even though the bulk of the labs clustered around the development end, the centers more toward the research side.

What this meant to the centers is that they too, like the labs, were caught in the different sets of expectations discussed in the previous chapter. Those who looked to the new institutions to bring new ideas and new persons, principally scholars and scientists, into the educational enterprise judged the centers harshly. The social planners expected the missions of USOE to be reflected in the centers and, not finding them, were equally as negative. What support outside USOE these new institutions did receive came from individual researchers with stature and from the universities that were committed to these new organizations in their midst. Even here, the support dwindled over the years so that by the mid 1970s, the centers, like labs, were largely on their own.

The Educational Research (Resources) Information Center

To most outsiders the Educational Research (later changed to Resources) Information Center (ERIC) was hastily constructed as one of the byproducts of the expanded research program authorized by the Elementary and Secondary Education Act. In fact, the notion of a centralized dissemination effort run out of the Office of Education had been on the drawing boards since the late 1950s.

When asked during hearings before a House Appropriations Committee in February of 1958 how the Office of Education informed the several thousands of school systems of the latest research findings, Assistant Commissioner Roy Hall could cite only two ways this was done: (1) by encouraging all the research contractors to report their findings at appropriate professional meetings, and (2) through the USOE magazine, *School Life*.[11] But Hall was well aware of the inadequacy (and the political liability) of this approach. So using NDEA funds he contracted with Murray Talber at the Columbia University Library for a study that documented the need for a more systematic information service. Later Dave Clark, Hall's successor, contracted with the Center for Documentation and Communication at Western Reserve University (now Case Western Reserve) to design some of the elements of a computerized document retrieval system. At the same time, an internal committee headed by Thomas Clemens was working at an USOE dissemination plan for which funds were requested but not granted at that time. Much of the spade work for ERIC had been done by 1965.

It took two events, however, to produce the ERIC system: increased funding for R&D as a result of the ESEA, and the arrival of Lee Burchinal. Burchinal was discovered by Fritz Ianni in the Vocational Rehabilitation Program in DHEW and brought to USOE originally to be his deputy. This kind of administrative job didn't suit Burchinal who earlier in his career had demonstrated his intellectual talents as a sociologist. Besides, as he explains it, he had an interest in communication and information processing. Also, Burchinal had more than a little entreprenurial-political talent. In the feverish milling about in USOE during the early ESEA days, he sensed that there were new program domains available for the asking. So he convinced Ianni to let him build a dissemination program. After accepting the stipulation that it initially not exceed a million dollars, he got right to work and a few months later, in July 1965, ERIC was announced.

Burchinal's operating style soon became apparent. He had a sense of system and was viewed as a good manager. But most important, he charted a course of action that was direct, relatively noncontroversial, and low profile. He sought out a few competent advisors like Fred Goodman from the University of Michigan and Gene Kennedy from the Federal Aviation Agency who plugged him into the latest thinking and the best thinkers about information systems, inside and outside the bureaucracy. In 1966, he contracted with North American Aviation-Rockwell to produce the monthly document, *Research in Education*, and with Bell and Howell to operate the Document Reproduction Service. Without an advisory committee and with relatively little guidance from the commissioners, Burchinal created in just a few years what was to become one of the more sophisticated and successful (at least by federal bureaucratic standards) federal information processing systems.

Burchinal found a way to operate successfully in the climate of the times in USOE. Consider again these comments:

One of the rules of the bureaucratic games is that there are upper limits set on any new program or agency. Given reasonable consistency of staff some increases can be expected. But there are limits; not hard and fast ones. These are determined in part by the outside appeal of the program, by the internal "efficiency" which usually means how well the staff and manager pay attention to the unwritten as well as written rules of OMB and how well they are perceived by their internal constituents, the administration, congressional staffs, persons like that.

To get above those limits you must move the program up to a much higher perceived level or get support from a higher level. It depends on the overall budget for the agency what those limits are. In the Bureau of Research any time a program would get above the five million mark, let's say, suddenly it is fair game, targeted for much more examination. In other agencies it might have to be 15 or 20 million. In NSF it is much lower.[12]

Burchinal took as his righthand man Thomas Clemens who had been on the staff of the NDEA research program since 1959. Clemens had the knowledge of both the inside characteristics of the USOE and the decentralized nature of the American educational system. Together they established clearinghouses at universities and professional organizations so that "leading experts in various fields of knowledge can remain active in their various professional roles and yet contribute to the development of information services for their respective professional fields."[13] The clearinghouses abstracted documents, indexed, prepared newsletters, bibliographies, reviews, and journal columns, and provided consultant services, reference work, and other forms of service. This decentralization of services served two vital purposes: specialists could serve ERIC, yet remain close to their career fields and institutions; and special interest groups developed a vested interest in ERIC. It is no wonder that by 1968 Burchinal bet that he could count on key school administrators and state school officers to come to his aid if the ERIC budget was threatened.

In sheer volume, the growth of the ERIC system is impressive. During the first six months of 1968, the Document Reproduction System distributed nearly 1.5 million microfiche and sold more than 7,500 hard-copy documents; *Research in Education* subscriptions climbed to nearly 5,000 in mid-1968 in an impressive increase from the 209 listed in the beginning of 1967. The total document collection for ERIC by mid-1968 exceeded 12,000.[14]

ERIC was not enthusiastically received by the R&D community, nor for several years by the practitioners.[15] Yet in every year up to 1975, the staff could point to annual increases in the use of the system. Howe points to it as one of the solid accomplishments of USOE,[16] and it was lauded within the bureaucracy, as Burchinal's career testifies. From the position of Director of the Dissemination and Training Division, he worked his way up to assistant commissioner and, in 1973, was appointed head of the Office of Science and Information Service, National Science Foundation. Burchinal and ERIC stand as examples of how a program can succeed even without wide-spread support by satisfying critical audiences within and outside the bureaucracy.

ES '70 Program

The fourth USOE program selected to illustrate how the staff of the Bureau of Research functioned is ES '70. This one, like ERIC, was largely the product of a handful of bureaucrats, led by the Director of the Division of Adult and Vocational Education Research, David Bushnell. He joined the Office in September 1964 after taking leave from the Stanford Research Institute to serve as a consultant for six months; his task was to plan and launch a new research program in vocational education. Section 4-c of the Vocational Act of 1963 (P.L. 88–210) had authorized 10 percent of future appropriations in vocational and technical education to be set aside for research, training, and experimental programs.[17] After serving a second six-month consultancy in 1965, Bushnell was appointed director of the newly created Division of Vocational Educational Research in the Bureau of Research.

This division had political problems as difficult as any in USOE. The lobby behind vocational education had been strong for years, and some in this group soon accused Bushnell of selling out what they saw was "their" research program to the academicians.[18] (This was not the attitude held by a small corps of researchers primarily interested in vocational education. They greeted the new program with an "excitement" that lasted for several years.[19]) But Keppel and then Howe kept the vocational education constituency reasonably satisfied. This provided the divisional staff with a framework of support that permitted them considerable freedom to innovate.

Bushnell had the training and the ambition to take advantage of the opportunity. He was led beyond administering an extra-mural R&D program to larger issues. How could the Division of Vocational Educational Research devise strategies that would better ensure the use of research results throughout school systems? Like Burchinal, his training in sociology had acquainted Bushnell with the agricultural experiment stations and the extension services; he pondered why education couldn't devise something similar.

In a speech before the state convention of New Jersey teachers in 1966, he proposed that schools change by altering several variables at once like teaching behavior, grading systems, use of technologies, and so forth. He speculated on the value of having "lighthouse" schools scattered throughout the nation. These would serve as models and would concentrate on total systems change. He advocated a new partnership arrangement between these model schools and the Office of Education with the federal government picking up the costs of the innovations.

Unexpectedly, the Associated Press picked up the story. The result was a "landslide of mail from superintendents around the country who wanted to participate."[20]

Within USOE he found a ready supporter in Lou Bright. Together they located the staff man they needed in Robert Morgan, the Director of Learning Resources, Litton Industries, and a former California colleague of Bushnell's. As Morgan said:

I was interested in working for the government for a couple of years and I wanted to work with a major systems experiment. Bright's missionary spirit appealed to me.[21]

Morgan's principal task assignment was to plan what was labeled "the ES '70" project.

Three months later, in November of 1966, Morgan and Bushnell presented their preliminary ideas to the Executive Committee of the Office of Education, the commissioner's internal policy "cabinet" that was made up of his principal line and staff assistants. Morgan remembers that he didn't have time to do detailed cost accounting for that meeting, but it was obvious that the project would be expensive. He and Bushnell set the figures between $200 and $600 million. In spite of the expense and the fact that they were advocating an unprecedented relationship between the Office of Education and local school districts, Morgan recalls that the project was "ratified" in about ten to fifteen minutes. "But it took about 40 minutes to decide on a name for it" he remembers; they settled on calling it the "organic curriculum."[22]

Morgan and Bushnell then set about to select the lighthouse schools from those districts who had written in response to the AP news release. After gathering more data, a series of meetings were scheduled to which representatives from seventeen school districts were invited after having been screened on criteria of size, location, and other educational and political variables. At the first of these meetings in Florida, two chief state school officers also were invited.

It was an intriguing idea. The superintendents themselves had to promise that they would give the project personal supervision. The staff of one comprehensive high school were to be involved from each district. The idea was to build a program that would expose all the students to both effective vocational training as well as academic preparation, so as to better prepare them both for work and further study after leaving high school. The Office of Education agreed to pick up all the costs of developing the new curricula and preparing the teachers, as well as the salary of a coordinator in each school.

It was to have been a long-term project; the subcontractors doing the development work were encouraged to plan for four to six years' lead time, and while no government agency legally could guarantee funds to anyone from future budgets, there clearly was a moral commitment made.[23]

At first, things went well for the project. The divisional staff was enthusiastic; Bright was giving it a lot of his time and support; and in FY 1968 about $3.5 million was allocated from the USOE budget.[24] To this was added funds from the National Science Foundation, private foundations, and local districts. USOE appeared to have launched a new and rather spectacular venture.

They were skating on very thin ice, as it turned out. Many vocational educators expected their research funds to be used for ideas that were closer to their interests.[25] The researchers most closely related to the vocational R&D saw ES '70 as another example of the growing tendency to allocate "their" funds to targeted priorities of a more developmental nature, and they were not enthusiastic.[26] Many of the staff in other divisions in the Bureau did not understand what the organic curriculum was, but they did understand that a lot of dollars that might otherwise go to their projects could be gobbled up with this seemingly over-expanding activity. "It cost too much," commented Lou Bright nine years later.[27]

It also was politically vulnerable. The chief state officers by and large didn't like having USOE going directly to local school districts, as they showed in 1967 by supporting the amendment to Title III of ESEA that restricted the authority of the commissioner in awarding funds for services.[b] They might have come around if the principals in the project had been more sensitive to the importance of the state agencies and paid them more heed; Lou Bright, Bob Morgan, and Dave Bushnell were from outside the educational enterprise and by their own admission were unfamiliar with the traditions and nuances of federal-state relations.

By the end of 1969, all of the principal staff had departed from the federal scene—and the project. True, the project was larger than those three persons;

---

[b]The 1967 amendments to ESEA reduced the authority of the commissioner. In the original act he approved all grants; the amendments restricted this right to 25 percent.

theoretically control and initiative rested with an executive committee composed of representatives of all the school districts and USOE representatives. But there also had been erosion among the original superintendents, and the real locus of control remained with the Office of Education who was footing the largest share of the bill. When Commissioner Allen had to choose among the USOE projects he would fund in 1969 and decided to go with the labs and centers, rather than the EX '70, the project lost much of its impetus. It limped along for a while, but by 1972, for all intents and purposes, it was dead.

USOE dared to tamper with one of its basic policies with the ES '70 Project—that is, federal-state relations—not from any expressed mandate from the secretarial level in DHEW (or the White House itself), but from a policy stance among the highest levels at that time that encouraged bureaucrats to step outside old boundaries. Both Presidents Kennedy and Johnson approved when federal agencies circumvented state governments and formed a partnership with cities and other local communities; OEO was only the best known example. Their postures were based on the liberal philosophy that looked to the federal government to rescue its citizens from the unimaginative, corrupt, or corroded state political system.

In USOE, this philosophy had taken a slightly different but no less expansive twist. The Gardner Task Force of 1964 recommended using federal funds to spur school districts to innovate. But to them, effective ideas for these innovations had to come from outside the system, which meant getting around the state governments. Title III of ESEA was written so that the Commissioner of Education, a federal official in a federal agency, would select which innovations in local schools were worthy of federal support. So while the source of this expanded federal role emanated from the issue of how to juice up the sluggish educational establishment, it was compatible with the ascendant liberal political beliefs of mid-1960s.

What specifically does ES '70 teach us about the Bureau of Research in the 1960s? Remember that the commissioner and his immediate staff in the years 1966 through 1969 were preoccupied with hot political issues of desegregation and equalizing educational opportunities. Divisional chiefs and their staffs were struggling with new programs and (for them) large appropriations. There was a gap in the middle; something was needed to deal more effectively with ideas that rose up from the staff, like ES '70. The implications of this program went far beyond the authority of David S. Bushnell and involved some of the fundamental policies on which our educational system is based. The fact that it got as far as it did is a reflection of the relative isolation of this (and almost all other) divisions in the Bureau—that is, isolation with considerable freedom. Looking back, ES '70 was doomed from the start; it was simply a matter of how long before the budget restrictions, the realization of the policy implications, and the full political implications of the proposal caught up with the program.

Two Research Activities Outside the Bureau of Research

Now let us turn to two research projects that received considerable publicity and attention from high figures in the federal government in the middle and late 1960s. These were the Equality of Educational Opportunity (EEO) Survey, most frequently called the Coleman study after its principal author, and the National Assessment of Educational Progress (NAEP). Neither were administered nor shaped by the Bureau of Research. To understand better why this was so and the implications for research support efforts in USOE, we shall examine each project in more detail beginning with the EEO Survey.

The Equality of Educational Opportunity Survey

Authority for the Educational Opportunity Survey can be found in Section 402 of the Civil Rights Act of 1964. It provided for a study "concerning the lack of availability of equal educational opportunity for individuals by reason of race, color, religion or national origin in public educational institutions at all levels . . . ." But USOE was slow in responding until Keppel hired Alexander Mood as Assistant Commissioner for Statistical Programs in August of 1964. The Civil Rights Survey was one of the first items they discussed.[28]

    Mood's appointment was a particularly fortunate one for USOE and for Keppel. The statistical services of the Office had been under almost constant fire from the Congress and from outside groups for years. Reports typically contained out-of-date information in difficult-to-use tabular form. Mood was an experienced statistician, a former professor of mathematics, an author of texts in statistics, and a proven administrator. He gained his managerial experience as Vice President of the Western Operations of CEIR, Inc., and as President of General Analysis Corporation.

    Both Keppel and Mood decided to interpret Section 402 in the "broadest way possible,"[29] and communicated this to the man they selected to do the job, James S. Coleman. Coleman at this time was still a rather obscure professor at Johns Hopkins University, although his first book, *The Adolescent Society*[30] published in 1961, received very favorable reviews. It was based on his dissertation study of peer-group influences on learning in five high schools.[31] He wasn't much interested in the survey at first, but he agreed to talk to them because he had the "highest possible regard for Mood," having used his text in graduate school.[32] He finally agreed to their offer, but only after he stipulated that they find a co-director. Ernest Q. Campbell of Vanderbilt was tapped to handle the higher education sections.

    Why did Coleman take the assignment? Consider his words:

Sociology and social research had been writing a lot of promisory notes about what they could do. They claimed to have the capability of saying something relevant about social policy. This seemed as good a time as any to show that the use of systematic methods could teach us something of interest in education.[33]

Coleman saw the survey as a possible turning point in the use of social science methodologies, and he viewed Mood as having the sophistication and integrity to back him up. By early Spring, those two were ready to go, but Keppel wasn't.

Finding resistence from a group of superintendents invited to react to the preliminary proposals of Coleman and Mood, Keppel delayed giving the O.K. until May of 1965, even though the law required that the results of the survey be reported to the Congress by July 1966!

The vississitudes of the survey and the actions taken to gather and process the millions of bits of data while gingerly skirting very touchy and hot political issues are too detailed to be reported here. What is important to note is that not only was the survey completed within the imposed time constraints but that it became a "landmark document in social science."[34] As Moynihan said: "It destroyed two generations of beliefs about policy and education."[35]

We cannot pass over so quickly, however, the difficulties the findings of the study caused Johnson administration officials. The results were so complex and open to such differing interpretations (or so it seemed to the readers of the original versions of the report) that USOE and other DHEW officials were fearful lest opponents of their desegregation policies seize on the report to support their views. After much pulling and tugging that resulted in three versions, a summary report was finally released that was "cast in such a way as to all but erase what, in Mood's version is clearly the heart of the survey."[36]

In spite of a few meetings with outside groups, USOE did little to publicize the findings. As a result, two years after its completion, it had had "no discernible effect on any program within the Office of Education [although it was cited occasionally by Howe in speeches], and plans for a followup study were quietly dropped when no one pressed for it."[37]

Out in the field interest in the report generated slowly. For example, even though it was released in July of 1966, there was no attention paid to it at the next annual meeting of the American Educational Research Association the following February. It was more than a year before reviews appeared in the journals of the psychologists or sociologists.

Not everyone was this disinterested, however. Thomas Pettigrew and Daniel P. Moynihan, who had returned to his professorship at Harvard from the Department of Labor, sought and received a modest grant from the Carnegie Corporation to operate an interdisciplinary seminar that reanalyzed and extended the original findings. When Moynihan accepted the offer to become President Nixon's advisor on urban affairs (which inevitably included education), the report was exumed in Washington. The education message of March 3, 1970, written principally by Moynihan, laid the groundwork for Nixon's approach to federal support by placing the emphasis on reform through the development of new, and proven, ideas. As Grant put it, "It was the Coleman Report writ large."[38]

The point to be made is that this survey is a prime example of what it takes to make a piece of research important at the highest policy levels of the federal government: attention from key officials and methodological and analytical sophistication of the highest order. Keppel saw to it that the study was aimed at educational issues that had significant federal policy implications. (In spite of the mandate of Congress, the survey could have bogged down in meaningless details about inconsequential aspects of education.) He also saw to it that the best possible researchers were tapped to do the job. A bookkeeping tabulation of buildings or degrees and years of experience of teachers, for example, would have won scant attention from experienced social scientists. Alexander Mood, a competent and respected staff man, was the key to setting and maintaining this level of sophistication.

The National Assessment of Education Progress

The NAEP story has some similarities with the EEO Survey. Keppel had an early hand in shaping it. In fact, it can be traced directly to Keppel himself.[39] To him, a national assessment "just made good sense," since that is what he viewed the Office of Education having been created to do in the first place—that is, to keep track of the state of American education.[40]

Early in 1963, Keppel discussed the idea with men like John Gardner and Roy Larsen. That summer they turned to Ralph Tyler and asked him to prepare a memo giving his views on a national assessment of education.

Using Carnegie funds they pulled together first a group of measurement people and then a group of educational and lay leaders. During 1964 they held a total of seven conferences with teachers, administrators, school board members, and others to test the substantive and political feasibility of such a survey; from these meetings emerged the Exploratory Committee on Assessing the Progress of Education (ECAPE). The study was beginning to jell, and in February 1965, Tyler convinced Jack Merwin, a professor at the University of Minnesota with wide test and measurement experience, to become the director of what at that time was intended to be a very small, part-time staff. In fact, ECAPE believed that the project probably would be ready to launch in about six months; after all, wasn't the project mostly a matter of picking up what tests were needed from those lying about? But as Merwin remarks:

No one realized that there was a technology to be developed. Everywhere we turned we had to do some research.[41]

More than technical matters slowed the project; political issues broke out early. In the spring of 1965, Harold Hand, at an address before the Association of Supervision and Curriculum Development (ASCD) convention, sharply critized the idea of a national assessment. He followed up with articles in educational journals.[42] He wasn't alone; that summer Parker reported:

By far the most provocative discussion at the 1965 (White House) conference. . . centered on a national assessment of educational performance.[43]

By the winter of 1966–67, some educational associations were taking official action. The Executive Board of the American Association of School Administrators (AASA) in a memo to all members and their institutions recommended that "they refuse to participate in the tryouts of these tests and in the eventual testing program—presently slated for the fall of 1967."[44] The President of the National Council of Teachers of English urged teachers to "fight tooth and nail to prevent a proposed plan to measure the quality of American education."[45] The furor spilled over into Congress, and during appropriations in February 1967, there was sharp questioning from members of the committee including Chairman Fogarty.[46]

All this was weathered, however, and cooler heads prevailed. AASA tempered its stand at the 1967 convention, and by that summer, most organizations had backed off from their criticisms. What finally resolved the major political issue was the decision of ECAPE and USOE to pass the administration of the project along to a quasi-legal agency, the Education Commission of the States. By that time Merwin could state that the half-million dollars granted by the Fund for the Advancement of Education had permitted the project to make "great progress in virgin territory—inventorying the status and progress of education in this country."[47] Congress gave its approval by appropriating $1,000,000 for the study in FY 1968. By FY 1970, this figure was doubled.

Of what value was this national assessment through these years to the policy shapers in the federal government? Not much. The decision to divide up the ten subject areas so that only three or four would be used for testing each year (and the retesting postponed for two years) meant that there could not be immediate implications for federal policies. This places the NAEP in direct contradiction to those who maintain that the government cannot support long-range policy studies; Commissioners Howe and Allen gave the Assessment their full support.

This support was all the more surprising since, as Merwin cites, there were many disappointments. But he cautions, "I'm not sure any of us had realistic expectations."[48] The advisory committee and staff discovered that the testing technology, as sophisticated as everyone believed it to be, was not up to the challenges of a national assessment. Constructing test items down from objectives didn't work well; nor were the writers able to produce items that had enough face validity to satisfy lay people. So the testing technicians learned much—about matrix sampling and its administration, for example,[c] or whether test items could be read to students or whether all students could read their own, and if they were read, whether regional voice made a difference.

What do these two projects (EEO and NAEP) show us by contrast about the Bureau of Research? We indicated in Chapter 6 that one of the frequent criticisms made of the Bureau was that little of the research it funded contributed to the larger missions of USOE. The EEO survey and the NAEP reveal some of the necessary tradeoffs that would result were the Bureau to become more mission and policy oriented. Let's examine some of these:

1. The Bureau would have had to serve more like a staff arm to the commissioner and through him to other high officials who shape high level educational policies.

2. Top priority would have had to been given to those major studies that are involved with the immediate and pressing policy issues, thereby committing more resources to the immediate over the long range and to the political issues over others.

3. The Bureau would have had to been staffed with more sophisticated bureaucratic-political directors with the know-how to steer through the kind of political turbulence that inevitably seems to surround educational issues at the federal level.

4. The Bureau would have had to maintained different ties with visible and influencial social and behavioral scientists and laymen: those with political influence would have had to have been more prominent in policy matters.

It is quite obvious to anyone who is aware of the difficulties of staffing USOE during the years we have covered so far in this book that the Bureau of Research was not up to these tasks, particularly since from the onset of the CRP, the Bureau was designed for different purposes. To have criticized it after the fact for missions it was not designed to accomplish was either stupid or politically motivated. To have expected the Bureau of Research to swing around rapidly to a different mission orientation was both foolhearty and naive.

Yet this was asked of it, and as we shall see in the next chapter, this was what the staff attempted to do. It is now time to turn to those events that will carry us through the final months of the Johnson administration, into the Nixon years, and up to the creation of the National Institute of Education.

---

[c]Matrix sampling, in brief, divides test items into packages so that each student takes only one package in a given subject area. With each student receiving only a fraction of the total set of items and with all packages not being given to the same student body, data cannot be compared by school. For more details, see *The National Assessment Approach to Sampling,* R. Paul Moore, James R. Chromy, and W. Todd Rogers (1974). National Assessment of Educational Progress, 700 Lincoln Towers, 1860 Lincoln St., Denver, Colorado 80203.

8 Nixon and Educational R & D

In 1969, a committee of the Organization for Economic Cooperation and Development (OECD) came to the United States to examine the state of educational research and development in this country. What they found impressed them:

> Our first conclusion is that American society has mounted an impressively large effort in educational research and development in a remarkably short period of time. Only, perhaps, in the U.S.A. would that effort be regarded as both trivially small and highly controversial.[1]

What the committee was referring to as controversial was that part of the federal effort conducted by the Office of Education. But since by 1968 this made up 60 percent of federal support for educational R&D it set the stamp on the entire area,[2] and controversial it had become.

Within the federal government, one way of measuring the degree of controversy of any program is by the number of times it has been investigated or studied. In the last eighteen months of the Johnson administration, educational research was the subject of more than a half-dozen major reviews. These were conducted by the Department of HEW, the Westheimer PSAC Committee, the Committee of Economic Development (CED), a group from the education products industry, and a USOE study in addition to the OECD review referred to above.[3] While there were some plaudits, there were more criticisms, and the most common conclusion was that many improvements were needed. The commissioner who would take over in 1969 obviously had to make some major changes.

Who would he be? Would he favor research and would he have the kind of support from the DHEW secretary and the president that Keppel and Howe had? Of the two major candidates in 1968, Hubert Humphrey seemed far more likely to give education a high priority. For one reason, he tapped as his advisors in education men like Francis Keppel, Wilbur Cohen, and Sam Halperin so that it was no surprise that he promised to continue and extend most of the breakthrough programs like ESEA.[4]

Nixon promised more for education in 1968[5] than he had eight years previously, but domestically he showed a preference for the areas of welfare and health. His appointment of Robert Finch as Secretary of DHEW gave little indication of what might happen in education. Finch had shown only modest interest in education while serving as Attorney General in California. After his first press conference in February 1969, the educational community breathed somewhat easier; it appeared then that he would not depart drastically from the policies of his predecessors, even as to desegregation of public schools.[6]

Spirits and eyebrows were raised with the announcement that the next commissioner (and Assistant Secretary of Education in DHEW) would be James E. Allen, then Commissioner of Education for the State of New York. Clearly, he was one of the most respected and prestigious men in education.[7] When he stated his conviction that both Nixon and Finch were going to give education a high priority, expectations among educationists began to climb.[8]

As for his part, Allen indicated that he saw the federal government as taking the "major share of the responsibility for the enhancement and renewal of the capabilities of our educational system."[9] He wanted the USOE to provide support in whatever form was needed to enable local and state governments to carry out their tasks with maximum effectiveness.[10] Research, development, planning, and dissemination comprised what he put as the first major area for action.[11]

In order to strengthen the Office for these tasks and as one step in his reorganization, he created a new staff organization in HEW to be headed by a deputy assistant secretary for Planning, Research and Evaluation (DASPRE), who also would be deputy commissioner. Reporting directly to the deputy would be an associate commissioner who would direct a new organization, the National Center for Educational Research and Development (NCERD). These moves were intended to signal a higher priority for research and related functions within DHEW and USOE.

To fill the DASPRE position, Allen sought out a prominent and highly respected scholar but was soon convinced that this was not practical. Several of those with whom he talked referred him back to a member of his own staff, the person temporarily assigned to the job, James E. Gallagher. Gallagher had chalked up an impressive record since 1967 as Associate Commissioner and Chief of the Bureau, Education of the Handicapped. While he was relatively unknown to the larger field of educational research, those who came in contact with him were impressed. And his own research, both as a student and colleague of James Kirk at the University of Illinois at Urbana, was substantial. Allen's selection augured well for research.

Gallagher faced tough prospects, however; he inherited a situation that would have been extraordinarily difficult for the wiliest and most experienced of bureaucrats. Gallagher was neither. To understand the complexities he faced it is necessary to step back and take stock of what was happening within and to the Office of Education itself in 1969.

USOE in 1969 and Beyond

Johnson may have lost some interest in improving the U.S. school system by the end of his administration, but the Office of Education was still a far more vibrant and important agency of the government in 1969 than it was when he assumed the presidency. But early in the Nixon administration USOE lost some of both. Leadership in desegregating schools was transferred to another agency, and USOE assumed a papershuffling role in equalizing educational opportunity.

Harold Howe II had continued and extended Keppel's efforts to desegregate the schools. But USOE was not meant to be an enforcement agency and had neither the personnel nor the tradition for the tasks it inherited under Title VI of the Civil Rights Act of 1964. Nevertheless, it accomplished more than many people thought it would.[12]

In 1968 Secretary Cohen tried to get the Congress to authorize transfer of this authority to the Justice Department, but failed. Finch succeeded in 1969, and USOE assumed a secondary role in the government's battles against segregation in the schools.

As for the other mission, USOE had been the primary agency for equalizing educational opportunity through the administration of Title I of ESEA. In 1968, this program was costing the federal government over $1.1 billion. Nixon retained this program but was not willing to put more money into it; he vetoed the appropriation bill when Congress did try to increase funds for Title I.[13] The White House was communicating two beliefs about this policy: (1) that the Johnsonian programs were not working and new ideas and initiatives were needed and (2) that USOE was an unlikely place to find these new ideas or to house new initiatives.[14] Ultimately, this reasoning would lead to the proposal for and the creation of the National Institute of Education.

So with the enforcement authority for Title VI of the Civil Rights Act transferred and USOE's place in the mission to equalize educational opportunity reduced largely to administrative matters, what was left for USOE to do? Plenty. Since 1965, the Office had taken on several new programs to increase the supply of teachers and to improve the way they were prepared. Title V of the Higher Education Act of 1965 (P.L. 89-329) created the Teacher Corps. In 1967, Congress passed the Education Professions Development Act (EPDA) (P.L. 90-35) that extended these provisions. To spearhead the EPDA was a new associate commissionership; Don Davies, formerly the director of National Commission on Teacher Education and Professional Standards, NEA, was induced to take the job in March of 1968.

There were other signs of vibrancy: in the education of the handicapped, vocational education, the National Assessment of Educational Programs, and higher education. One of the most visible and successful of USOE-funded projects was the Sesame Street TV series to which it was granting $2,000,000 in FY 1969.[15]

Did all this add up to success? Wasn't the Office of Education viewed by this time with favor? Hadn't it managed to increase both its popularity and prestige? Hadn't the effective leadership for more than five years by the highly respected teams of Gardner and Keppel, and Gardner and Howe paid off? Unfortunately, the answer was an unequivocal "No."

First of all, it continued to have a bad reputation for managing its own affairs. Edith Green's investigation of USOE in 1967 and the audit by the General Accounting Office in 1971 found it burdened with paperwork, bungling, and mismanagement.[16] Apparently it had grown too fast and taken on too much too quickly.

The Bureau of Research came in for its share of the criticism. It never had been granted enough positions, the staff maintained. Edith Green learned from her study what many men and women in the field had known before: it took months for proposals to be processed, many were lost in the process, and there was little continuity in staff decisions.[17]

These critics of the management only added to a growing audience of persons who were unhappy with the Bureau, outside the government as well as inside. In fact, it is no exaggeration to say that by 1969 the Bureau could find little support from any quarter. When Gallagher tried to establish more effective liaison with the leading educational associations, the so-called "big six" (Association of Elementary School Principals, Council of Chief State School Officers, American Association of School Administrators, National Association of Secondary School Principals, National Association of State Boards of Education, and the National School Boards Association) he found disinterest and even some hostility.[18] Even most of the leaders of the very audience being served by the Bureau, the educational research community, had concluded that USOE did not know how to operate an extra-mural R&D program.

Of course, part of this criticism was a knee-jerk reaction to the curtailment of project funds. Over the years, there had been a notable shift in the percentage of funds made available for field initiated projects of the kind that had characterized the early years of the Cooperative Research Program.[a] From Bright's time on, the policy had been to polarize the R&D effort—that is, to stimulate more basic research in the disciplines of relevance to education on the one hand[b] and to emphasize more large-scale development and product

---

[a]Changes in the definitions and reporting procedures makes it difficult to trace shifts of priorities of any kind. The term research as used in the early CRP years later was broken into several categories: applied research and development were reported separately yet some of what remained in the fundamental or general research category could also be described as applied research. Nevertheless, there was a trend from investigator-initiated research toward mission-oriented development work as USOE itself admits in its report, "Highlights of Cooperative Research and Development in Education," Fiscal Year 1971, NCERD, Washington, D.C., June 1972.

[b]Since its inception the CRP staff had sought out discipline-based scholars, but in 1967 and 1968 they announced two "programs" to reach this goal: the Committee on Basic Research in Education (COBRE) operated through the National Research Council (and was co-sponsored by the National Academy of Education); and the Multidisciplinary Research Program operated within and by the Office itself. For a description of COBRE, see "Final Report of the Committee on Basic Research in Education," Division of Behavioral Sciences, National Academy of Sciences, National Research Council, Washington, D.C., September 1972.

engineering work on the other. A small grants program was initiated in 1966
in part to compensate those researchers from the traditional educational research community (and their students).[19] In 1970, the regional offices, through
which this program was administered after 1968, funded 207 projects, but
because of the $10,000 limitation (originally set at $7,500) per project, this
obligated only $1,800,000.[20] This figure was smaller than the entire CRP
budget had been ten years previously; by 1972, this program constituted
virtually the only project funding available.

Under Nixon, the trend away from individual small scale projects was
hastened largely because of new planning procedures. As we noted in Chapter
7, the "science" of program management and planning had considerable impact in the mid-1960s in the federal government when Johnson had directed
all departments to emulate the DOD; Nixon went another step. Each agency
was required to formulate policy recommendations and program evaluations
in different ways. There was a shift from assessing programs by how well they
used their funds to what they produced with those funds, an emphasis on the
output.[21] The White House wanted "analytical studies of options rather than
single policy recommendations."[22] The ultimate effect of these policies for
educational research can be seen in the 1972 budget: $3,000,000 was allocated
for basic research, down from nearly $7,000,000 the year before. To make
matters worse, in the course of the year over three-fourths of this amount was
reprogramed to other efforts like the Right to Read, leaving only $690,000
for field-initiated projects.[23]

However it was reported, many researchers in the field were well aware
that a vital source of support was drying up. Gallagher could not expect enthusiastic support from this quarter. So what about the audiences within the
government?

Criticism from Within the Government

Precious little support for educational R&D was to be found in theCongress.
As noted in Chapter 6, in spite of the efforts of Secretary Gardner in 1968,
the R&D budget was cut by $52 million in 1969.[24] Gallagher reports that when
he made his first visit, as deputy assistant secretary, to Chairman of the Senate
Appropriations Subcommittee for DHEW Warren Magnuson, he was met with
a virtual diatribe against educational research. "I could hardly finish a sentence," he recalls.[25]

How about within the Department of HEW? Before Allen arrived in March
(he took a well-deserved vacation between positions), Finch turned to a Ford
Foundation official recommended by Keppel, Edward Meade, Jr., to help him
shape priorities. Meade convened a dozen task forces made up of outsiders
and DHEW–USOE officials on topics like school finance and vocational educa-

tion. One of these groups recommended the Experimental Schools Program.[26] This rather vague notion of a partnership arrangement with states and local authorities was meant to design and demonstrate new and different model schools. The intention was, apparently, to form a network of these schools so that the neighboring systems would more readily adopt those "tested" innovations. Originally, Finch wanted $25 million the first year, but later the department requested and received one-tenth of that amount for planning purposes.

Other than this, Meade found "little enthusiasm" for USOE's research program in DHEW. "People were asking what had prior funds bought and they were not getting satisfactory answers," he recalls.[27] But then, the same question had been asked in the planning offices of DHEW under William Gorham and Alice Rivlin, Lew Butler's predecessors (see Chapter 6). So there was little support for the Bureau of Research from this quarter.

That left the White House and its supporting agencies, BOB (changed in 1972 to the Office of Management and Budget) and OST. Little had changed here: John Mays was still assigned to OST and still showed little enthusiasm for USOE programs. Emerson Eliott promoted in the fall of 1970 to Deputy Chief of Human Resources Division, and Bernard Martin, principal examiner for education in BOB still found the Bureau's performance below acceptable standards. These two men, along with Michael O'Keefe in the ASPE office formed what O'Keefe himself labeled the "Unholy Trinity."[28] Because they were frequently appointed to policy, planning, and review committees of various kinds, but more importantly, becuse of their roles in the budget building and review processes, these men "made life miserable for the Bureau of Research."[29]

In fact, the new administration only made matters worse for the Bureau. During the Johnson administration, there was little response from the White House and the DHEW Secretary to the criticism about educational R&D. It wasn't so much that the president or John Gardner were protecting these programs as much as no one seemed willing to take the time to marshall the resources needed to call for a policy shift. In a bureaucracy, this can be, and frequently is, a tortuous and exhausting procedure. But in 1969, since the White House staff was in the process of reviewing programs, the burden of proof had shifted from the critics to the operators. As it turned out, no one would defend R&D as administered by USOE, least of all, its principal reviewer, Daniel Patrick Moynihan.

Moynihan and his assistant, Chester Finn, arrived in the White House from their Harvard–MIT positions at the Joint Center for Urban Studies and shared the skepticism of educational research and USOE prevalent on those campuses.[c]

---

[c]This attitude toward educational research I found typified by three comments that appear in separate letters written in response to the first draft of the RAND proposal

To them, research in education had been "inadequate, probably incompetent, and certainly disappointing."[30] Moynihan himself had recently emerged from a several month study of the Coleman report, a work that he viewed as "epic" and "of promethean daring."[31] He and his staff believed that this single study and a few others like the Westinghouse evaluation of Headstart[32] provided more information for policy purposes than all the rest of the research funded by USOE.[33]

With this dismal scene confronting the Bureau, why did Gallagher (or anyone) want to take on the DASPRE job? Part of the answer lies in some other events of those early Nixon months.

The Early Nixon Months

In 1969 Finch appeared to be in a strong position in the new administration. There were frequent references in the press to his "friendship" with Nixon and how he had open access to the Oval Office in the White House.[34] And he had moved early to establish departmental policies in education.

During his very first week in DHEW, he brought in Meade who organized fifteen review teams on such topics as moving desegregation enforcement to the Justice Department; transferring the responsibility for operating the school lunch program; and organizing troubleshooters to help college and school administrators with school disorders, experimental schools, and vocational education.[35] Several of these recommendations were acted on quickly—for example, legislation to transfer the desegregation authority and the experimental school program. So it seemed to follow in those early months that whoever Finch would bless personally in education would be in a strong position in the administration.

Gallagher reports that when he first presented his ideas for R&D the Secretary approved.[36] What Gallagher proposed, in essence, was a hard-nosed weeding out of what was good—that is, eliminating both projects and people that didn't measure up, but retaining what was commendable. These were the assumptions on which he and Allen built their first budget. Confident that he was on solid ground, he asked for more funds for R&D for FY 1970.

---

for an NIE. The first is by Christopher Jencks, then at Harvard, who states, "Unfortunately, I have pretty much lost whatever faith I once had in educational research making a difference to anyone other than educational researchers." The second, also from a Harvard faculty member, Sheldon H. White, was, "There are precedents for effective and meaningful R&D efforts in education, although one always associates them with particular talented people standing outside the profession of "educational researcher." The corroborating comment comes from a psychologist who at that time was at the Institute for Advanced Study at Princeton, George A. Miller who described himself as a "skeptic that there is anything in education to spend [large amounts] of research money on." See letter and responses to 30 October and 15 December, 1970, drafts of the NIE Preliminary Plan for the Proposed Institute, NIE Library, NIE A-000003.

That very first meeting with the BOB budget examiners was disasterous. Gallagher explains what happened:

They cut the R&D budget $20 million from what it had been the previous year. Their attitude was, "Let's wipe the slate clean, let's start over, let's bring in all new characters." That just didn't make sense to me; I wanted to keep the best, like the best labs and centers and put them on longer-term support, give them five-year commitments.[37]

The BOB and DHEW staff were adamant, and Gallagher is reported to have lost his cool and attacked them; one of the senior BOB officials angrily left the meeting.[38] That cast the die; Gallagher and his dreams for NCERD were as good as dead from that moment on. As Sproul reports:

Gallagher, and with him the fledgling NCERD, had completely fallen from the good graces of the Unholy Trinity. So it was that, by the end of 1969, key representatives of [these agencies] had reluctantly concluded that educational research was beyond salvation as long as it was controlled by OE.[39]

Gallagher might have been protected by the commissioner and the Secretary who hired him if they too had remained strong but by mid-summer 1969, it was increasingly obvious that power in educational matters, as in so many other affairs in the government, was being consolidated within the White House.

One manifestation of where the locus of control was coming to rest was who was making the decisions on personnel. In the first six months, key personnel were being located and hired by Allen and Finch. The commissioner (himself a Democrat) could and did employ a Democrat as DASPRE, but a few months later, when Allen nominated Peter P. Muirhead, an old-line USOE bureaucrat, to be his deputy commissioner, the White House said "No" even though Muirhead was of recognized competence and was supported by the leading associations of higher education. By the winter of 1969–70, it was increasingly obvious that the White House was doing the hiring even at second-echelon levels.[40] Gallagher learned this when he tried to fill the associate commissionership vacated by Boyan in June; his candidate was not cleared by the White House.[41]

Policy initiatives also emenated from White House sources. A task force was organized to put together new educational initiatives; its chairman was Edward Morgan from John Ehrlichman's staff.[42] In addition to Moynihan from the White House, there were Chester Finn, Lee Dubridge (the president's science advisor) and John Mays; Richard Nathan, an associate director, and Bernard Martin from BOB; James Allen; and Thomas Glennan, Director of Research and Evaluation from OEO.

Allen was accustomed to being a leader and did not feel comfortable being in the backwash of the Nixon administration. So he followed the kind of advice that he got from Chairman of the House Subcommittee on Appropriations Daniel P. Flood:

You better use your elbows and claws in that Department because they did a job on education this year.[43]

In September 1969, Allen at the National Association of State Boards of Education Convention announced a national crusade to teach all Americans to read; it became labeled the "Right to Read" program. It caught Nixon and his staff off guard.[44] But while Allen was successful in having the idea adopted as an administration policy statement (it was included in the Nixon education message to Congress) in the White House it never got far beyond rhetoric. In the 1971 budget, it was not made a line item, which meant that it had to be funded from other programs, like the commissioner's discretionary funds[45] and other funds from the Cooperative Research Program. For example, in June of 1970, three "basic projects" in the reading were funded for the total amount of $753,000.[46]

It soon became obvious that Right to Read only confirmed what everyone was suspecting: Allen was not part of the in-group that was shaping the administration's new policy initiatives in education.

The Nixon Administration's Proposal for Educational R&D: NIE

If it weren't to be the Right to Read Program, what would the new program in education be like? This question was made more difficult for the White House Task Force by Nixon's insistence that he would not continue to fund any program that did not prove to be effective; this meant that the TF had to devise something that, by 1972 or earlier, could be demonstrated as having "worked." This is a nearly impossible job in government, and Moynihan with his prior experience in the Labor Department knew it better than anyone in that group. Further complications arose from Nixon's fiscal stringencies for education; what extra funds he was willing to request for domestic programs were going first to welfare reforms.[47] Intensifying matters were the pressures that resulted from Nixon's veto of the educational appropriations bill that Fall and the growing influence of the educational lobbyists.[48] The task force had to come up with something, but what could fulfill all these requirements?

How that "something" materialized as the proposal for a National Institute of Education (NIE) is open to interpretation. One story has it that at a meeting of the task force in the office of Lew Butler the issue being discussed was not new legislative initiatives but what could be done with the hopeless NCERD in USOE. One member of the group who had been assigned the task of reviewing the presidential campaign promises recalled that Nixon had advocated creating a National Institute for the Educational Future. Here was a chance to kill two birds at once; start fresh in educational R&D and give Nixon a major plank in a new educational platform.

Moynihan liked the idea. He had concluded that too little was known about the processes called education and, therefore, that "the time had come for long-term, sustained, controlled research."[49] After due deliberation, and after they discovered that most of those to whom they "floated" the idea approved, the proposal became the first and prime recommendation of the president in his Educational Message to the Congress in March 1970.[50] NIE was intended to become the "focus for educational research and experimentation in the United States" and eventually to oversee the expenditure of a quarter of a billion dollars.

Those who are unfamiliar with the workings of the government at the White House level may not realize the full implications of a presidential announcement of this magnitude. As Finn reports, the idea for an NIE was argued at some length at cabinet meetings and staff meetings: "No one doubted that the Institute was the Message's central proposal...."[51]

Could not this have been a glorious way to end this book and begin what could be essentially a new chapter in the federal government's involvement in educational research? A new agency to rival in excitement and hope, the National Institutes of Health and the National Science Foundation, a new effort to plot the way for the educational enterprise as it tried to extricate itself from the issues of the 1960s that common sense and workbench inventions couldn't solve. Yes, what a finish that would have been—if only!

If only conditions had remained in the White House as they were that winter of 1969–70, and Moynihan had retained his influence.[52]

If only the educational associations could have become convinced that NIE was a once-in-a-lifetime opportunity for the enterprise they served.

If only the educational researchers could have found a way to organize themselves so they could have helped develop high interest and support.

The facts are: a few weeks after the president's message there were so few reactions that it was as if the proposal had never been made. What most of the educational profession read from that message was not a new initiative but another example of Nixon's evasiveness.[53] For NIE to be considered seriously, a climate of excitement and hope was needed. Nixon's veto of the educational appropriations, his threats to impound funds appropriated by Congress, his continued involvement in the Vietnam conflict that again sparked campus unrest—all these factors and more created a climate of incredulity. Faced with this growing riff from the educational community, Nixon soon appeared to lose whatever interest he had in educational reform. And by 1971, Moynihan was gone. With him went any real interest in the White House for NIE.

In fact, one of the greatest paradoxes of this story is that the main thrust of the Republican president became fact only through the persistence of a

Democratic congressman, John Brademas of Indiana. How he persevered and
how NIE did in fact become created is another story (and told much better
in other sources[54] than can be reported in the few paragraphs left in this chapter). But one final point must be made.

Remember that the idea for an NIE was generated because of two concerns
held by members of the task force. A new presidential initiative was only one
of them. When Nixon lost interest and with Moynihan's departure, the residual
effect was to leave those who were mostly interested with closing down the
USOE effort and creating an agency with which they would have more sympathy,
more influence, and closer working relationships. Brademas may have wanted
to create an edifice; the "Unholy Trinity" was more concerned with the nuts
and bolts of putting together an operating program, one this time that would
not slip into the control of those who had so effectively managed to run—or in
their eyes, bungle—matters.

It may have been coincidence that Emerson Elliott, John Mays, and Bernard
Martin, three of the most visible members of the network built around the
"Trinity" ended up as principal staff members of the NIE. (There is no evidence
that they ever set out to create a new agency to which they could transfer.)
It was no coincidence, however, that they kept a firm hand on the planning
and that "their" candidate, Thomas Glennan, was chosen as the first director;
Elliott became the deputy director. NIE in many ways became "theirs," not
Nixon's and certainly not Brademas'.

NCERD in the Interim

A coda can be described as a final repetition of an oft-heard phrase (of music
usually); NCERD becomes the coda in our story. By the end of the summer of
1970, Gallagher had resigned; Allen denounced the bombing of Cambodia
and left thereby with some honor a few months later. Finch, too, had gone
by the end of the year.

A caretaker crew in NCERD tried desperately to recoup and threw together
or arranged for bundles of planning documents aimed at clarifying the missions
and the goals of educational research. Some of these, like the AIR review of
products of the labs and centers[55] had merit but never received serious attention. Others like the document, "Directed Research Program,"[56] which was
distributed widely to persons in the field for reactions, were noted mostly for
their bulk and incomprehensibility.

The NCERD staff found themselves in an increasingly untenable position:
for two years the NIE legislation languished in Congress. The center obviously
was on its way out and certainly was not being granted many favors. Many
career bureaucrats turned elsewhere and vacancies could not be filled easily.
The Bureau of Research in 1967 had a staff of approximately 270.[57] By

February of 1971, this had dropped to 150, and by the end of that year, it was further reduced to 118.[58] Yet they were called upon to perform like bureaus in the Department of Defense and other agencies that had longer histories of mission management. NCERD obviously needed help and direction.

They recruited as director someone from one of the think-tank agencies, Systems Development Corporation, where there was a tradition and experience in sophisticated planning and evaluation of bureaucratic activities. But Harry Silverman, the new associate commissioner for Research, as of January 1, 1971, was given two jobs: run a caretaker NCERD and direct the planning for the new NIE. It must have been the latter task that appealed to him because he had been offered and refused the position under Gallagher before NIE was proposed. As it turned out, within the year, he turned over the caretaking chores to his hand-picked deputy, Richard McVity, to devote just about full-time to the NIE tasks.

In June 1972, NIE was authorized in Title III of the Education Amendments act of 1972 and signed into law by President Nixon. Those events caused no more stirring in the field than had the original proposals two-and-one-half years earlier. Maybe educational researchers were too experienced with federal programs by then to revive the religious fevor they felt in the mid-1960s. Maybe it was the almost surreptitious way NIE had been created: the administration's approach seemed to be, "Don't call attention to it!" Or maybe it soon became obvious that NIE would inherit most of NCERD's programs, thereby beclouding its image as a "new effort."

What effect would NIE have on the other agencies that were still funding R&D in education? That was not at all clear in 1972. NSF continued to fund curriculum projects by men like Zacharias at EDC and Edward Beagle at Stanford. A "second generation" was taking over even though the curriculum approach to educational reform had lost many of its adherents. As USOE and the newly created Office of Child Development increased their funding for research related to schools, there was less interest in this area in NIMH. And OEO found its educational programs transferred to OCD and later to NIE.

While the map in Washington was changing—that is, which agency was responsible for what initiative—the creation of NIE reaffirmed an important principle: educational R&D was important for the federal government. Then and increasingly as the 1970s wore on, DHEW officials and congressmen showed displeasure with what they were getting for their money. But they couldn't bring themselves to close out their efforts.

So we end our far-from-glorious tale of the involvement of the federal government in educational R&D at a convenient place: A new agency promising to start a new phase at least as far as the government is concerned. This affords the opportunity for us to stop our descriptive narrative to reflect and speculate about the future. That is the purpose of the last chapter.

9

What We Need to Do

In the first two chapters was stated the proposition that the support of educational R&D by the federal government was less effective than it could have been because the bureaucratic-professional complex was not fully functioning. The task in this chapter is to propose ways to improve that situation. But first, in order to lay the groundwork for those recommendations, let us review and highlight the ways in which the complex was dysfunctional and some of the causes of those difficulties.

Problems of the Educational R&D Complex

To begin with, the reader is reminded that the educational R&D complex is composed of two parts: the bureaucratic side includes agency officials, elected politicians and their staffs, policymakers and their staff assistants; the professional side refers to educational researchers and developers whether they are located in universities, public schools, or private research companies, selected officials of foundations, and certain educational administrators at the state and local levels who are involved in R&D processes.

A complex functions best when each side pursues policies and programs that complement the other. This does not mean that the research community and the bureaucracy need to have the same goals; this is an unrealistic expectation. Bureaucrats must respond to forces and powers that researchers have little or no knowledge of, and vice versa. But the essence of a complex is that there are common values and common objectives that can be used to keep the interests of both parties from becoming contradictory. Some of these common elements are fashioned during the professional training of both bureaucrats and researchers, and these can be reinforced and further shaped throughout their careers by frequent interactions. Take as an example the medical research complex. The bureaucratic side of this complex is most in evidence at the National Institutes of Health, the staff of which contains many eminent and respected scientists and former scientists now turned bureaucrat.

This was not the case with educational R&D in the 1960s. As was shown in the preceding chapters, the bureaucrats in the R&D sections of the USOE were selected from many fields, and most of them never adopted the R&D community as their reference group. The commonalities that characterize a complex were missing. The bureaucrats and researchers ended up by pursuing different policies. I can best illustrate this statement by first describing the policies under which the R&D community was operating in the early 1960s.

Policies of the Educational R&D Community

This fact, that the R&D community does operate under "policies," may surprise some readers. They see researchers as a disorganized collection of disparate individuals and groups, and in many ways, as acknowledged in Chapter 2, this is an accurate observation. But Chapter 2 also described the structure of the research community, which includes a kind of governance. The elite group that acknowledges and controls the growth of knowledge also shapes opinions and therefore, decisions on matters such as how best to recruit and train young graduate students, or how to best organize around specific issues and for different R&D functions. These are called here the logistical and managerial issues. Largely through informal discussions and in other almost mysterious ways, prevailing views emerge that serve as policies on these matters.

I can cite four such policies in the early 1960s that led to a number of decisions and activities. In somewhat over-simplified fashion, these policies can be stated as follows:

1. The quality of educational research and its prestige among the social and behavioral sciences had to be improved.
2. The study of education would benefit from more input by the social and behavioral scientists.
3. Educational development had to be made more sophisticated, tied more closely to research, and made to play a more prominent part in the life of the educational system.
4. The educational R&D community had to expand, but slowly.

How were these policies evidenced? What decisions and activities were made that reflected them? A review of the decisions of the USOE Cooperative Research Program in the period 1956–1965 shows a remarkable consistency with these policies. But the research community had other ways of expressing them. Five separate events, only one of which involved the federal government, illustrate how the community can operate. These events were:

1. The inclusion of "educational researchers" among those who were eligible to be invited to the Center for Advanced Study in the Behavioral Sciences.
2. The creation of the National Academy of Education.
3. Policy changes in the American Educational Research Association.
4. The work of the Committee on Basic Research in Education.
5. Changes in the research personnel in certain schools of education.

Let us examine each of these in more detail.

1. *Inclusion of "educational researchers" among those invited to the Center for Advanced Study in the Behavioral Sciences.* The Center for Advanced Study grew out of the interest of the Ford Foundation in fostering post-doctoral scholarship in the behavioral and social sciences. Upon the advice of a group of distinguished scholars, the Ford Foundation created the Center in 1964. By November 1975, the Center could count as its alumni 963 persons in more than 17 separate fields of study who had each spent a year pursuing his/her own intellectual interests. Thirty-seven of these alumni list education as their field of study. While this is only 4 percent of the total, it is about equal to the number of biologists, lawyers, linguists, philosophers, and psychiatrists.[1]

Being at the Center for a year does not guarantee anything. Some men and women let the year slip by with little to show for it, but most get to know more about the work of at least some of the 40-odd compatriots who are there with them. And these relationships can provide access to new networks and vital sources of new knowledge. The Center offers a group of leaders in educational research the opportunity to interact with their counterparts in other fields, thereby establishing a new precedent for some and making such interaction easier for others who have already begun it on their own.

2. *Creation of the National Academy of Education.* For years, many of the better scholars in education had discussed the need for a new and more scholarly organization in education. In 1964, a nominating committee was formed and the first eight members were selected by a committee of persons who did not consider themselves eligible: James B. Conant, John Gardner, Clark Kerr, and Sterling McMurrin. These first eight members consisted of Jerome Bruner, Roald Campbell, Lawrence Cremin, Lee Cronbach, William Frankena, Richard Hofstadter, Theodore Schultz, and Ralph Tyler. Thirteen more persons were added soon thereafter and the first meeting was held in March 1965. Ralph Tyler was elected the first president.

To most outsiders, the NAE has not appeared to be particularly active. It sponsored two formal "studies," one of which examined the state of research on education and the second of which looked at the way education policy is shaped at all levels of government. It co-sponsored CoBRE, and at its regular semi-annual meetings, heard reports and papers from its members and invited guests.

But NAE was not created to conduct studies or engage in other public, formal activities so much as to serve its members and the rest of the scholarly community in other ways. This is how the Academy is described in its statement of purpose:

It is hoped that the proposed Academy will give that [group of distinguished investigators] form and structure, making it a forum for conversation, debate, and mutual instruction, a rostrum for the communication of scholarly information and opinion, a stimulus for imagination and fruitful research.[2]

This stimulus was being provided in part by mixing easily identifiable educational researchers like Benjamin Bloom, George Counts, and Robert Havighurst with researchers more readily identifiable with other fields, such as Robert Merton in sociology, Gary Becker in economics, and Bernard Bailyn in history.

3. *Policy changes in the AERA.* In the 1930s, AERA sought and was granted departmental status in the National Education Association. For the next thirty years the NEA played an integral and at times dominant position in the affairs of the smaller organization. As long as educational research was viewed primarily as an activity of professors of education and directors of testing and/or research in local or state school systems, that alliance made sense.

By the 1960s, the beliefs and perceptions of what was needed to improve scholarship in education that had led to the creation of NAE also began to have implications for AERA's activities. There was no grand design, but there was a sense that the Association could and should help to improve the quality and range of research activities. The governing board launched a number of new publications, beginning with *The Handbook of Research on Teaching.*[3] (a well-received single volume edited by N.L. Gage), a new journal for the publication of original research called the *American Educational Research Journal* (that within a few years was viewed as the most prestigious quarterly in educational research), and a monthly newsletter (excluding summer) that included new items on activities in federal agencies supporting educational R&D. They expanded the annual meeting and set up more controls so as to improve the quality of the work being reported. They also accepted the responsibility for helping to train researchers through short courses held in conjunction with the annual meeting. And they left the NEA.

If the activities of the organization demonstrated higher intellectual competency, better scholars might be induced to interact with educational researchers, it was argued. At the same time, by creating a division for social scientists and sponsoring several meetings and training programs for them, the Association encouraged members of "other" disciplines to interact with those doing educational research.

4. *Committee on Basic Research in Education.* As an idea, CoBRE has been attributed to R. Louis Bright while he was Associate Commissioner for Research in USOE. Bright saw most of the USOE R&D funds going to support applied research, so he endeavored to strengthen other research activities—that is, development, dissemination, and basic research.

Basic research to Bright was an activity primarily conducted by scholars and scientists in the disciplines. To entice more of them to do work in education, he knew he had to work through their channels. So he turned to one of the most prestigious of the scholarly organizations, the National Academy of Sciences. There he found Henry David, then (in 1966) the newly appointed Director of the Behavioral Sciences Division. Together, Bright and David shaped the idea of a committee whose membership would consist of highly reputable scholars from education as well as the behavioral and social sciences. As chairman they selected Patrick Suppes, a mathematician and philosopher from Stanford who had turned his attention only a few years before to experimenting with the use of the computer in elementary classroom instruction. Others who were familiar to educational researchers were John C. Carroll, Robert Gagne, and James S. Coleman. Bright and David also invited persons like Ernst Caspari, a biologist, and Julius Richmond, from the Harvard Medical School, who were relatively unknown to educators.

CoBRE operated in two distinct phases. At first they devoted their attention to identifying and encouraging young scholars from the disciplines whose work had significance to education to draft research ideas; the best of these they eventually supported, spending $1,990,000 all told for 46 projects. In the final year of its three-year history, CoBRE shifted tactics. They sponsored eight workshops, the purpose being to "stimulate basic research in the behavioral sciences in areas of potential relevance to education." The topics for the workshops were:

1. Cognitive Organization and Psychological Process;
2. Politics of Elementary and Secondary Education;
3. Grammar and Semantics of Natural Language;
4. Language Comprehension and the Acquisition of Knowledge;
5. Sociological Theory and Research in Education;
6. Higher Education: Equity and Efficiency;
7. Coding Theory in Learning and Memory;
8. Genetic Endowment and Environment in the Determination of Behavior;[4]

The final activities of the committee were to distribute approximately $500,000 to 46 small grant projects.

5. *Changes in research personnel in schools of education.* This concern for improving the form and level of scholarship in education was not universally adopted throughout the educational enterprise. Most of the teacher-preparation institutions made minimal changes. Their response to the advent of federal funding in research was often superficial: appointing a "house scholar"; creating a research coordinator to teach other faculty members how to write proposals; creating a paper research organization. But in a few institutions there was notable change.

At Stanford University, for example, where the research tradition from the years of Cubberly had never completely died out, there was a remarkable renaissance that eventually blossomed under the deanship of H. Thomas James. From within the field of education, Stanford lured men like N.L. Gage; from outside, it enticed persons like James March from political science, psychologists Robert Hess and Lee Cronbach, Henry Levin, an economist, and Michael Kirst from public administration.

While there was no other institution that could point to so many new and visible faces, there was a ripple effect that touched many institutions in all parts of the country, and at places that did not have a tradition of scholarship in education: Florida State University, U.C.L.A., Michigan State University, Washington University at St. Louis, to mention but a few. And in others, the research tradition was extended or revived, such as at the University of Chicago, the University of Illinois at Urbana, and Teachers College, Columbia University.[a]

Policies of the Bureaucracy

While these activities were taking place within the research community, what was happening in the federal government? There had grown up in the late 1950s parallel efforts to support educational R&D: one located in the National Science Foundation, and the second in the USOE. The NSF program was an outgrowth of and related to some of the complexes in the physical and chemical sciences; in USOE there were several programs, but the dominant one, labeled the Cooperative Research Program (CRP) was shaped and largely controlled at first by the educational research community.

From the period between the launching of the CRP and the passage of the Elementary and Secondary Education Act, the R&D policies of the USOE and the research community were remarkably compatible. For example, the research community favored a slow but steady growth in the numbers of researchers and in the number and types of R&D institutions, and federal policies were intended to produce such growth. But when education, and with it R&D, were catapulted into the political arena nationally, the research governing elite was not able to maintain its high level of influence on federal policies. Funding leaped from $25 million to nearly $100 million in one year; training fellowships were granted to more than a thousand people; and the plans for new institutions shot up from the four or five originally envisioned to the thirty that eventually materialized.

When the research elite lost its influence on federal policies, no other outside group was able to take its place. The resulting vacuum was filled by the USOE bureaucrats themselves, whose knowledge and exposure to educational R&D was limited. (In NSF, the staffs were more closely associated with the scientific community, and the history of those projects in the Course Contest Improvement Program show much more consistent support from the outside.)

What were the policies of the bureaucrats? To them the external validity of any program or piece of research became critically important. How would it be judged by practitioners, politicians, and policymakers? Would it be likely

---

[a]I apologize to my many (former) friends who find their institutions omitted. Will there be an educational researcher of any prominence who wouldn't believe that his or her presence has reestablished or extended the research tradition in that institution? Not I!

to "make a difference" in schools, particularly with respect to the major educational issues of the moment? Increasingly during the latter half of the decade of the 1960s, the bureaucrats tried to use their mechanisms of control to point the researchers toward the issues of most importance to them. The result was to further alienate the research community.

So the two sides of the complex found themselves running on divergent tracks. It is no wonder that when the Nixon administration proposed a new research agency, the National Institute of Education, that there was virtually no opposition from researchers. By that time, 1970, there was a sense of hopelessness toward the USOE programs; NIE seemed to hold promise because few researchers believed that the USOE programs could be reshaped so as to again reflect R&D values.

If they hoped that NIE would be much different, they were soon discouraged, for NIE was shaped by persons and issues that emerged victorious from the internal bureaucratic power struggle more than by anthing else; the research community in the beginning found itself as divorced from NIE's operations and policies as it had been from USOE. Ironically, many more respectable researchers were appointed to NIE staff positions than had ever been found on USOE rosters, but they appeared to have little influence on NIE policies. The cadre staff around the director remained distant from the educational research community and the formal advisory bodies were filled mostly with persons from other fields.

Proposals for Change

So the educational R&D complex in the mid-1970s is still dismembered. And it is time to propose some changes that will put it into a more effective operating condition.

Change in the Bureaucracy

As a first corrective step, we must do whatever we can to ensure that more key government positions are filled by persons from the R&D community itself. The locale of prior professional experience is not nearly as important as the position that any NIE appointee holds within the R&D community. Such appointees should be from the elite, or in a working relationship with the elite. They should have widespread knowledge of the field, substantively and in terms of who is doing what where, and how well. They should understand how to ply the communication networks so they can seek the best advice on any issue.

NIE appointees need to have a sense of perspective on education and educational research, and they must be aware of the issues of the day and the debates about those issues. In short, in addition to being as knowledgeable as they can be about substantive and methodological matters in the social and behavioral sciences, they must have some "common sense" about the field.

In all agencies that support educational R&D, but particularly in the NIE, a cadre of top-ranking staff must be created consisting of persons like those described above. They must be willing to commit a sizeable portion of their careers to government service, for only then will they become fully integrated into the culture mentioned in Chapter 1.

The key position in this cadre is obviously the director. It is possible in some governmental settings, where the cadre staff is of sufficient competence and grounded in the field represented by the agency, to fill the directorship with part-timers, persons who devote only two to four years to government service. Our need in educational R&D is so great that this will not do. The model for the kind of person I have in mind in James S. Shannon, who served as Director of the National Institutes for Health for thirteen vibrant, exciting, and often turbulent years. He was a man with respectable research credentials for his work in renal physiology and electrolyte metabolism, but government service became his second, and highly successful, career.

The director is particularly important in fusing the work of the agency to the field, and vice versa. He not only has to know who is doing research work, but also how to reach them and how to command their loyalty. Edward Zigler, Director of the Office of Child Development from 1972 to 1974, although no career bureaucrat, showed he understood this principle when he said:

You see, I knew who to contact for help. I could telephone, say, Nick Hobbs at Peabody, or George Miller, and say, 'Hey, I need some of your time on this one' and, if they were available, they would respond.[5]

The director and this cadre of men and women around him need many kinds of support, such as career managers, short-term in-and-out R&D specialists, and advisors of many kinds. As important as all these persons are, however, they must remain support staff for the director and the cadre of research-bureaucrats. It is this core group who will make the critical decisions.

Why must these men and women, the research-bureaucrats, be asked to commit themselves to a long tenure in government service? Isn't it enough if good persons serve for a few years? Unfortunately, no, for the bureaucrats must perform another badly needed task—to educate the field about the political realities of public policies and public affairs. We researchers have been lectured to on several occasions by bureaucrats about our naivete, but accurate as the messages are they have fallen, by and large, on deaf ears. Why? Either because the messages themselves were from the "temporaries," who revealed their own naivete, or they were from persons outside the R&D community who were labeled "administrators" or "political types." We need to grow our own crop of bureaucrats who understand the value systems, the vicissitudes, the foibles, and the aspirations of researchers, but who develop a sympathy for and an understanding of the political world. Only then will we have the basis for developing a really effective R&D complex.

Change in the Research Community

Let us turn our attention now to the opposite side—to the R&D community, and specifically to the way its policies are fashioned and implemented. *We need to improve the way the R&D community shapes its policies.* The kind of slow, "bubbling up" (or filtering down) process that has characterized policy shaping heretofore needs to be augmented.

The changes are necessitated not merely because of the faster pace of events, although that is a factor; the R&D complex has grown large and, pardon me, complex. No longer can a handful of advisors gather at first hand all the necessary data from which to make sound policy decisions. In the early 1960s, a man or woman could hope to visit all the relevant research organizations and stay in touch personally with the leading investigators. He/she also was confident that he/she could keep up with what the bureaucrats were doing. No more. Lacking other sources, advisors have come to rely unnecessarily upon the bureaucrats themselves for vital data. Who controls the data controls the program, it is said.

Two changes are recommended:

1. The research community should develop other sources of data collection and analysis on matters that relate to the operation of that community.
2. There should be more, and more profitable, interaction on policy matters between the elite of the research community and the middle level R&D producers.

Data Collection

There are more data being generated all the time about the operations of the educational R&D field—that is, data on substantive matters (including methodological) and on matters of community functioning. It is much easier today than ten years ago to gain a competent overview of the work going on in various specialties within the field. The AERA publication, *Review of Research on Education,* an annual, supplements the quarterly *Review of Educational Research.* The ERIC system allows quick inventories of ongoing work, as do *Psychological Abstracts* and *Sociological Abstracts.* Granted, there are gaps in the system, but the point is that it is more convenient today to draw a substantive map of the field than it has been previously.

Studies in the mechanics of the field also have been increasing. I refer now to the early studies of the kind completed by Lazarsfeld and Sieber, which examined the organization of educational research. Since that time there have been a host of evaluations of government-sponsored programs. But there still is a lack of continuing collections of data on issues such as manpower requirements and utilization, institutional organizations for R&D, organization of schools or colleges of education for R&D, relationships of public schools to the R&D system. This need may be met if NIE decides to continue the publication of the Databook annually.

The dimension that is missing from these studies, and that no government agency can provide adequately, is the assessment of the *quality* of events and activities in the field. How well are students being trained? Which innovative ideas for preparing evaluators holds the most promise? In which research areas is the most competent work being performed? Which should be granted the most support in the future? Questions such as these again require data and researchers must have access to the facts.

There are university research groups that will respond if there is a call for more qualitative studies of the R&D community. Other sources might help with quantitative studies. Professional associations, for example, are in an advantageous position to do annual audits of the content of meetings and to trace the topics being reported in their journals. They also have data about membership that can be useful. But it is highly unlikely that they will contribute much to the qualitative assessment of research products, if past experience is any guide.

Policy Shaping

More than new and different kinds of data are needed, however. The R&D community must find better ways of shaping their policies. How does this occur now? The most common way is through a slow process of accretion; policies gradually evolve out of many informal discussions. Frank Chase remarked during his interview for this study that his advice about the regional labs was grounded in discussions with colleagues that extended back further than he could remember. These policy-shaping processes have served us well in the past. What is now called for, however, is a more systematic, time-telescoped way of producing these policies—that is, a way of forcing out those issues that are of most concern to the researchers themselves.

Let me hasten to add that the call is not for researchers to attempt to anticipate what issues will be commanding the attention of most politicians and practitioners five to ten years hence; nor is it for a statement of "research priorities," that dreary task that so frequently ends up with a lising of every conceivable question that might be asked of anyone. Rather, researchers should meet regularly to consider the needs of the research community in light of the most likely future events: (1) in the educational enterprise; (2) in the social and behavioral science communities; and (3) in the federal government.

Let me cite just one example. It is becoming increasingly apparent to some of us that the continued professionalization and bureaucratization of public, formal education, coupled with the disintegration of the conventional family life in this country, is producing high anxieties among many parents. We have become one of the few societies in the history of the world, perhaps the only one, where parents have become shaky about child raising and socialization practices. Some researchers already have anticipated this and are putting together research staffs and organizing to concentrate on the relationship between schools and families. There are implications here for the kind of researcher who needs to be produced, where he/she might best be housed (in schools of education? schools of home economics?), and so forth. We can wait for the slow evolution of some issues that relate to these areas of study, or we can hasten them along and thereby, as researchers, have more to say when they become policy considerations.

I am not necessarily calling for more formal reports or for a new science of predicting the future. I am asking that associations like NAE and AERA, foundations, university departments, and government agencies sponsor and organize more informal gatherings so that more researchers can keep abreast of (1) the present and likely state-of-the-art in various research specialties, and (2) the present and probable events in the educational enterprise. Let us bring together more often the keen observers with the thoughtful analyst.

Many readers will immediately respond by commenting that there are many opportunities now for the *leadership* to meet in this way: at NAE gatherings, when invited to attend the "Cleveland Conferences" (a self-appointed group of practitioners and scholars who meet once a year to discuss major issues in education), and at meetings called at "think tanks" such as the Center for Humanistic Studies at Aspen and the Center for Advanced Study in the Behavioral Sciences. What else is needed then? More of the same? Yes, but also more meetings that include researchers (and others concerned with R&D who are called upon to advise educators) at *all levels* of the enterprise. Far too often, the policies that are shaped and understood by the elite have not been communicated to their younger or less influential colleagues. Let me cite a personal example.

I was used frequently as an advisor to the laboratory program: four times I was chairman of a site review team and reviewed and/or advised eight labs altogether. As an executive officer of AERA, I also was frequently exposed to those top level advisors who were influencing the entire program. Yet I had limited knowledge and not well-shaped views about what those labs could become and what education needed from them. My opinions were formed, by and large, by the information passed on to me by the staff of the laboratory program. Most of my fellow advisors and I had only one formal meeting with the National Advisory Committee for the Regional Laboratories.

Critical issues must be made more public and more public debate must take place on them. Fortunately, this is beginning to happen. AERA, APA, and other associational meetings have far more sessions devoted to discussion of policy-related issues than was the case ten years ago. And there are more printed channels now available for discussion of these issues, such as the AERA news magazine, *The Educational Researcher.*[6] Yet communication on these matters still is constricted. Take one example: NIE has been struggling ever since its creation with the issue of what to do with the R&D institutions created by USOE. It established a blue-ribbon panel to recommend new policies. These were devised, discussed by the National Council on Educational Research, the official advisory body to NIE, and by the NIE staff, some of whom, in turn, consulted outsiders for reactions. There was no organized effort by outside groups (except for the organization of research institutions themselves, CeDAR) to debate among themselves the issues that were faced by this panel. There are many researchers who may be called upon by individual labs or R&D centers who will have little notion of what these organizations now are expected to become, or why.

Recapitulation

On the basis of this review of the federal role in educational R&D, I have proposed two basic recommendations for change in the complex: filling key government positions with persons from the R&D community and improving the policy-shaping procedures of the R&D community. But what are the themes that underlie these recommendations?

First, I am reaffirming the need for the elitist system that governs our community. I see no other way that the best minds can be kept at work in our field. And from this review there is evidence that they have functioned quite well under very trying circumstances. Forced to struggle in academic departments that, with rare exceptions, were not receptive to scholarship and faced with issues that were both intellectually defying on the one hand, yet potentially politically explosive on the other, they have fashioned ways of operating and have selected and encouraged talented assistants thereby giving some of us additional hope for the future.

I am also saying that there are some improvements that can be made. The process of shaping policies needs to be systematized and broadened, to include more people. And that calls for a change in attitude. Some of our elite have been arrogant toward certain issues. They have ignored for too long the need for the external validation of their work. The better educational practitioners are imbued with the kind of common sense that Campbell discussed in his 1975 APA address.[7] I have participated in several meetings where competent scholars developed a new respect for the wisdom, collective and individual, of schoolmen.

The reasons for the hope to which I referred are several fold at this point. Let me share some impressions. No, I do not yet seen an abundance of printed research reports that contain great import for public school practices. But I do see that the conditions under which researchers are operating are changing for the better. In the first place, we are now, and have been for about a decade, it seems to me, receiving our fair share of bright young people. They have not known the deprivation, both intellectual and financial, of the generation ahead of them. They interact more freely and are more freely accepted by colleagues in the social and behavioral sciences. They publish more widely and in better journals, interact more extensively with colleagues, have more opportunities to learn within their own other fields, and are far more productive overall.

Furthermore, they are more accepting of the researchers from the other modes of research. Historians, anthropologists—those who observe and describe man's activities—are being accepted for making valid contributions to the study of education. I recall quite vividly the reasoning, and the emotion, of those in 1968 who did not want to form the division on history and historiography in AERA; few would support these views today. This attitude is best exemplified by Cronbach when he said:

Scientific discipline is what we uniquely add to the time-honored ways of study-ing man. Too narrow an identification with science, however, has fixed our eyes upon an inappropriate goal. The goal of our work . . . is not to amass generali-zations atop which a theoretical tower can someday be erected. . . . . The special task of the social scientist in each generation is to pin down the contempor-ary facts. Beyond that he shares with the humanistic scholar and the artist in the effort to gain insight into contemporary relationships, and to realign the culture's view of man with present realities.[8]

This is a statement of equality among professionals. It can be extended to include practitioners—and bureaucrats, to acknowledge practice as a source of knowledge. It is the basis for the researcher to regard practitioners, including his bureaucratic counterparts, as equals. Government workers need not be regarded as "researchers gone to waste." It is this kind of acceptance that is integral to the building of a fully functioning educational R&D complex. Without it, all that can be learned from this book will go for naught. With it, perhaps there are some helpful hints contained herein as to where we can most profitably go from here.

Appendix A: Persons Interviewed*

Date of Interview and Institutional Affiliation, if any, at that time

J. Myron Atkin, University of Illinois, Urbana, April 16, 1974.

Stephen K. Bailey, American Council on Education, November 19, 1973.

James W. Becker, National Foundation for the Improvement of Education, Washinton, D.C., February 20, 1974.

Edward Beagle, Stanford University, August 1, 1974.

Laurence O. Binder, National Science Foundation, June 10, 1975.

Benjamin S. Bloom, University of Chicago, February 8, 1974.

Eli M. Bower, University of California, Berkeley, July 5, 1974.

Norman J. Boyan, University of California, Santa Barbara, June 28, 1974.

John Brademas, U.S. Congress, February 28, 1974.

R. Louis Bright, President, Western Institute for Science and Technology, May 8, 1974.

Glen Bryan, Office of Naval Research, November 26, 1974.

David S. Bushnell, Human Resources Research Organization, November 29, 1973.

Lee G. Burchinal, National Science Foundation, November 1, 1973.

William Cannon, University of Chicago, September 30, 1974.

William G. Carr, retired, May 21, 1975.

Francis S. Chase, retired, April 16, 1974.

David L. Clark, University of Indiana, May 6, 1974.

Thomas D. Clemens, National Institute of Education, October 29, 1973.

James S. Coleman, University of Chicago, February 8, 1974.

Lawrence A. Cremin, Teachers College, Columbia University, March 7, 1974.

Leonard Duhl, University of California, Berkeley, August 7, 1974.

Ralph Dungan, State of New Jersey, December 9, 1974.

James A. Dunn, American Institute for Research, September 26, 1975.

Emerson Elliott, National Institute of Education, February 14, 1974.

Richard E. Emory, National Institute of Education, May 12, 1975.

John C. Flanagan, American Institute for Research, April 1, 1974.

James J. Gallagher, University of North Carolina, May 30, 1974.

John W. Gardner, Common Cause, May 28, 1974.

Jacob W. Getzels, University of Chicago, February 9, 1974.

Hendrick D. Gideonse, University of Cincinnati, March 29, 1974.

Thomas K. Glennan, National Institute of Education, November 14, 1974.

Shana Gordon, National Institute of Education, November 9, 1974.

Roy Hall, Georgia State University. Atlanta, April 18, 1974.

Gary E. Hanna, U.S. Office of Education, September 18, 1975.

*Includes both telephone and face-to-face interviews.

145

Samuel Halperin, Institute for Educational Leadership, September 19, 1973.

Fred R. Heckinger, New York Times, July 16, 1974.

John K. Hemphill, Far West Educational Laboratory, July 15, 1974.

Howard F. Hjelm, U.S. Office of Education, September 17, 1973.

Harold Howe, II, Ford Foundation, February 5, 1974.

Laurence Iannaccone, University of California, Riverside, April 15, 1974.

Francis A.J. Ianni, Teachers College, Columbia University, November 21, 1973.

Francis Keppel, General Learning Corporation, November 8, 1974.

Michael W. Kirst, Stanford University, April 2, 1974.

David R. Krathwohl, Syracuse University, April 17, 1974.

Charles W. Lee, Committee for Full Funding, March 14, 1974.

Roger E. Levian, Rand Corporation, February 27, 1974.

Sidney P. Marland, College Entrance Examination Board, March 14, 1974.

Bernard H. Martin, National Institute of Education, October 16, 1974.

Ward S. Mason, National Institute of Education, September 25, 1974.

John M. Mays, National Institute of Education, March 25, 1974.

Richard A. "Skip" McCann, University of California, Los Angeles, April 4, 1974.

Gretchen McCann, Unaffiliated, April 4, 1974.

Edward J. Meade, Ford Foundation, February 5, 1974.

Jack C. Merwin, University of Minnesota, April 16, 1974.

Robert M. Morgon, Florida State University, October 3, 1974.

Edith K. Mosher, University of Virginia, February 14, 1974.

Salvatore J. Rinaldi, U.S. Office of Education, April 24, 1974.

Wade M. Robinsin, Central Midwestern Regional Laboratory, October 3, 1974.

Sherman Ross, National Academy of Sciences, May 3, 1974.

William J. Russell, American Educational Research Association, October 14, 1975.

E. Joseph Schneider, Council for Educational Research and Development, November 12, 1974.

Alice Y. Scates, U.S. Office of Education, February 6, 1973.

Richard E. Schutz, Southwestern Regional Laboratory for Educational R&D, April 5, 1974.

Harry Silverman, University of California, Los Angeles.

Arthur Singer, Sloane Foundation, March 14, 1974.

Richard Smith, U.S. Senate Staff, February 19, 1974.

William G. Spady, National Institute of Education, October 17, 1974.

Patrick Suppes, Stanford University, April 5, 1974.

Marc Tucker, National Institute of Education, October 15, 1974.

Ralph W. Tyler, Retired, February 7, 1974.

John N. Williamson, National Institute of Education, September 24, 1974.

Jerold Zacharias, Massachusetts Institute of Technology, March 7, 1974.

Edward Zigler, Yale University, June 17, 1975.

Appendix B: Regional Educational Laboratories as of 1969

Appalachia Educational Laboratory
Charleston, W. Va.

Center for Urban Education
New York, N.Y.

Central Atlantic Regional Educational Laboratory
Washington, D.C.

Central Midwestern Regional Educational Laboratory
St. Ann, Mo.

Cooperative Educational Research Laboratory, Inc.
Northfield, Ill.

Eastern Regional Institute for Education
Syracuse, N.Y.

Education Development Center, Inc.
Newton, Mass.

Far West Laboratory for Educational Research and Development
Berkeley, Calif.

Michigan-Ohio Regional Educational Laboratory
Detroit, Mich.

Mid-Continent Regional Educational Laboratory
Kansas City, Mo.

Northwest Regional Educational Laboratory
Portland, Oreg.

Regional Educational Laboratory for the Carolinas and Virginia
Durham, N.C.

Research for Better Schools, Inc.
Philadelphia, Pa.

Rocky Mountain Educational Laboratory
Denver, Colo.

South Central Region Educational Laboratory
Little Rock, Ark.

Southeastern Educational Laboratory
Atlanta, Ga.

Southwest Educational Development Laboratory
Austin, Tex.

Southwestern Cooperative Educational Laboratory
Albuquerque, N. Mex.

Southwest Regional Laboratory for Educational Research and Development
Inglewood, Calif.

Upper Midwest Regional Educational Laboratory
Minneapolis, Minn.

Appendix C: Research and Development Centers, Policy Centers, and the National Laboratory on Early Childhood Education, as of 1969

Center for Research & Development for Cognitive Learning
Wisconsin

Center for the Advanced Study of Educational Administration
Oregon

Center for Research & Development in Higher Education
Berkeley

Research & Development Center in Teacher Education
Texas

Learning Research & Development Center
Pittsburgh

Research & Development Center in Education Stimulation
Georgia

Stanford Center for Research and Development in Teaching
Stanford

Center for the Study of the Evaluation of Instructional Program
UCLA

Center for the Study of the Social Organization of Schools and the Learning
  Process
Johns Hopkins

National Laboratory on Early Childhood Education

Educational Policy Research Center (SRI)

Educational Policy Research Center (SURC)

Notes

Notes

Chapter 1
The Bureaucratic-Professional Complex: The Federal Side

1. Samuel H. Beer, "The Modernization of American Federalism," *Publius,* Vol. 3, No. 2, Fall 1973 (Center for the Study of Federalism, Temple University).

2. Ibid., p. 75.

3. See the analysis through 1967 in "Educational Research and Development in the United States," National Center for Educational Research and Development, U.S. Department of Health, Education and Welfare, December 1969.

4. Anthony Downs, *Inside Bureaucracy* (Boston: Little, Brown, 1967), p. 27.

5. Robert S. Merton, *Social Theory and Social Structure* (Glencoe, Ill.: The Free Press, 1949), p. 151.

6. Downs, *Inside Bureaucracy,* p. 24

7. William A. Niskanen, Jr., *Bureaucracy: Servant or Master?* Hobart Paperback, (Levittown, N.J.: Transatlantic Arts, Inc., 1973).

8. Ibid.

9. William A. Niskanen, Jr., *Bureaucracy and Representative Government,* (Chicago: Aldine Atherton, 1971), p. 5

10. Arnold Brecht, "How Bureaucracies Develop and Function," *The Annuals of the American Academy of Political and Social Science,* March 1954, p. 3

11. Downs, *Inside Bureaucracy,* p. 6

12. Richard F. Fenno, *The Power of the Purse* (Boston: Little, Brown, 1966), p. 212.

13. See Peter M. Blau and W. Richard Scott, *Formal Organizations* (San Francisco: Chandler Publishing, 1962).

14. Fenno, *The Power,* p. 212.

15. Diana Crane comments on style and sees it for certain fields analogous to theory in the sciences. In art and literature, for example, she points out the importance of agreement among key members of a field; see her *Invisible Colleges* (Chicago: University of Chicago Press, 1972).

16. Fenno, *The Power,* p. 289

17. Interview with Richard Emory, May 12, 1975.

18. Interview with Edward Zigler, June 17, 1975.

19. Francis E. Rourke, *Bureaucracy, Politics, and Public Policy* (Boston: Little, Brown, 1969), p. 43.

20. James J. Gallagher, "Unfinished Educational Tasks," *Exceptional Children,* Summer 1970, pp. 709-716.

21. Interview with Harold Howe II, February 5, 1974.

22. Ibid.

23. See the *Wall Street Journal,* June 28, 1974, p. 30: "The Institute is perilously close to flunking the test that matters most: gaining political support in Congress."

24. See Fenno, *The Power,* pp. 303-13.

25. Daniel S. Greenberg, *The Politics of Pure Science,* (New York: The New American Library, Inc., 1967).

26. From interviews with Francis A.J. Ianni, November 21, 1973, and Leonard Duhl, August 7, 1974.

27. See Stephen P. Strickland, *Politics, Science and Dread Disease* (Cambridge: Harvard University Press, A Commonwealth Fund Book, 1972); and Fenno, *The Power.*

28. Strickland, *Politics,* p. 124

29. See also Stephen K. Bailey and Edith K. Mosher, *ESEA, The Office of Education Administers a Law,* (Syracuse: Syracuse University Press, 1968).

30. Interview with Richard Smith, February 18, 1974.

31. Ibid.

32. Interview with Roger Levien, February 27, 1974.

33. Lee Sproul, Stephen Weiner, and David Wolf, "Organizing an Anarchy: Belief, Bureaucracy and Politics in a New Federal Agency," Stanford University, unpublished manuscript, 1975, p. 26.

34. John Mays, Michael O'Keefe, and Emerson Elliott did present some of their views of educational research at an invited symposium of the American Educational Research Association in 1968.

35. "Educational Research and Development in the U.S. Office of Education," A Report of the Task Force on Educational R&D of the President's Science Advisory Committee, Washington, D.C., October 1968.

36. See Sproul et al., "Organizing an Anarchy."

37. See "The Office of Economic Opportunity During the Presidency of Lyndon B. Johnson," Volume I, Administrative History, Part I, Office of Economic Opportunity, Washington, D.C., undated p. 16.

38. For a description of the Cosmos Club and its importance, see Gene M. Lyons, *The Uneasy Partnership* (New York: Russell Sage Foundation, 1969).

39. See Stephen P. Strickland, *Politics,* and Daniel S. Greenberg, *The Politics.*

40. Ibid., p. 50.

41. Ibid., p. 50.

42. See Niskanen, *Bureaucracy.*

43. Ibid., p. 27.

44. Ibid., p. 26.

45. Interview with Lee Burchinal, November 1, 1973.

Chapter 2
The Bureaucratic-Professional Complex, Continued:
The Outsiders

1. I use the term "constituencies" as does Rourke: "Groups that regard themselves or that are regarded by an agency as benefitting from its work"; see Francis E. Rourke, *Bureaucracy, Politics and Public Policy,* (Boston: Little, Brown, 1969). However, to me, most of these groups must consist of voters or potential voters.

2. Ibid.

3. See Stephen P. Strickland, *Politics, Science and Dread Disease* (Cambridge: Harvard University Press, 1972), for a case history of how Senator Elliott and Congressman Fogarty were assisted by the medical health complex.

4. Robert S. Merton, *Social Theory and Social Structure* (Glencoe, Ill.: The Free Press, 1968), p. 265.

5. Paul E. March and Ross A. Gortner, *Federal Aid to Science Education, Two Programs,* The Economics and Politics of Public Education (Syracuse: Syracuse University Press, 1963), p. 43.

6. Eugene Eidenberg and Roy D. Morey, *An Act of Congress* (New York: W.W. Norton, 1969), p. 4.

7. Francis E. Rourke, *Bureaucracy.*

8. See Strickland, *Politics,* and Richard F. Fenno, *The Power of the Purse* (Boston: Little, Brown, 1966).

9. "Report of the study for the Ford Foundation on Policy and Program," Ford Foundation, New York, November 1949.

10. See Roald F. Campbell, "Antecedent Expressions of Educational Policy at the National Level," Educational Research Bulletin, Vol. 38, No. 6, September 9, 1959, p. 141-150.

11. Interview with Francis Keppel, November 8, 1974.

12. See Waldemar A. Nielsen, *The Big Foundations* (New York: Columbia

University Press. 1972); as James C. Stone, *Breakthrough in Teacher Education* (San Francisco: Jossey-Bass, 1968), put it, "Officials charged with the responsibility for funding the Breakthrough curricula (at Ford) had a negative attitude toward research and evaluation" p. 169.

13. Stone, *Breakthrough,* says: "To a large extent, the Foundation bet on people as much as on the intrinsic worth of a program" p. 17.

14. 1969 Annual Report, The Ford Foundation, New York, N.Y.

15. Stone, *Breakthrough,* p. 15.

16. See Stephen K. Bailey and Edith K. Mosher, ESEA: *The Office of Education Administers a Law* (Syracuse: Syracuse University Press, 1968).

17. Administrative History of the Office of Education, Transcript, Henry Loomis Oral History Interview, LBJ Library, p. 45.

18. Dwight Waldo, "Epilogue: Public Service Professional Associations in Context of Socio-Political Transition," *Public Service Professional Associations and the Public Interest,* Monograph 15, Don L. Bowen, Ed. (Philadelphia: American Academy of Political and Social Science, 1963), pp. 295-308.

19. Harvey Brooks, "The Scientific Adviser," in *Scientists and National Policy Making,* Robert Gilpin and Christopher Wright, Eds. (New York: Columbia University Press, 1964).

20. Robert Gilpin and Christopher Wright, *Scientists and National Policy-Making* (New York: Columbia University Press, 1964).

21. Waldo, "Epilogue," and Robert C. Wood, "Scientists and Politics: The Rise of an Apolitical Elite," in *Scientists and National Policy Making,* Robert Gilpin and Christopher Wright, Eds. (New York: Columbia University Press, 1964).

22. See Daniel S. Greenberg, *The Politics of Pure Science* (New York: The New American Library, Inc., 1967).

23. Ibid., p. 152.

24. Willard Libby, the Nobel laureate chemist who served as a commissioner for the Atomic Energy Commission, described how he viewed the process: "You see, here's what you do: it's a kind of modern piracy. When I was on the AEC I carefully 'ground in' all the top talent I could find in the physical sciences—and you give them everything they need and they get loyal to you and pretty soon you've got them, you see." Quoted in Greenberg, *The Politics,* p. 137. See also, Martin L. Perl, "The Scientific Advisory System: Some Observations," *Science,* Vol. 173, 24 September, 1971, pp. 1211-15.

25. Rae Goodell, "The Visible Scientists," Ph.D. Thesis, Department of Communication, Stanford University, July 18, 1974, p. 77.

26. For a description of both projects and the controversies surrounding them, see Greenberg, *The Politics.*

27. For a description of PSAC, see Robert Kreidler, "The President's Science Advisors," in *Scientist and National Policy Making,* Robert Gilpin and Christopher Wright, Eds. (New York: Columbia University Press, 1964).

28. See Michael Polanyi, *Knowing and Being* (Chicago: Chicago University Press, 1969); and Florian Znaniecki, *The Social Role of the Man of Knowledge* (New York: Columbia University Press, 1940).

29. There are many exceptions to the statement; see, for example, Goodell, "The Visible Scientists."

30. Strickland, *Politics.*

31. Ibid., p. 279.

32. Ibid., p. 286.

33. Richard A. Dershimer, Ed., "The Educational Research Community: Its Communication and Social Structure," ERIC # ED 057 275, Washington, D.C., April 1970.

34. Charles Bidwell, "Effect of the Socialization Process on Decisions Related to the Training of Educational Researchers, *Preparing Researchers for Education,* David L. Clark and Blaine R. Worthen, Eds., (Bloomington: Phi Delta Kappa, Inc., 1967, pp. 45-50.

35. Norman Storer, "The Organization and Differential of the Scientific Community: Basic Disciplines, Applied Research, and Conjunctive Domains," in *The Educational Research Community: Its Communication and Social Structure,* Richard A. Dershimer, Ed., ERIC # ED 057 275, Washington, D.C., April, 1970, p. 193.

36. Znaniecki, *The Social Role,* p. 12

37. See Merton, *Social Theory,* and Polanyi, *Knowing and Being.*

38. Diana Crane, *Invisible Colleges,* (Chicago: University of Chicago Press, 1972), p. 14.

39. Polanyi, *Knowing and Being.*

40. Holtan P. Odegard, *The Politics of Truth* (University: The University of Alabama Press, 1971

41. A term used by I.I. Rabi and quoted in Greenberg, *The Politics,* p. 3.

42. Ibid., p. 12.

43. Polanyi, *Knowing and Being,* p. 49.

44. See Derek J. de Solla Price, *Little Science, Big Science* (New York: Columbia University Press, 1963); also Crane, *Invisible Colleges.*

45. A few examples: Harvey Brooks, "Physics and the Polity," *Science,* Vol. 160, 26 April 1968, pp 394-400; "The Need for Priorities" Editorial, *Science,* Vol. 163, 3 January, 1969; Don K. Price, "Pursuits and Politicians," *Science,* Vol. 163, 3 January 1969, pp 25-31.

46. For a description of COSPUP, see "National Research Council (II); Answering the Right Questions?" *Science,* Vol. 172, 22 April 1971, p. 354.

47. Daniel P. Moynihan, "The Education of the Urban Poor," in *Coping: On the Practice of Government* (New York: Random House, 1973), p. 178.

48. Outsiders also had to contend with some problems indigenous to advisory committees in general. See Thomas E. Cronin and Norman C. Thomas, "Federal Advisory Processes: Advice and Discontent," *Science,* Vol. 171, 26 February 1971, pp 771-79.

49. Interview with Richard Smith, February 19, 1974.

Chapter 3
Education and Educational Research, Circa 1960

1. Paul Woodring, *Investment in Innovation* (Boston: Little, Brown, 1970), p. 79.

2. See Research Division #36, 1958-59 NEA Research Division, Network Education Association, 1201 16th Street, N.W., Washington, D.C.

3. James L. Sundquist, *Politics and Policy, the Eisenhower, Kennedy and Johnson Years* (Washington, D.C.: The Brookings Institution, 1968).

4. Raymond E. Callahan, *Education and the Cult of Efficiency* (Chicago: University of Chicago Press, 1962).

5. Cited in Woodring, *Investment.*

6. "Report of the Study for the Ford Foundation on Policy and Program," Ford Foundation, New York, November 1949, p. 38.

7. Pamilla Roby, *The Poverty Establishment* (Englewood Cliffs, N.J.: Prentice-Hall, 1974); and David Halberstam, *The Best and the Brightest* (New York: Random House, 1969).

8. Halberstam, Ibid. p. 6.

9. Roby, *The Poverty Establishment,* p. 5.

10. Vannevar Bush, *Pieces of the Action* (New York: William Morrow, 1970).

11. "Paying for Better Schools," A Statement on National Policy by the Research and Policy Committee of the Comittee for Economic Development, New York, December 1959, p. 9.

12. Ibid., p. 12.

13. "Innovation in Education: New Directions for the American School," A Statement by the Research and Policy Committee of the Committee for Economic Development, New York, July 1968, p. 31.

14. For a description of the relationship of modern corporations to science

and technology, see *Science in American Society,* by George H. Daniels (New York: Alfred A. Knopf, 1971).

15. Vannevar Bush, *Science the Endless Frontier* (Washington, D.C.: National Science Foundation, Reprinted, July 1960), p. 148.

16. Paul E. Marsh and Ross A. Gortner, *Federal Aid to Science Education: Two Programs,* The Economics and Politics of Public Education, Syracuse (New York: Syracuse University Press, 1963).

17. All figures in this paragraph taken from "Status Report on the Course Content Improvement Activities of the National Science Foundation," National Science Foundation, Washington, D.C., March 1965.

18. John I. Goodlad, *School Curriculum Reform in the United States,* The Fund for the Advancement of Education, The Ford Foundation, New York, March 1964, p. 9.

19. The effects of these programs on American education remain a debatable issue but few dispute that they have had impact. As Cremin noted, these discipline-based course developers broke the "increasingly exclusive hold" of the professional curriculum-makers on determining both the content and the processes of curriculum development in American education. See Lawrence A. Cremin, *The Transformation of the School* (New York: Vintage Books, 1961), p. 21.

20. Sundquist, *Politics and Policy.*

21. See Peter Marris and Martin Rein, *Dilemmas of Social Reform* (Chicago: Aldine Publishing, 1973).

22. Ibid., p. 24.

23. We must be cautious when we talk about OEO "experiments" based on social science knowledge, however. As Piven points out, it is just as easy to deduce that politicians merely used the social scientists to justify what they, the politicians wanted to do in the first place. See Frances Fox Piven, "Social Scientists and the Poor," in *The Poverty Establishment,* Pamela Roby, Ed. (Englewood Cliffs, N.J.: Prentice-Hall, 1974), pp. 211-17.

24. Daniel P. Moynihan, "The Professors and the Poor," in *On Understanding Poverty, Perspectives from the Social Sciences,* Daniel P. Moynihan, Ed., (New York: Basic Books, 1968).

25. Ibid., p. 14.

26. Transcript, Francis Keppel Oral History Interview, April 21, 1969, LBJ Library.

27. Sundquist, *Politics and Policy.*

28. Bush, *The Endless Frontier.*

29. James Conant, *Slums and Suburbs* (New York: McGraw-Hill, 1961).

30. The ferment in education during the fifties was not limited just to

the issues articulated by these networks. For a more complete description of the social, economic, and political forces that were operating during those years, see *Social Forces Influencing American Education,* 60th Yearbook, Part II, NSSE (Chicago: University of Chicago Press, 1961); also David B. Tyack, *The One Best System,* A Harvard Paperback, (Cambridge, Massachusetts 1974).

31. Carter Good, "Educational Research after Fifty Years," *Phi Delta Kappan* 37, January 1956, pp 145-52.

32. Benjamin S. Bloom, "Twenty-Five Years of Educational Research," *The American Educational Research Journal,* Vol. 3, No. 3., May 1966.

33. John B. Carroll, "Neglected Areas in Educational Research," *Phi Delta Kappan* 42, May, 1961, p. 339.

34. Cremin, *The Transformation.*

35. See the 37th Yearbook, Part II, *The Scientific Movement in Education,* National Society for the Study of Education, Guy M. Whipple, Ed. (Chicago: University of Chicago Press, 1938).

36. A.E. Traxler, "Some Comments on Educational Research at Mid-century," *Journal of Educational Research* 47, January 1954, pp. 359-36.

37. Arthur P. Coladarci, "More Rigorous Educational Research," *Harvard Educational Review,* Vol. 30. No. 1, Winter 1960, pp. 3-11.

38. David V. Tiedeman and Morris L. Cogan, "New Horizons in Educational Research," *Phi Delta Kappan* 34, March 1958, 286-91.

39. Carroll, "Neglected Areas."

40. Lee J. Cronbach and Patrick Suppes, Eds., *Research for Tomorrow's Schools: Disciplined Inquiry for Education* (New York: MacMillan, 1969).

41. N.L. Gage, Ed., *Handbook of Research on Teaching* (Chicago: Rand McNally, 1965).

42. Orville Brim, *Sociology and the Field of Education* (New York: Russell Sage Foundation, 1965).

43. Neal Gross, "The Sociology of Education," in *Sociology Today,* Robert Merton, Leonard Brown and Leo Cottrell, Eds. (New York: Basic Books, 1959).

44. "Psychological Research in Education," National Academy of Sciences National Research Council Publication #643, Washington, D.C., 1958. Included on the committee were several persons who in the 1960s were to become closely identified with the educational research community or whose work was to be frequently cited in the educational research literature: Robert Gagne, John Carroll, B.F. Skinner, Arthur Melton, Lloyd Humphreys, and Henry Dyer. They supplemented some of the "old timers" at educational research, men like Guy Buswell, Chester Harris and Philip Rulon.

45. Warren G. Findley, "The Impact of Applied Problems on Educational Research," in *First Annual PDK Symposium on Educational Research* (Bloomington: Phi Delta Kappa, Inc., 1960), pp. 43-53.

46. Philip H. Coombs, "A Vice President in Charge of Heresy," *Phi Delta Kappan* 41, March 1960, pp. 243-47.

47. See Paul F. Lazarsfeld and Sam D. Sieber, *Organizing Educational Research* (New York: Prentice-Hall, 1964).

48. Nicholas A. Fattu, "A Survey of Educational Research at Selected Universities," in *First Annual Phi Delta Kappa Symposium on Educational Research,* (Bloomington: Phi Delta Kappa, Inc., 1960), pp. 1-22.

49. Lazarsfeld and Sieber, *Organizing Educational Research;* p. 9.

50. P.M. Symonds, "The Organization of Educational Research in the United States," *Harvard Educational Review* 27, No. 3., Summer, 1957, p. 166.

51. See Lazarsfeld and Sieber, *Organizing Educational Research;* also Egon Guba, "Operational and Training Problems in Traditional Bureau of Research, Organizations for Research and Development in Education," *Phi Delta Kappa,* Bloomington, Indiana, 1966; and Warren O. Hagstrom, "Educational Researchers, Social Scientists and School Professionals" in *The Educational Research Community: Its Communication and Social Structure,* Richard A. Dershimer, Ed., ERIC # ED 057275, Washington, D.C., April 1970.

52. See, for example, Herbert S. Conrad, "Research—Education's Gilbraltar," *School Life* 34, April 1952; Traxler, "Some Comments"; J. Cayce Morrison, "A More Effective Instrument," *Phi Delta Kappan* 35, October 1953, pp. 63-66; David P. Ausubel, "The Nature of Educational Research," *Educational Theory* III, October 1953, pp. 314-20.

53. David L. Clark, "Educational Research: A National Perspective," *Educational Research: New Perspectives,* Jack A. Culbertson and Stephen P. Hencley, Eds., (Danville, Ill.: Interstate Printers and Publishers, Inc., 1963), p. 7.

54. Symonds, "The Organization."

55. Carroll, "Neglected Areas," p. 339.

56. Brim, *Sociology.*

57. Gross, "The Sociology of Education."

58. See, for example, Theodore W. Schultz, *The Economic Value of Education* (New York: Columbia University Press, 1963).

59. N.L. Gage, "New Directions in Educational Research," in *New Directions in Educational Research,* The University of the State of New York, State Education Department, 1963, p. 51.

60. See, for a more detailed description, "The First Twenty-Five Years," (Battle Creek, Mich.: W.K. Kellogg Foundation, 1955).

61. See *Behavioral Science and Educational Administration,* 63rd Year-

book of the National Society for the Study of Education, Part II (Chicago: University of Chicago Press, 1964).

62. Edgar Dale, *Historical Setting of Programmed Instruction,* 66th Yearbook of the National Society for the Study of Education, Part II (Chicago: University of Chicago Press, 1967).

63. The editors in their introduction to *Historical Setting of Programmed Instruction.*

64. See Cremin, *The Transformation.*

65. See Lazarsfeld and Sieber, *Organizing Educational Research.*

66. From correspondence from David L. Clark dated October 8, 1974.

67. See H. Kursh, *The U.S. Office of Education: A Century of Service* (New York: Chilton Book, 1965), for the complete law and interpretations.

68. From conversations with the author.

69. Conference on Cooperative Research and Demonstration held on February 21, 1950 in Washington, D.C., of which there are only incomplete records on file in the U.S. Office of Education.

70. Hearings before the Subcommittee on Education of the Committee of Labor and Public Welfare, U.S. Senate, 83rd Congress, 2nd Session on S 2856, A Bill to Authorize Cooperative Research in Education, April 2, 1954.

71. See the remarks of Representative John Fogarty, Hearings before the Subcommittee of the Committee on Appropriations, House of Representatives, 85th Congress, 1st Session, Washington, D.C. February 11, 1958, pp. 230-231. Cooperative research also was one of the items cut out of the HEW budget by the Chairman of the full committee, Representative Cannon to "discipline John Fogarty." See Richard F. Fenno, *The Power of the Purse* (Boston: Little, Brown, 1966).

72. Don E. Kash, "Politics and Research," *The Social Context of Research,* edited by Saad A. Nagi and Ronald G. Corwin, (New York: Wiley Interscience, 1972), pp. 97-127.

73. Interview with Leonard Duhl, August 10, 1974. Of the $1,020,190 provided for CRP in FY 1957, $675,000 was earmarked for research on problems of the handicapped. Hearings before the Subcommittee of the Committee on Appropriations, House of Representatives, 85th Congress, 1st Session, Washington, D.C., February 12, 1957, p. 22.

74. Francis A.J. Ianni, "The United States Office of Education, *The Encyclopedia of Education* (New York; Macmillan 1970).

75. In the Research Advisory Committee meeting, December 14-15, 1956, Acting Commissioner Wayne Reed maintained that the CRP was "never conceived as a grant program" pp. 10 and 11, RAC minutes.

76. For a description of the NIMH system, see "Research in the Service

of Mental Health," Report of the Research Task Force on the National Institute of Mental Health, Julius Segal, Editor-in-Chief, National Institute of Mental Health, Rockville, Md., DHEW Publication # (ADM) 75-236, 1975.

77. "Educational Research and Development in the United States," U.S. Office of Education, National Center for Educational Research and Development, Washington, D.C., 1965.

78. From interview with Laurence Iannaccone, April 15, 1974.

79. Stephen K. Bailey and Edith K. Mosher, *ESEA: The Office of Education Administers a Law* (Syracuse: Syracuse University Press, 1968), p. 73.

80. Public Law 85-864, September 2, 1958, 72 Statutes, 1959.

81. Ibid.

82. From interview with Donald White, May 8, 1974.

83. See Frank J. Munger and Richard F. Fenno, Jr., *National Politics and Federal Aid to Education, The Economic and Politics of Public Education* (Syracuse: Syracuse University Press, 1962); and Sundquist, *Politics and Policy.*

84. "Educational Research and Development in the United States," p. 114.

85. Interview with Thomas Clemens, as cited.

86. Robert T. Filep and Wilbur Schram, "The Impact of Research on Utilization of Media for Educational Purposes Sponsored by NDEA, Title VII, 1958-1968," Institute of Educational Development, New York, July 15, 1970.

87. Hearings before the Subcommittee of the Committee on Appropriations, House of Representatives, 86th Congress, 2nd Session, Departments of HEW, February 1960.

88. Interview with Glen Bryan, Office of Naval Research, November 26, 1973.

89. Interview with Eli Bower, August 6, 1974.

90. See Jeanne L. Brand, "The National Mental Health Act of 1946; A Retrospect," *Bulletin of Medicine,* Vol. 39, No. 3, May–June, 1965: "From the start, it was recognized that, lacking definite clues to the etiology or best methods of treatment of mental illness, it is wisest to support the best research in any and all fields related to mental illness . . . " p. 244.

91. "Research in the Service of Mental Health," p. 35.

92. Fenno, *The Power.*

93. See Gene M. Lyons, *The Uneasy Partnership* (New York: Russell Sage Foundation, 1969), p. 133.

94. "Status Report on the Course Content Improvement Activities of the National Science Foundation," Education Division, NSF, March 1965.

95. Interview with J. Myron Atkin, April 16, 1974.

96. Interview with Larry Binder, June 10, 1975.

97. Transcript of Research Advisory Committee meeting, DHEW, Office of Education, 10th meeting, February 14, 1959, p. 78.

98. Transcript of Proceedings, "Conference on the Status of Educational Research Activities sponsored by the U.S. Office of Education." San Francisco and Washington, D.C., Fall 1965.

99. USOE Files.

100. Herold C. Hunt, "Some Questions Educators Ask," *Phi Delta Kappan* 35, October 1953, pp. 51–58.

Chapter Four
Research and the Breakthrough in Federal Aid for Schools

1. Interview with William G. Carr, May 21, 1975.

2. James L. Sundquist, *Politics and Policy, the Eisenhower, Kennedy and John Years* (Washington, D.C.: The Brookings Institution, 1968).

3. Stephen K. Bailey and Edith K. Mosher, *ESEA: The Office of Education Administers a Law* (Syracuse: Syracuse University Press, 1968).

4. Interview with Jerold Zacharias, March 7, 1974.

5. Bailey and Mosher, *ESEA*, p. 18.

6. Donald W. Robinson "Commission of Education Our Least Most Important Government Post," *Phi Delta Kappan*, December 1962, p. 109.

7. Bailey and Mosher, *ESEA*, p. 23.

8. Sundquist, *Politics*, p. 205.

9. Bailey and Mosher, *ESEA*, p. 35.

10. Franklin Parker, "The White House Conference on Education and the Emergence of the New Guard," *School and Society*, November 13, 1965, p. 426.

11. Bailey and Mosher, *ESEA*, p. 35.

12. U.S. Budget, 1960, PR 34.107:960, p. 585, and DHEW Publication No. (OE) 74-11104.

13. Hearings before the Subcommittee of the Committee on Appropriations, House of Representatives, 87th Congress, 1st Session, Washington, D.C. April 12, 1961, pp. 438 and 480.

14. Robinson, "Commissioner of Education," *Phi Delta Kappan*, p. 108.

15. Calendar Year Report, 1962, U.S. Office of Education Files.

16. Richard F. Fenno, *The Power of the Purse* (Boston: Little, Brown, 1966), p. 11.

17. DHEW Publication OE 74 11104.

18. Interview with Francis A.J. Ianni, November 21, 1973.

19. Interview with David L. Clark, May 6, 1974.

20. Paul F. Lazarsfeld and Sam D. Sieber, *Organizing Educational Research* (Englewood, N.J.: Prentice-Hall, 1964).

21. Hearings before the Subcommittee of the Committee on Appropriations, House of Representatives, 87th Congress, 1st Session, Washington, D.C., April 12, 1961, p. 503.

22. "Research: Education's Neglected Hope," Address by Commissioner Francis Keppel to the Congress on Instruction of the NEA, Washington, D.C., April 27, 1964.

23. U.S. Budget 1960-1964, 20 US.C., 331-332.

24. Ralph Tyler remembers that the RAC was well aware of those facts throughout those early years; interview, February 7, 1974.

25. Interview with David S. Clark.

26. Interviews with David S. Clark, and Roy M. Hall, April 18, 1974.

27. These were "Regional Educational Media Research Organization," The National Planning Committee of the Council of Chief State School Officers, April 1962, and "A Research Report on Operational Plans for Developing Regional Educational Media Research Centers," C. Ray Carpenter and others, ERIC No. ED 0003-632, April 1962.

28. Interview with Francis A.J. Ianni, previously cited.

29. From interviews with Lawrence Cremin, Benjamin S. Bloom and Jacob W. Getzels, March 7, 1974; February 8, 1974; February 9, 1974.

30. Study No. 1, Administration of Research and Development Grants, Report of the Select Committee of Government Research of the House of Representatives, 88th Congress, Washington, D.C., July 31, 1964.

31. See Francis A.J. Ianni and Lois S. Josephs, "The Curriculum Research and Development Program of the U.S. Office of Education: Project English, Project Social Studies and Beyond," in *New Curricula,* Robert Heath, Ed. (New York: Harper Row, 1964), pp. 161-212.

32. Interview with Francis A.J. Ianni.

33. Ward S. Mason and Howard F. Hjelm, "The Research and Development Center Program of the U.S. Office of Education," Paper presented at AERA Annual Meeting, 1965.

34. See Egon G. Guba and David L. Clark, "The Configurational Perspective: A View of Educational Knowledge Production and Utilization," (Washington, D.C.: Council for Educational Development and Research, Inc., November 1974).

35. Francis A.J. Ianni, "Research and Experimentation in Education, *Phi Delta Kappan,* Vol. 48, No. 10, June 1965, p. 490.

36. See David L. Clark and Egon G. Guba, "An Examination of Potential Change Roles in Education," Essay Six in *Rational Planning in Curriculum and Instruction,* Ole Sand, Ed. (Washington, D.C.: NEA, Center for the Study of Instruction, 1967), p. 116.

37. From conversations with the director, Robert Glaser.

38. Francis Keppel, "Research: Education's Neglected Hope."

39. Hearings before the Subcommittee of the Committee on Appropriations, House of Representatives, 88th Congress, 2nd Session, Washington, D.C., February 17, 1964, p. 460. An internal staff memo dated November 23, 1964, "Research and Development Centers" proposed to establish twenty centers by 1966 and five each year thereafter until by 1970 there would be forty-five requring an estimated 17,125 full-time equivalent positions at a total cost of $318,916,250. From U.S. Government Records, DHEW 1965–1969, Box 97, LBJ Library, Austin, Texas.

40. Interview with Francis Keppel, November 8, 1974.

41. Interview with William Cannon, September 30, 1974.

42. "Innovation and Experiment in Education," Panel on Educational Research and Development, President's Science Advisory Committee U.S. Government Printing Office, Washington, D.C., March 1964, p. vii.

43. "Status Report on the Course Content Improvement Activities of the National Science Foundation, NSF, Washington, D.C., March, 1965, Tab O.

44. See James B. Conant, *The Education of American Teachers* (New York: McGraw-Hill, 1963).

45. Paul Woodring, Investment in Innovation (Boston: Little, Brown, 1970). But others disagreed; Cremin saw the new developers accepting the "paradigm of curriculum-making that had prevailed for three-quarters of a century" (see "Curriculum-Making in the United States, *Teachers College Record,* Vol. 73, No. 2, December 1971, p. 16.

46. Status Report on the Course Content Improvement Program Activities, National Science Foundation, Washington, D.C., March 1965, p. 10.

47. Interview with William Cannon.

48. See Sundquist, *Politics and Policy.*

49. Daniel P. Moynihan, "The Education of the Urban Poor," in *Coping* Daniel P. Moynihan, Ed. (New York: Random House, 1973), p. 5.

50. David Halberstam, *The Best and the Brightest* (New York: Random House, 1969), p. 302.

51. See Bailey and Mosher, *ESEA,* p. 27.

52. Sundquist, *Politics and Policy,* p. 211.

53. Transcript, James Gaither Oral History Interview, p. 12 LBJ Library.

54. Bailey and Mosher, *ESEA.*

55. Interview with Francis A.J. Ianni and Francis Keppel.

56. Interview with William Cannon.

57. John W. Gardner, "Innovation and Leadership in American Education," *NASSP Bulletin,* March 1965, p. 36.

58. "Report of the President's Task Force on Education," June 14, 1965, Executive FG 600/Task Forces File, Ed. Box 1, LBJ Library, p. 3.

59. Gardner, "Innovation," p. 2.

60. "Report of the President's Task Force on Education," p. iii.

61. Ibid., p. 33.

62. Ibid., p. 38.

63. Interview with Ralph Tyler, February 7, 1974.

64. Interview with John Gardner, May 28, 1974.

65. Interview with William Cannon; his emphasis.

66. "Report of the President's Task Force on Education," p. 34.

67. Ibid., p. 35.

68. Ibid., p. 37.

69. Interview with Ralph Tyler.

70. "Report of the President's Task Force on Education," op. cit., p. 12.

71. See Bailey and Mosher, *ESEA.* This strategy also kept the bill from being referred to the House Rules Committee through which it had to pass if a joint House-Senate Committee were appointed to reconcile differing versions of the bill. Representative Smith of Virginia, Chairman of the Rules Committee at that time was likely to bottle up the bill. What amendments were made occurred in the subcommittee of the House; Wayner Morse was able to convince his Senate colleagues to go with that version.

72. Administrative History of the Office of Education, Transcript, Frances Keppel Oral History Interview, July 18, 1968, LBJ Library.

73. Remarks of the President at Reception for Members of Congress on Occasion of the Passage of the Education Bill, April 13, 1965, FG 16504 Files, Office of Education, LBJ Library, Austin, Texas.

74. From conversations with the author.

Chapter Five
Gearing Up to Go

1. Daniel P. Moynihan, *Coping: On the Practice of Government* (New York: Random House, 1973), p. 8.

2. David Halberstam, *The Best and the Brightest* (New York: Random House, 1969), p. 452.

3. Remarks of the President to the White House Conference on Education, July 21, 1965, Executive and General File, SP 2-3, 1965, Education, Box 2, Lyndon B. Johnson Library, Austin, Texas.

4. "Toward Full Education Opportunity," President's Education Message to Congress, January 12, 1965, Executive and General File, SP 2-3, 1965, Education, Box 2, LBJ Library, Austin, Texas.

5. Transcript, S. Douglass Cater Oral History Interview, Volume I, Part IV, Oral History of Francis Keppel, p. 1-30.

6. Francis Keppel, "The National Commitment to Education," *Phi Delta Kappan* Vol. 47, No. 4, December 1965, p. 167.

7. "Educational Research and Development in the United States," National Center for Educational Research and Development, U.S. Department of Health, Education and Welfare, Office of Education, Washington, D.C., December 1969, p. 28.

8. Stephen K. Bailey and Edith K. Mosher, *ESEA, The Office of Education Administers a Law* (Syracuse: Syracuse University Press, 1968), p. 69.

9. Office of Education Report, September 1965, FG 165-4 Files, Office of Education, LBJ Library.

10. Hearings before Subcommittee on Appropriations, House of Representatives, 89th Congress, 2nd Session, Part 2, Department of Health, Education and Welfare, Washington, D.C., Feb. 7, 1966.

11. Stephen K. Bailey, "The Office of Education and the Education Act of 1965," Inter-University Case Program #100 (Indianapolis: The Bobbs-Merrill Company, 1966).

12. H. Kursh, *The United States Office of Education* (New York: Chilton Books, 1965), p. 51.

13. Administrative History of the Office of Education, Transcript, Henry Loomis Oral History, Interview, August 15, 1968, LBJ Library, p. 5.

14. Ibid., p. 8.

15. Transcript, S. Douglass Cater Oral History Interview, pp. 1-32.

16. Transcript, Francis Keppel Oral History Interview, April 21, 1969, LBJ Library, p. 22.

17. Halberstam, *The Best,* p. 437.

18. Memo from Francis Keppel to John Macy, December 23, 1965. File 31, FG 165-4, LBJ Library.

19. Interview with Michael Kirst, April 2, 1974.

20. Bailey, "The Office of Education."

21. Transcript, Henry Loomis Oral History Interview.

22. Memo, FG Files 165-4, LBJ Library.

23. Transcript, Francis Keppel Oral History Interview.

24. Transcript, Henry Loomis Oral History Interview.

25. History of the Department of Health, Education and Welfare, Volume I, Part IV, LBJ Library.

26. Interview with Thomas Clemens, October 29, 1973.

27. For a more detailed description of this reorganization plan, see Bailey, "The Office of Education."

28. Ibid., p. 14.

29. Transcript, Henry Loomis Oral History Interview.

30. Ibid.

31. Ibid., p. 15. Loomis explained that he was looking for persons "who are used to striving for the best, who go around with the best" as opposed to the professional educator "who knows he is second class and most of the people around him are second class and he doesn't want to admit that to himself and I think that where you happen to go to college is relatively immaterial."

32. Administrative History of the Office of Education, Transcript, Ralph Flynt Oral History Interview, LBJ Library, p. 12-13.

33. Bailey, "The Office of Education."

34. Transcript, Henry Loomis Oral History Interview.

35. Transcript of Proceedings, "Conference on the Status of Educational Research Activities Sponsored by the U.S. Office of Education," San Francisco and Washington, D.C., Fall 1965, p. 21.

36. Ibid., p. 22.

37. History of the Department of Health, Education and Welfare, Vol. I, Part 4, p. 513.

38. Memo from Keppel to John Macy.

39. See Charles E. Silberman, "Technology is Knocking at the Schoolhouse Door," Fortune, August 1966.

40. Cited by J. Myron Atkin, "Federal Government, Big Business and Colleges of Education," The Educational Forum, XXXI, No. 4, May 1967, p. 397.

41. "Leadership for Education," Saturday Review, January 15, 1966, p. 58.

42. Atkin, "Federal Government"; also Carl Hanson, "Giants in the Schoolhouse," Phi Delta Kappan 49, November 1967, pp. 113-14.

43. Hearings before a subcommittee of the Committee on Appropriations, House of Representatives, 89th Congress, 2nd Session, for the Department of Health, Education and Welfare, Washington, D.C.

44. Interview with R. Louis Bright, May 8, 1974.

45. See Transcript of Proceedings, Conference on the Status of Educational Research Activities." pp. 3–11. Of this amount, $70 million was authorized under the Cooperative Research Act, $20 million of which was part of the funds authorized over a five-year period for construction, acquisition, remodeling and equipment facilities for R & D; $17,750,000 was for vocational research; the remaining $12,800,000 was for NDEA titles VI and VII and Handicapped Research. The total was $100,550,000.

46. See transcript of Hearings before a Subcommittee on Appropriations, House of Representatives, 89th Congress, 2nd Session, part 2, Department of Health, Education and Welfare, Washington, D.C.

47. Transcript, Francis Keppel Oral History Interview.

48. Transcript, Henry Loomis Oral History Interview.

49. Transcript, Francis Keppel Oral History Interview.

50. Ibid.

51. For a brief description, see Bailey and Mosher, *ESEA,* p. 152.

52. Transcript, S. Douglass Cater Oral History Interview.

53. Halberstam, *The Best.*

54. "Leadership for Education," p. 57.

55. Interview with Michael Kirst, April 2, 1974.

56. Interview with Salvatore Rinaldi, April 24, 1974.

57. April 1966 issue.

58. Interview with Laurence Iannaccone, April 15, 1974.

59. See, for example, Simon Marcson, *The Scientists in American Industry* (Princeton, N.J.: Princeton University Press, 1969); and William Kornhauser, *Scientists in Industry: Conflict and Accommodation* (Berkeley: University of California Press, 1962).

60. Private conversations with the author.

61. See Chapter 4.

62. Interview with Francis A.J. Ianni.

63. See Transcript of Proceedings, "Conference on the Status of Educational Research Activities," p. 7. An illustration: "In keeping with the need to involve the research interest and efforts of all parts of the community—not just the education community—we have broadened our list of consultants accordingly. If a few years ago I had found the name of a vice president of a bank on our list of consultants, I would have been sure somebody was pulling a joke on me. Today, if our list of consultants included only educational researchers, I would wonder how we could adequately cover the interests of the teachers and ad-

ministrators—and parents and employers—during the process of reviewing research directed toward the improvement of education.

64. Interview with Hendrick Gideonse, March 29, 1974.

65. See the January 1966 Bureau of Research, Report to the Commissioner, NIE files.

66. Stenographic Transcript, Department of Health, Education and Welfare, Office of Education, Bureau of Research, NIE Files.

67. Summary of Transcript, Research Advisory Council Meeting, October 7, 1966 meeting, NIE Files, p. 4.

68. See Chapter 1 for definitions.

69. See Chapter 1, "The Colloquium: A Recapitulation" in *The Educational Research Community: Its Communication and Social Structure,* Richard A. Dershimer, Ed. ERIC Document # ED. 057275, April 1970.

70. See Derek J. de Solla Price, *Little Science, Big Science,* (New York: Columbia University Press, 1963); and Diana Crane, *Invisible Colleges* (Chicago: University of Chicago Press, 1972).

71. Don E. Kash, "Politics and Research," in *The Social Context of Research,* Saad A. Nagi and Ronald G. Corwin, Eds., (New York: Wiley Interscience, p. 106.

72. Thomas E. Cronin and Norman C. Thomas, "Federal Advisory Processes: Advice and Discontent," *Science,* Vol. 171, 26 February, 1971, p. 771.

73. Summary of Transcript, RAC, p. 48.

74. Interview with David R. Krathwohl, April 17, 1974.

Chapter 6
Some Bureaucrats and How They Fared: The Division of Educational Laboratories

1. Interview with David L. Clark, May 6, 1974; his emphasis.

2. "Educational Research and Development in the United States," National Center for Educational Research and Development, U.S. Department of Health, Education and Welfare, Office of Education, Washington, D.C., December 1969, p. 118.

3. Ibid., p. 114.

4. Ibid.

5. Interview with Francis Keppel, November 8, 1974.

6. Ibid.

7. Hearings before the Subcommittee of the Committee on Appropriations, House of Representatives, 87th Congress, 1st Session, Washington, D.C., April 12, 1961, p. 330.

8. Stephen K. Bailey and Edith K. Mosher, *ESEA: The Office of Education Administers a Law* (Syracuse: Syracuse University Press, 1968), p. 93.

9. Transcript of Proceedings, "Conference on the Status of Educational Research Activities Sponsored by the U.S. Office of Education," San Francisco and Washington, D.C., Fall, 1965, p. 17.

10. Interview with Michael W. Kirst, April 2, 1974.

11. Interview with Arthur Singer, March 14, 1974.

12. Interview with John W. Gardner, May 28, 1974.

13. "Report of the President's Task Force on Education," June 14, 1965, Executive FG 600/Task Force File, Education, p. 34. Box 1, LBJ Library, Austin, Texas.

14. Ibid. p. 15.

15. Interview with Arthur Singer.

16. See Daniel S. Greenberg, *The Politics of Pure Science* (New York: The New American Library, Inc., 1967).

17. Interview with William Cannon, September 30, 1974.

18. Stenographic Transcript, Research Advisory Council, Bureau of Research, Office of Education, Department of HEW, December 17, 1965, p. 129.

19. Interview with Ralph W. Tyler, February 7, 1974.

20. Interview with Francis A.J. Ianni, November 21, 1973.

21. Hearings before the Subcommittee on Education of the Committee on Labor and Public Welfare, U.S. Senate, p. 862.

22. Ibid., p. 884.

23. See Stenographic Transcript, Research Advisory Council, pp. 33 and 36. Ianni expected the funding level for each lab to reach two to three million a year. Gideonse saw them reaching $17 million each.

24. Interview with Richard McCann, April 4, 1974.

25. Monthly reports to the Commissioner, Bureau of Research, Office of Education, Office of Education Files, July 1965, p. 6.

26. Interview with Hendrik D. Gideonse.

27. Memorandum, Office of Education, July 8, 1965, Folder III-D, Administrative File IV, National Institute of Education.

28. Memorandum, Office of Education, Folder III-D, Administrative File IV, National Institute of Education, July 29, 1965.

29. Monthly reports to the Commissioner, Bureau of Research, Office of Education, Office of Education Files, October 1965.

30. "The USOE and Research in Education: An Interview with Richard Louis Bright," *Phi Delta Kappan*, Vol. 48, No. 1 September 1966, p. 4.

31. Interview with William Cannon.

32. "The USOE and Research in Education: An Interview with Richard Louis Bright," p. 3.

33. The reasons for the resignation are now obscured but the panel was bothered by Bright's decision about staff prerogatives. At the April 28, 1966, meeting of the RAC Cremin said: "There is also a compelling problem of the Office of Education staff itself. You cannot send a civil servant to argue with a man like Bowker. Even if Dr. Bright could recruit bright youn men, it must be someone at Bright's level to oversee the program. And I must confess, our committee members have been doing some of the staff's work." Transcript of Proceedings, p. 19.

34. Interview with Gretchen McCann, April 4, 1974.

35. Elwin V. Svenson, "Observations on Emerging Relations Between Regional Educational Laboratories and State Departments of Education," Central Midwestern Regional Educational Laboratory, Inc., 10646 St. Charles Rock Road, St. Ann, Missouri 63074, October 1969, p. 23.

36. Ibid., p. 25. In a report from a staff member in October 1965 after visiting eight prospective labs we find, "Program is often not mentioned at all or alluded to only in the 'glitteringest of all possible generalities', " Memo from James Gillis, October 13, 1965, Administrative File IV, III-B File Folder, National Institute of Education.

37. Correspondence from John I. Goodlad, July 3, 1975.

38. "A National Program in Early Education, Final Report, Project No. 6-2937, Department of Health, Education and Welfare, Office of Education, Bureau of Research, November 14, 1966, p. 3.

39. Correspondence from John I. Goodlad.

40. Interview with Hendrik D. Gideonse.

41. Memorandum to Members of the Lab Steering Committee from Hendrik Gideonse and Dale Mann,"The Attached Paper," October 14, 1965, U.S. Government Records, Department of Health, Education and Welfare, 1963-1969, Box 96, LBJ Library. The National Program on Early Childhood Education lasted as a separate entity until 1970 at which time it was transferred to the CEMREL laboratory. For all intents and purposes that marked the end of the only national laboratory.

42. Press release dated July 5, 1965, LBJ Library.

43. Reported to the RAC, Meeting of June 17, 1965, from the Transcripts, p. 5.

44. Interview with Emerson Elliott, February 14, 1974.

45. From transcript of RAC Meeting, April 29, 1966.

46. Interview with Harold Howe II, February 5, 1974.

47. Interview with Francis S. Chase, April 16, 1974.

48. Interview with Arthur Singer.

49. From interview with Gary Hanna, September 18, 1975.

50. Interview with Francis S. Chase.

51. Ibid.

52. Francis S. Chase, "The Educational Laboratories: How do they fit into the Future of American Education?" Paper delivered at New Orleans Meeting of the Laboratory Directors, January 15, 1967.

53. "The National Program of Educational Laboratories," Bureau of Research, Office of Education, Department of Health, Education and Welfare, Washington, D.C., December 17, 1968.

54. Interview with Francis S. Chase.

55. "The National Program of Educational Laboratories," p. 8.

56. Ibid., p. 22.

57. Ibid., p. 37.

58. Interview with John M. Mays, March 25, 1974.

59. Interview with Harold Howe II.

60. Memo, "A Brief Chronology of the National Program of Educational Laboratories," Mimeo, undated, NIE Files.

61. Hearings before the Subcommittee of the Committee on Appropriations, House of Representatives, 90th Congress, 1st Session, Department of Health, Education and Welfare, Part 3, Washington, D.C., March 1967, p. 524.

62. Interview with James W. Becker, February 20, 1974.

63. Many of the most visible researchers, those who formerly had supported the Bureau of Research, were pulling back. See, for example, Lee J. Cronbach, "The Role of the University in Improving Education," *Phi Delta Kappan* 67, June, 1966, pp. 539-45.

64. See Transcript of RAC Meeting, April 29, 1967, p. 8.

65. See Stephen D. Strickland, Politics, *Science and Dread Disease* (Cambridge: Harvard University Press, 1972).

66. Richard F. Fenno, *The Power of the Purse* (Boston: Little, Brown, 1966), p. 402.

67. Interview with David L. Clark.

68. Conversations with the author.

69. "Study of the United States Office of Education," Report of the Special

Committee on Education, Committee on Education and Labor, House of Representatives, 85th Congress, 2nd Session, House Document, No. 193, Washington, D.C., 1967.

70. Ibid., p. 228.

71. Quoted in Greenberg, *The Politics,* p. 5.

72. See Don E. Kash, "Politics and Research," in *The Social Context of Research,* Saad A. Nagi and Ronald G. Corwin, Eds. (New York: Wiley-Interstate, 1972), pp. 97–127. This view seemed to be well documented by the publication of Project Hindsight. For a review of this report, see Chalmers W. Sherwin and Raymond S. Isenson, "Project Hindsight," *Science,* Vol. 156, 23 June 1967, pp. 1571–77.

73. Greenberg, *The Politics,* p. 159.

74. Ibid., p. 159.

75. Alice Y. Rivlin, *Systematic Thinking for Social Action* (Washington, D.C.: The Brookings Institute, 1971), pp. 23 and 24. Also George L. Perry, "The '66 Budget," *The New Republic,* December 25, 1965.

76. "Educational Research and Development in the United States," p. 116.

77. Memorandum and reports in Exec-FG 600/Task Forces/Education, Box 2, LBJ Library.

78. Interview with Jacob W. Getzels, February 9, 1974.

79. Interview with Norman J. Boyan.

80. "A Review of Planning and Programs of the Bureau of Research, Office of Education," Office of the Assistant Secretary for Planning and Evaluation, Department of Health, Education and Welfare, Washington, D.C., October 1968, Appendix F, Five-Year Program and Financial Plan, Bureau of Research.

81. Interview with Norman J. Boyan.

82. Interview with Richard Emory, May 12, 1975.

83. Interview with Stephen K. Bailey.

84. Annual Report, 1967, Education Development Center, 55 Chapel Street, Newton, Massachusetts 02160.

85. See Rivlin, *Systematic Thinking.*

86. Bailey and Mosher, *ESEA,* p. 181.

87. Interview with James W. Becker.

88. Interview with Salvatore J. Rinaldi, April 24, 1974.

89. Interview with Stephen K. Bailey.

90. Interview with Francis S. Chase.

91. "A Review of Planning and Programs of the Bureau of Research, Office of Education," p. 5.

92. Ibid., pp. 4–5.

93. Interview with Stephen K. Bailey.

Chapter 7
Other USOE R&D Efforts In and Outside the
Bureau of Research

1. See "Proposed Plan for the Review and Evaluation of Research and Development Centers," Division of Laboratories, Bureau of Research, Office of Education, dated March 28, 1968; personal files of author.

2. Working paper submitted to the PSAC Task Group on Education Research and Development, by F.H. Westheimer, Mimeo, August 8, 1968; personal file of author.

3. See Neal Gross, Ward Mason, and Alexander W. McEachern, *Explorations in Role Analysis: Studies of the School Superintendency Role* (New York: John Wiley, 1959).

4. S.M. Brownell, "R&D Centers and the Schools: A Reaction to Progress Reports," *Journal of Research and Development in Education,* Vol. 1, No. 4, Summer 1968, p. 174.

5. Benjamin S. Bloom, "Research and Development Centers: Promise and Fulfillment," *Journal of Research and Development in Education,* Vol. 1, No. 4, Summer 1968, p. 186.

6. Interview with Benjamin S. Bloom, February 8, 1974.

7. See "Proposed Plan for the Review and Evaluation of Research and Development Centers," p. 25. By 1968, local support from all sources averaged about 28 percent of total center funds.

8. Working paper submitted to the PSAC Task Group on Educational Research and Development.

9. "Proposed Plan for the Review and Evaluation of Research and Development Centers," p. 17.

10. Interview with Ward Mason, September 25, 1974.

11. Hearings before the Subcommittee of the Committee on Appropriations, House of Representatives, 85th Congress, 2nd Session, Washington, D.C. February 11, 1958, p. 206.

12. Interview with Lee G. Burchinal, November 1, 1973.

13. "ERIC Development through June, 1968," Mimeograph Report, undated, FG 600, LBJ Library.

14. Ibid.

15. See Peter Greenwood and Daniel Wexler, "Alternative Models for the

ERIC Clearinghouse Network, R-951-HEW (Santa Monica: The Rand Corporation, 1972).

16. Interview with Harold Howe II, February 5, 1974.

17. See Carl J. Schaefer, "Helter-Skelter: Vocational Education R & D," a paper prepared for the Committee on Vocation Educational Research and Development, National Academy of Science-National Research Council, Washington, D.C., June 15, 1975. The funding for vocational R&D never reached that level, but more funds were appropriated in the years after P.L. 88-210 became law than ever before. In FY 1966, $17.5 million was approved; that dropped to $10 million the next year but this still was a considerable sum for what was essentially a young specialty in education research.

18. Interview with David S. Bushnell, November 29, 1973.

19. Schaefer, "Helter-Skelter," p. 4.

20. Interview with David S. Bushnell.

21. Interview with Robert M. Morgan, October 3, 1975.

22. Ibid.

23. Interview with David S. Bushnell.

24. Ibid.

25. Interview with David S. Bushnell.

26. Schaefer, "Helter-Skelter," p. 22.

27. Interview with R. Louis Bright, May 8, 1974.

28. Gerald Grant, "Shaping Social Policy: The Politics of the Coleman Report," *Teachers College Record,* Vol. 75, No. 1, September 1973, p. 19.

29. Interview with Francis Keppel, November 8, 1974.

30. James S. Coleman, *Adolescent Society* (New York: The Free Press of Glencoe, 1961).

31. Interview with James S. Coleman, February 8, 1974.

32. Ibid.

33. Ibid.

34. Gerald Grant, "On Equality of Educational Opportunity: Papers Deriving from the Harvard University Faculty Seminar on the Coleman Report," edited by Frederick Mosteller and Daniel P. Moynihan, Essay Reviews, *Harvard Educational Review,* No. 1, 1972, p. 42.

35. "Not Damn Fools," Letter to the Editor, Daniel P. Moynihan, *Wall Street Journal,* July 8, 1974.

36. Grant, "Shaping Social Policy: The Politics of the Coleman Report," p. 29.

37. Ibid., p. 32. The EEO Survey was not the only study that caused the bureaucracy these difficulties. Moynihan points out the problems caused by

the findings of the National Advisory Commission on Civil Disorders, the Kerner Commission. Officials could not accept the predictions that civil disorders would grow worse. See Daniel P. Moynihan, *Coping: On the Practice of Government* (New York: Random House, 1973).

38. Grant, "Shaping Social Policy: The Politics of the Coleman Report," p. 33.

39. Roy Larsen, in the Introduction to Paul Woodring's book, *Investment in Innovation* (Boston: Little, Brown, 1970) attributes the ideas of the assessment to Keppel. John Gardner said, "The idea of the national assessment came from a phone call from Frank Keppel" (interview with John Gardner, May 28, 1974).

40. Interview with Francis Keppel.

41. Interview with Jack Merwin, May 16, 1974.

42. See, as example, Harold C. Hand, "National Assessment Viewed as the Camel's Nose," *Phi Delta Kappan* 47, September 1965, pp. 8-12.

43. Francis Parker, "The White House Conference on Education and the Emergence of the New Guard," *School and Society,* November 13, 1965 p. 427.

44. Memo to the members of AASA from the Executive Committee, "AASA Opposes National Assessment," AASA Files, January 9, 1967.

45. Cited in Hearings before a Subcommittee on Appropriations, House of Representatives, 89th Congress, 2nd Session, Part 2, Department of Health, Education and Welfare, Washington, D.C., February 1967, p. 161.

46. Ibid.

47. Jack C. Merwin and Frank B. Womer, "Evaluation in Assessing the Progress of Education to Provide a Basis of Public Understanding and Public Policy," Chapter XIII in *Education Evaluation: New Roles, New Means,* the Sixty-eighth Yearbook of the National Society for the Study of Education, Part II, Ralph W. Tyler, Ed. (Chicago: University of Chicago Press, 1969), p. 331.

48. Interview with Jack C. Merwin.

Chapter 8
Nixon and Educational R&D

1. "Educational Research and Development in the United States, Examiners Report and Questions," Committee for Scientific and Technical Personnel, Educational Policy Review, 12th November 1969, Paris, Organization for Economic Co-operation and Development, STP (69) 10, p. 241. (Hereafter referred to as OCED Report).

2. "Educational Research and Development in the United States," National Center for Educational Research and Development, Department of

Health, Education and Welfare, Office of Education, Washington, D.C., December 1969.

3. OECD Report (Chapter X) cites ten studies undertaken between the years 1967 and 1969 (pp. 155-76).

4. See the summary of Humphrey's platform for education in "Washington Monitor," *Education USA*, October 28, 1968, p. 53.

5. Ibid.

6. See "Washington Report," *Phi Delta Kappan* 50, February 1969, pp. 360-61.

7. See "Education: Nixon Nominates a Schoolman as Commissioner," *Science,* Vol. 163, February 28, 1969, pp. 912-15.

8. See "Interview with James E. Allen, Jr.," *Phi Delta Kappan* 50, April 1969, p. 473.

9. James E. Allen, Jr., "Federalism in Education–the Role of the Federal Government," Address before the Annual Meeting of the Education Commission of the States, ERIC, ED-031-797, Denver, Colorado, July 8, 1969.

10. James E. Allen, Jr., "Strengthening Educational Research and Development," Remarks at Conference on American Educational National Network of Regional Educational Laboratories, ERIC ED 032-640, Washington, D.C., July 17, 1969.

11. James E. Allen, Jr., "Federalism in Education–the Role of the Federal Government."

12. See Gary Orfield, *The Reconstruction of Southern Education.* (New York: Wiley-Interscience, 1969).

13. See "Nixon Vetos Education Bill," *The New York Times,* Education Supplement, January 30, 1970.

14. Chester E. Finn, Jr., "The National Institute of Education," *The Yale Review,* Winter 1975, pp. 227-43.

15. House Special Subcommittee on Education 1967, "Study of the United States Office of Education," House Document No. 193, 90th Congress, 1st Session, Washington, D.C., and General Accounting Office, "Need for Improving the Administration of Study and Evaluation Contract: Office of Education," (Washington, D.C.: U.S. GPO, 1971).

16. House Special Subcommittee on Education 1967, "Study."

17. House Special Subcommittee on Education 1967, "Study."

18. Interview with James E. Gallagher, May 30, 1974.

19. For a history and evaluation of the small grants program, see Theresa Rogers, Lois Saunders and Bernard Levenson, "Small-Project Grants of the Regional Research Program," Final Report No. 8-B-901-ED 054074, Washington, D.C., 1969.

20. "Research for Progress in Education," Annual Report, FY 1970, National Center for Educational Research and Development, USOE, Washington, D.C., p. 25.

21. See Daniel P. Moynihan, "Policy vs. Program in the 70's," *The Public Interest,* No. 20, Summer 1970, pp. 90-100.

22. "Nixon's White House Staff: Heyday of the Planners?" *Science,* Vol. 167, February 27, 1970, p. 1233.

23. "NIE Briefing Papers, Research, Development, Institutional Support and Research Training Programs Administered by NCERD," National Center for Educational Research and Development, USOE, Washington, D.C., June 6, 1972.

24. Lee Sproul, Stephen Weiner, and David Wolf, "Organizing an Anarchy: Belief, Bureaucracy, and Politics in a New Federal Agency," Stanford University, unpublished manuscript, 1975, p. 17.

25. Interview with James Gallagher.

26. Finn maintains that the experimental school idea was left over from the Johnson administration and dusted off for use by Finch. See Finn, "The National Institute of Education," p. 236.

27. Interview with Edward J. Meade, Jr., February 5, 1974.

28. Reported in Sproul, et al., "Organizing an Anarchy."

29. Ibid., p. 26.

30. Finn, "The National Institute of Education," p. 240.

31. See Daniel P. Moynihan, "The Education of the Urban Poor," *Coping: On the Practice of Government* (New York: Random House, 1973), pp. 167-84. The results of this analysis were published in *On Equality of Educational Opportunity.* Daniel P. Moynihan and Frederick Mosteller eds., (New York: Random House, 1972).

32. "The Impact of Head Start: An evaluation of the effects of Head Start on children's cognitive and affective development," PB 184328, Westinghouse Learning Corporation, Bladensburg, Md., 1969.

33. Finn, "The National Institute of Education."

34. See William Safire, *Before The Fall* (Garden City, N.Y.: Doubleday and Co., Inc., 1975).

35. See "Experimental Schools Urged by Finch Team," *The Washington Post,* February 24, 1969.

36. Interview with James Gallagher.

37. Ibid.

38. Sproul, et al., "Organizing an Anarchy."

39. Ibid., p. 34.

40. See "Party Loyalty Decides Who Gets HEW Positions," *Phi Delta Kappan* 51, February 1970, p. 338. When it came time to fill the vacancy

left by Gallagher's resignation, the White House was fully in charge of the process. Harry Silverman reports that his contacts were from this source and that he had contact with acting Commissioner Bell or commissioner-to-be Marland only when it came time "for the paperwork" (interview with Harry Silverman).

41. Interview with James J. Gallagher.

42. Prior to taking office, Nixon had organized a task force chaired by Alan Pifer of the Carnegie Corporation. But their recommendations were not well received by the White House. See "Washington Report," *Phi Delta Kappan* 50, January 1969.

43. Hearings before the Subcommittee of the Committee on Appropriations of the House of Representatives, 91st Congress, 2nd Session, Part 4, Washington, D.C., p. 8.

44. From telephone conversations on April 2, 1976 with Gregory Amreg who formerly was an administrative assistant to Commissioner James Allen.

45. Since Keppel's time up to $1 million was set aside each year for activities that required only the Commissioner's approval. It was tapped to initiate Sesame Street and to fund some of the activities of the Exploratory Committee for Assessing Educational Progress.

46. See the June 1970 monthly report of NCERD, Office of Education Files.

47. Finn, "The National Institute of Education."

48. See "Nixon at Odds with Congress," *Education USA,* September 1, 1969. By 1969, the educational associations had become better organized than ever before though the work of the Committee for Full Funding of Educational Programs. See Stephen K. Bailey, *Education Interest Groups in the Nation's Capital* (Washington, D.C.: American Council on Education. 1975).

49. Letters to the Editor of the Journal, *Wall Street Journal,* July 8, 1974.

50. "Message on Educational Reform," White House, Washington, D.C., March 3, 1970.

51. Finn, "The National Institute of Education," p. 242.

52. See Dan Rather and Gary Paul Gates, *The Palace Guard,* Warner Paperback, 1975.

53. See "Nixon's Cut Rate Rhetoric is No Substitute for Money," Editorial *Phi Delta Kappan* 51, May 1970, p. 461–62.

54. See Sproul, et. al., "Organizing an Anarchy," and Finn, "The National Institute of Education."

55. "Effectiveness of Educational Laboratories and Centers: A System for the Evaluation of Educational Research and Development Products," Final Report, Contract No. OEC-0-4891, February 1973.

56. "Directed Research Program," NCERD, Office of Education Files, May 1970.

57. House Special Subcommittee on Education, 1967, p. 37.

58. Current Staff Assignment by Major Budget Categories, Line Items and Associated Programs, mimeo report, USOE, Washington, D.C., December 1971.

Chapter 9
What We Need to Do?

1. Annual Report, Year Ending August 31, 1974, Center for Advanced Study in the Behavioral Sciences. Also, "Lists of Alumni by Fields, 1954–55 through 1975–76" (mimeograph), Center for Advanced Study in the Behavioral Sciences, November 1975.

2. "National Academy of Education," Background/Activities/Constitution/Membership," Brochure, Spring 1969, p. 4.

3. N.L. Gage, Ed., *The Handbook of Research on Teaching,* (Chicago: Rand McNally, 1965).

4. "Final Report of the Committee on Basic Research in Education," Division of Behavioral Sciences, National Academy of Sciences, National Research Council, Washington D.C., September 1972, p. 12.

5. Interview with Edward Zigler, June 17, 1975.

6. A recent example of how this magazine can be used is illustrated by the article in the December 1975 issue by Sam Sieber, "The Requirements of a National Educational R&D System."

7. Donald I. Campbell, "On the Conflicts Between the Biological and Social Evolution Between Psychology and the Moval Tradition," *American Psychologist,* 30, December 1975, pp. 1103-1126.

8. Lee J. Cronbach, "Beyond the Two Disciplines of Scientific Psychology," *American Psychologist,* 30, February 1975, p. 126.

Index

Index

185

About the Author

Richard A. Dershimer served from 1964 to 1974 as the Executive Officer of the American Educational Research Association. Before that he was a special assistant for research and development to the State Superintendent of Public Instruction, the Commonwealth of Pennsylvania; associate professor of education, the University of Delaware; and executive secretary of the Delaware School Study Council. He received the Doctor of Education degree at the Harvard Graduate School of Education and the B.A. degree from Cornell College, Iowa.